Henry Alford

Sermons on Christian Doctrine

Henry Alford

Sermons on Christian Doctrine

ISBN/EAN: 9783743349131

Manufactured in Europe, USA, Canada, Australia, Japa

Cover: Foto ©Lupo / pixelio.de

Manufactured and distributed by brebook publishing software (www.brebook.com)

Henry Alford

Sermons on Christian Doctrine

SERMONS

ON

CHRISTIAN DOCTRINE.

SERMONS

ON

CHRISTIAN DOCTRINE,

PREACHED IN

Canterbury Cathedral,

ON THE AFTERNOONS OF THE SUNDAYS IN THE
YEAR 1861-1862.

BY

HENRY ALFORD, D.D.
DEAN OF CANTERBURY.

LONDON:
RIVINGTONS, WATERLOO PLACE.
1862.

TO THE

CHRISTIAN MEMORY

OF

JOHN HAMPDEN GURNEY.

WHEN the former of these Sermons were preached, I anticipated what has ever been one of my chief pleasures on the publication of a new work,—the sending it to my beloved friend;—the receiving the looked-for letter of thanks, with his warm approbation where he could give it, and his manly and unsparing criticism where he thought me wrong.

But he is gone where doctrines need no proof, and thoughts no words to express them. We have lost from among us the living example of his noble character,— of his scorn of party watchwords, and his contempt of the time-serving and the self-seeking. We shall no more hear his generous outbursts of admiration for those who differed from him,—no more be awakened to our own duties by his stern refusal to praise and to follow after the world's favourites. Truthfulness, guilelessness, fearlessness,—these were the thoughts of his heart: and as he thought, so he spoke. A good man, a powerful man, a bold man,—he narrowly missed being a great man. But his goodness was often drowned in the voice of his power; and his power was too liable to spring forth at the call of generous impulse, for greatness to be achieved, or high position safely sustained. Himself a rigid Sabbatarian, he once incurred, at the hands of those who cared not to understand him, the imputation of opposite sentiments, rather than be party to an over-stated and ill-reasoned memorial.

As a preacher, he was, as might have been expected, earnest and even fiery in manner,—unsparing in denunciation of wrong,—rising into high eloquence and enthusiasm in fervid admiration of all that is noble and good.

But it was in the pulpit that that side of his character shone so brightly, for which some hardly credited him. His sermons were full of tenderness. He was a great master of description of the social affections, and of the softer feelings of the individual heart. It was a rich feast of enjoyment, to hear him draw out, in graphic touches, such subjects as the family histories in the Old Testament, or the return of the Prodigal in the New: to trace with him the progress of the softening of the once hard heart, or the kindling of high and noble desires in a character once incapable of them.

It was hardly perhaps in a course like that of the present volume that he preferred bestowing his labour. But the great doctrines of our holy faith, though not often treated of as subjects, were ever present, ever underlying his whole fabric of exhortation and description. His preaching, though seldom what is known as doctrinal, was always essentially Christian. If theological terms were not there, that which they imperfectly strive to represent, was; and thus the work of building up in the faith was, if not ostensibly, yet perhaps after all, the more really and safely accomplished.

Speaking in human weakness, looking at the blank place left in our defences where he fell, we seem to feel that we can ill spare him; we cannot tell where to look for one who shall be to London, who shall be to the Church, exactly what he was.

But speaking and feeling more worthily, because more trustfully, we are satisfied that his work was done: and that God, who has taken him to His rest, can fill his place with others, whose fitness He knows, but we do not.

Thun, Switzerland,
   July 21, 1862.

CONTENTS.

SERMON I.

(PREACHED ON THE SECOND SUNDAY IN ADVENT, DEC. 8, 1861.)

SIN AS A FACT.

Rom. iii. 23.

PAGE

All have sinned 1

SERMON II.

(PREACHED ON THE THIRD SUNDAY IN ADVENT, DEC. 15, 1861.)

THE DECEITFULNESS OF SIN.

Heb. iii. 13.

The deceitfulness of sin 13

SERMON III.

(PREACHED ON THE FOURTH SUNDAY IN ADVENT, DEC. 22, 1861.)

THE GUILT AND CONSEQUENCE OF SIN.

Ezek. xviii. 4.

The soul that sinneth, it shall die 28

SERMON IV.

(PREACHED ON CHRISTMAS DAY, 1861.)

GOD'S REMEDY FOR SIN.

Rom. iii. 3.

What the law could not do, in that it was weak through the flesh, God sending His own Son in the likeness of sinful flesh, and for sin, condemned sin in the flesh 42

SERMON V.

(PREACHED ON SUNDAY, JAN. 5, 1862.)

THE RIGHTEOUSNESS OF ONE MAN.

Rom. v. 18, 19.

As by the offence of one, judgment came upon all men to condemnation: even so by the righteousness of one the free gift came upon all men unto justification of life. For as by one man's disobedience many were made sinners, so by the obedience of one shall many be made righteous 54

SERMON VI.

(PREACHED ON THE FIRST SUNDAY AFTER EPIPHANY, JAN. 12, 1862.)

THE UNIVERSALITY OF THE GOSPEL.

Gal. iii. 28.

There is neither Jew nor Greek, there is neither bond nor free, there is neither male nor female: for ye are all one in Christ Jesus 68

SERMON VII.

(PREACHED ON THE SECOND SUNDAY AFTER EPIPHANY, JAN. 19, 1862.)

MIRACLES : WATER MADE WINE.

JOHN ii. 11.
PAGE
This beginning of miracles did Jesus in Cana of Galilee, and manifested forth his glory 82

SERMON VIII.

(PREACHED ON THE THIRD SUNDAY AFTER EPIPHANY, JAN. 26, 1862.)

MIRACLES OF HEALING.

MATT. viii. 13.

And Jesus said unto the centurion, Go thy way; and as thou hast believed, so be it done unto thee. And his servant was healed in the selfsame hour 97

SERMON IX.

(PREACHED ON THE FOURTH SUNDAY AFTER EPIPHANY, FEB. 2, 1862.)

MIRACLES OF POWER.

MATT. viii. 27.

What manner of man is this, that even the winds and the sea obey him ? 108

SERMON X.

(PREACHED ON THE FIFTH SUNDAY AFTER EPIPHANY, FEB. 9, 1862.)

PARABLES: THE TARES OF THE FIELD.

MATT. xiii. 3.

PAGE

He spake many things unto them in parables 120

SERMON XI.

(PREACHED ON SEPTUAGESIMA SUNDAY, FEB. 16, 1862.)

PARABLES: THE LABOURERS IN THE VINEYARD.

MATT. xx. 16.

So the last shall be first, and the first last 134

SERMON XII.

(PREACHED ON SEXAGESIMA SUNDAY, FEB. 23, 1862.)

PARABLES: THE SOWER.

LUKE viii. 15.

That on the good ground are they, which in an honest and good heart, having heard the word, keep it, and bring forth fruit with patience 150

SERMON XIII.

(PREACHED ON QUINQUAGESIMA SUNDAY, MARCH 2, 1862.)

WHY CHRIST SUFFERED.

LUKE xviii. 31.

PAGE

Then Jesus took unto him the twelve, and said unto them, Behold, we go up to Jerusalem, and all things that are written by the prophets concerning the Son of man shall be accomplished . . 166

SERMON XIV.

(PREACHED ON THE FIRST SUNDAY IN LENT, MARCH 9, 1862.)

OUR LORD'S TEMPTATION.

HEB. iv. 15.

He was in all points tempted like as we are, yet without sin . . 179

SERMON XV.

(PREACHED ON THE FIFTH SUNDAY IN LENT, APRIL 6, 1862.)

THE HIGH PRIESTHOOD OF CHRIST.

HEB. ix. 11.

Christ being come an High Priest of good things to come . . 193

SERMON XVI.

(PREACHED ON THE SUNDAY NEXT BEFORE EASTER, APRIL 13, 1862.)

CHRIST CRUCIFIED.

1 COR. i. 13.

We preach Christ crucified 210

SERMON XVII.

(PREACHED ON GOOD FRIDAY, APRIL 18, 1862, ALSO AT ST. MARY'S, OXFORD, ON FRIDAY EVENING, APRIL 11, 1862.)

OUR LORD IN DEATH.

JOHN x. 17, 18.

PAGE

Therefore doth my Father love me, because I lay down my life, that I might take it again. No man taketh it from me, but I lay it down of myself. I have power to lay it down, and I have power to take it again. This commandment have I received of my Father 223

SERMON XVIII.

(PREACHED ON EASTER DAY, APRIL 20, 1862.)

IN CHRIST ALL MADE ALIVE.

1 COR. xv. 12.

Now if Christ be preached that He rose from the dead, how say some among you that there is no resurrection of the dead ? . 242

SERMON XIX.

(PREACHED ON THE FIRST SUNDAY AFTER EASTER, APRIL 27, 1862.)

THE RESURRECTION OF THE BODY.

1 COR. xv. 20.

Now is Christ risen from the dead, and become the first-fruits of them that slept 251

SERMON XX.

(PREACHED ON THE SECOND SUNDAY AFTER EASTER, MAY 4, 1862.)

THE HOPE OF THE RESURRECTION.

Titus ii. 13.

PAGE

Looking for that blessed hope 266

SERMON XXI.

(PREACHED ON THE THIRD SUNDAY AFTER EASTER, MAY 11, 1862.)

JUSTIFICATION BY FAITH.

Rom. i. 17. Heb. x. 38.

The just shall live by faith 281

SERMON XXII.

(PREACHED ON THE SUNDAY AFTER ASCENSION DAY, JUNE 1, 1862.)

THE DOCTRINE OF THE LORD'S SUPPER.

John vi. 53.

Except ye eat the flesh of the Son of man, and drink his blood, ye have no life in you 294

SERMON XXIII.

(PREACHED ON WHIT-SUNDAY, JUNE 8, 1862.)

THE GIFT OF THE SPIRIT.

Acts ii. 33.

Being by the right hand of God exalted, and having received of the Father the promise of the Holy Ghost, He hath shed forth this which ye now see and hear 309

SERMON XXIV.

(PREACHED ON TRINITY SUNDAY, JUNE 15, 1862.)

THE HOLY TRINITY.

Matt. xxviii. 19.

PAGE

Baptizing them in the name of the Father, and of the Son, and of the Holy Ghost 319

SERMON XXV.

(PREACHED ON THE FIRST SUNDAY AFTER TRINITY, JUNE 22, 1862.)

KNOWLEDGE AND PRACTICE.

John xiii. 17.

If ye know these things, happy are ye if ye do them . . . 331

SERMON I.

(PREACHED ON THE SECOND SUNDAY IN ADVENT, DEC. 8, 1861.)

SIN AS A FACT.

Rom. iii. 23.

"All have sinned."

THE Gospel of Christ may be described as a glorious remedy for a disease fatal and otherwise incurable, with which our whole race is tainted. And the first step in treating of the Gospel must ever be to lay open, and make us sensible of, that disease. For one of its most dangerous symptoms is, that it makes men insensible to its own presence: so that the worse a man is afflicted with it, the less he knows that he has it at all. And, seeing that the remedy is not one which can be simply taken once and then all will be well, but one which requires long and painful and self-denying application, a man must be very thoroughly persuaded that he has the disease, and that he is likely to perish from it, before he will take the necessary trouble to be cured of it. Now this disease we call SIN. And in consequence of what has been said you will see, that in beginning a course of sermons on Christian doctrine, I must deal first with this fact which lies at the bottom of all Christian doctrine, that all men are sinners. I may be at once met with the question, Who does not know that? Who does not confess himself to be a sinner? Doubtless, all do this by profession and with the lips. But, my brethren, there is as much difference between confessing with the lips and feeling intensely in the depth of the heart, as there is between confessing and not confessing at all. "Miserable sinners:" "Have mercy upon us miserable sinners." But what do we mean by sinners?

Let us try and lay hold of this—let us try to-day and see what sin means—what "all having sinned" means.

When any of us looks out upon mankind, or looks within himself, with ever so little attention, one thing can hardly fail to strike him. It is, the presence of Evil. We at once see that there is a something in the world, and within us, rebellious, destructive, altogether unwelcome, and which we would gladly be rid of. We want harmony among men, harmony in ourselves, for all purposes of human improvement, for all purposes of our own progress and enlightening. But instead of harmony, we find discord every where. From the first, man's history has been a history of going wrong and doing wrong: from the first, our own personal history has been a history of interrupted good and interfering bad. Now observe, I am not at this moment speaking as a minister of the Gospel: I am speaking merely as man,—as a citizen of the world, as one of you, or one of any band of men gathered out of any age and any place upon earth. I am dwelling upon what is matter of universal observation. Who can deny this presence and this working of an unwelcome and a hostile element in all human matters? What deceit will ever enable a man to hide from himself this dark shadow which falls upon the fairest prospects and purest courses in life? What mind looking into itself is not found to confess that there is this *night side* of its thoughts and ways?

Now it is not my purpose, at all events not at present, to say a word about the reason why this evil ever came into God's universe. I am concerned to-day with the *fact*, and the importance of knowing and acknowledging the fact, that it has come into it and is every where present. Some may say — some have said, conceal the fact, and you will get rid of it. Don't tell people that there is evil in the world; forget that there is evil about and in yourself; and you and they will become good. It may be true, they continue, that there is such a dark spot in nature; that there are these black shadows amidst the shining of the Face of the universal Father: but gazing upon them is painful and useless: look at the bright side of every thing: believe things to be innocent and right, and infinitely more good will be done than by dwelling on the gloom and so increasing it. This, my brethren, not only has been the published advice of a whole school of writers,— it is also the view taken by many loose and shallow thinkers in every place at our own time. But let me ask you, do you suppose that the unquestioned evil in universal nature, and in our nature, can be thus got rid of? "Believe the world to be good, and it will become good," says one of these writers: "Believe yourself to be good, and you will become good." I answer, Try it. Try it for a day, for an hour. Then go into your chamber, and take strict unsparing account. And if it is urged that more time is wanted, try it for a year: shut your eyes to all that is bad in the world—to all that is bad in you: refuse to believe, refuse to entertain any suspicion of evil in yourself, or in others, for that time: then retire and trace your path during the time. Does not every man see what would be the result? Do not we all know, that it would be simply the tale of the silly ostrich over again, which imagines itself safe from the hunter by shutting its eyes, and by hiding him from its own sight? Do we not see, that such a person would only be delivered up far more and far more helplessly into the power of evil?

No, my brethren: a man who wants to get rid of evil in himself must open his eyes to the evil, not hide it: must not shrink from any pain which the sight may give him, if it also gives him the knowledge, what the danger is, and how to meet it. And he who wants to overcome evil in others, must not shrink from the gloomy and unwelcome task of speaking of it, exposing it, probing its extent and measuring its strength, that so they may be the more deeply and earnestly convinced of its existence, and the more active in combating it.

There is then this evil all about us and in us: and we must make up our minds to see it, to recognize it, to stand face to face with it, and conquer it. Now here come in two most important remarks. This evil is not the only disagreeable thing in life. There are bodily pain, discomfort, misery, common to us and all mankind —nay, common to us and the lower animals. And there is this circumstance about all these, worthy of our present notice. If we can manage to forget them, to flee away from them, to hide them from us, we thereby get rid of them. We need not look at them, nor study their nature. A man who wants to avoid breaking a limb, need not be always gazing on or describing broken limbs: he has but to avoid those risks which might occasion the mischief. A man who would avoid death will follow the ordinary instinct of self-preservation: he would not be for ever studying all the possible ways of dying. Such knowledge is not necessary; nay, it would be an incumbrance and a nuisance. But the man who wishes to avoid *evil* in this world, must be awake and alive to the forms and accesses of evil. He cannot do without such knowledge: his very safety consists in it. Therefore—and mark the inference as an important one in our progress to-day—evil is a matter of a *totally different kind* from bodily pain, misery, or death.

Again: evil is not by any means our only *inward* source of annoyance and hindrance. You have—I have —every one has—defects, infirmities, in his or her mind and disposition: things of which we would willingly be rid if we could: bars to our progress and hindrances to our perfection. But none of these do we look upon as we look upon evil. Let it be shewn that we are dull, or feeble, or inferior to some others, we put up with it, we excuse it, we make ourselves as comfortable as we may under the knowledge of it: but let it be once shewn by others or by our own conscience that we have wished, said, done, that which is *evil*, and we know at once that there is *no excuse* for it. We may try to shew that we did it inadvertently, or by force of circumstances; or in some way to lessen our own share in it: but the very labour to construct an excuse shews that we hold the evil itself, as evil, to be inexcusable. Evil itself no one attempts to excuse: all take for granted that it is a loathsome thing, all desire that their character and their conscience should stand free from it.

So far then this evil is something which our nature itself teaches us to revolt from and abhor. We do not, we cannot excuse it; we cannot contentedly put up with it, we cannot be happy under its influence. Now do not mistake me. Many a man, as we have seen, excuses *his share* in evil, excuses his evil deed as *not being evil*, plays the self-deceiver and hides the evil of his ways from himself, abandons his helm and lets himself drift into evil, and so is contented, and fancies himself happy, under evil. But again, and for all this, the *thing itself* is simply a deadly enemy to us, whenever and wherever detected, and exposed as being what it is. No son of man ever said or could say, from his inmost heart, what the great poet sublimely represents Satan as saying, " Evil, be thou my good." It requires more than man ever to say this.

Well now, my brethren, what does all this shew? Does it not testify to there being a law within us, implanted in our nature, by which evil is avoided, and by consequence good sought and desired? And observe that this is true, quite independently of and previous to all circumstances in which a man is placed, all interests in which he is involved. Our abhorrence of evil as evil does not spring from our finding it to be hurtful to us: we know that it is hurtful to us, the moment we know any thing. The little child for the first time detected in evil, is as much ashamed of it as the experienced and mature man. Now this is exceedingly important: all-important, in our present enquiry. A law within us tells us what is good, tells us that we ought to be good, to say good, to do good. Mind I only assert this fact. That this law is broken in upon, that it is not always distinctly or properly or effectively asserted, is nothing to my present purpose. I know all this, and shall have to use it by and by. But I only care now for this great fact, that there is this law: that we all know it, all judge by it, all act upon it as a familiar and confessed thing. All our enacted laws, all our public opinion, even all our ways of thinking and speaking in words, are founded on there being such a law within man, sanctioning good, prohibiting evil.

Now then it is time for us to ask, when man becomes, says, acts evil, *what sort of a thing* does he do? For that such is the case, is but too plain. Evil thoughts, evil words, evil acts, are but too often to be found in the course of all of us; evil men unhappily abound in every place and society. How are we to look upon such evil thoughts, words, acts, and men? Are they necessary? In plain words, is it a condition of our lives that we must enter into compact with evil, as it is that we must eat and sleep? Certainly not. This is clear from what has already been said. Every protest against evil, every resistance to evil, every victory over evil, proves that evil is not necessary to our being; that He who made us has made us *capable* of existing without evil, and all the better for existing without evil. But now let us listen to what follows. True as this is, we must always remember, that this great and blessed state of our being, the freedom from and victory over evil, is not that after which all men are striving. There are all kinds of lower forms of our being, which satisfy men, and in some cases constitute their chief good. One man seeks the gratification of his bodily appetites and lusts: another, the heaping up of wealth: a third, the gaining of power: a fourth, the rising in the esteem of those about him: another again, several, or all of these together: and so, not man's brightest aim, to be good and pure and calm and wise, but an aim very far below this, is followed by the worse part of mankind always,—by even the best of mankind sometimes.

Now, my brethren, every one of these lower and unworthy objects, if followed as an object, does necessarily bring a man into contact and compromise with evil. To be bent on gratifying lust, is of itself evil: to amass selfishly, is evil: to promote our own influence and push for precedence, is evil. Greed, intemperance, injustice to others, unkindness, overweening opinion of self, and a hundred other evil things beset every one of such courses of life; every one of such thoughts, words, actions.

Now we have advanced, I think, close to our point. When a man lives such a course, when any one of us gives way to such thoughts or words, or commits such deeds, he is disobeying that great first law of our being by which, as I shewed you, we choose the good and abhor the evil. How it is that men got the wish so to go wrong and so to disobey the law of their being, it is not my present object to enquire. But though it is not, I must simply remind you that we Christian believers know how this was; and more than this,—that our Bibles give us the only satisfactory account that ever was given of it. We know that it was by a taint at the root and spring of our race; by our first parents using that freedom in which their Creator made them, not to please Him by remaining in good, but to please themselves by entering into a compromise with evil. But I say no more, as to enlarge on this is beyond our subject to-day. Men are (there is no doubt of this) liable, every man is liable, thus to enter into compact with his worst enemy, evil, in order to serve his present lower purposes. We all do this continually.

Now whenever we do this, we SIN. "All sin," says St. John, "is transgression of law." Where there is no law, there is no sin; wherever there is a law, there he who disobeys that law commits sin. And we have seen that this inward law which teaches us to abhor evil and choose good is broken and set at nought by us all.

We do not choose the good which we know we ought to choose: we do choose the evil which we very well know we ought not to choose. The propensity to do this, the entertaining the temptation to do it, the doing it, all these are sin. Now sin is not, like evil, a mere general quality: it is committed *against a person*. And there is, properly speaking, but one Person, against whom sin is, or can be committed. There is One who is the source and fountain of all law, all right, all purity, all goodness. And this law of good and evil of which we have been speaking, this above and before all others, springs from that Holy and Just one who hath made us and to whom we are accountable. All sin is against Him: is a violation of His law, is a thwarting, by His mysterious permission, of His holy and blessed purposes with regard to man.

ALL HAVE SINNED. And in dwelling on this, the fact, that all men have inherited the disposition to sin, necessarily comes first. And this is no fiction: this is not, as the unbeliever of our day would try to persuade you, an exploded fallacy of a gone-by system; but it is sober and fearful truth. It is moreover agreeable to the analogy of all God's works in nature and in spirit: a truth, as matter of experience, undeniable by any who is aware of even the most common phænomena of our nature. And, inheriting this disposition, but with it inheriting also the great inward law of conscience warning us against evil, we have again and again followed, not the good law, but the evil propensity: in wayward childhood this has been so: in passionate youth: in calm deliberate manhood. We have not chosen evil; we have hated evil by our very nature; but we have followed evil, fallen into sin, by reason of our lusts and our passions blinding us, dragging us onward and downward, and delivering us tied and bound into the power of the enemy whom we naturally shun and detest. We have done this,—we are doing it, continually: we shall ever be doing it more or less, in our manifold weaknesses, our besetting dangers, our abounding temptations.

Now then, this being so, what follows? Can sin be safe? Can a sinner be happy? Can a sinful man be gaining the ends of his being? The full answer to this question does not belong to our subject to-day; but I cannot and ought not to conclude without slightly anticipating it.

Sin is and must be the ruin of man, body and soul, here and hereafter. The born sinner—the tainted child of a tainted stock, living under that taint, with it working and spreading in him and through him,—how shall he be safe? how shall he be happy? how shall he ever grow on to good and to a blessed eternity? Without going any further into the matter to-day, do you not see that this cannot be so? Whoever sins, goes wrong: lays up grief, shame, all that is dreadful, for himself, by thwarting the gracious ends for which God created him, viz. to love, obey, and imitate Himself, that he may become like Him, and one day see Him as He is.

No more then at present but this. Every man's work in life, sinners as we all are, is this: to find out his sins, to confess his sins to God, to struggle with

God's help against his sins, year by year and day by day to gain victories over his sins through Him who overcame sin for us; to believe in, and live in the reality of, the Atonement which His Blood has made for all and every sin. All the glorious process of that which He hath accomplished for us, will come before us as we proceed.

But now in this season of Advent, when we are to cast away the works of darkness, I must detain you some Sundays longer on our own need of Him for whose coming we are to prepare; and shall therefore, by God's help, speak to you on the next two Sundays on the manifold nature of sin, and on its guilt and consequences.

Now to Him who hath loved us and washed us from our sins in His own blood, to the Son of God, with the Father and the Holy Ghost, be honour and glory for ever. Amen.

SERMON II.

(PREACHED ON THE THIRD SUNDAY IN ADVENT, DEC. 15, 1861.)

THE DECEITFULNESS OF SIN.

HEB. iii. 13.

"The deceitfulness of sin."

WE are warned, in the passage in which these words occur, to beware lest any of us be hardened through the DECEITFULNESS OF SIN. It is to this last quality of sin, as connected with its manifold working, that I would to-day bespeak your attention.

I described it last Sunday as one of the worst symptoms of our spiritual disease, that the more a man is affected with it, the less, in many cases, does he know that he has it at all. And herein consists the *deceitfulness* of sin: not in making itself appear more important, but in making itself appear less important, than it really is. It is, as we saw, a deadly taint in our nature, ever stealing onward, requiring ever the most active check to be put upon it; never shrinking back, or declining, as a matter of course, but, on the contrary, as a matter of course always waxing, always flourishing: creeping about our pure thoughts, entangling our good resolves, binding down our holy aspirations; even until all becomes overborne by it, and confusion and helplessness and hopelessness set in, and self is exalted as supreme, and God is forgotten in the chambers of the heart, and the voice of the good Spirit becomes silent, and the darkness of the night gathers round, and the spoiler only waits without, certain of his prey. And mind I am not speaking now, I do not mean to speak to-day, of what men call great sinners, or of what are known as deadly and shameful sins: I speak of us all, I want to benefit all: I speak of the course of sin, its manifoldness, its deceitfulness, in us who, I will suppose, abstain at least from its outward and grosser manifestations: us, who are not murderers, not adulterers, not defrauders, not false swearers, but who are lovers of self, vain, envious, seekers of applause from men, careless, indolent, unwatchful, unfaithful to Christ. It is of the ordinary character of the average Christian man that I speak; in its infirmity, in its capriciousness, in its unwariness. May I be guided to speak aright, and you to judge what I say.

It will be plain to you that, in order to deal with such a subject profitably, I must not linger amidst mere general matters, but must enter into particulars, and exhibit sin in some of its various modes of attack and access to us. I must divide our life and its energies into its several departments, and shew how the manifoldness and deceitfulness of sin beset us in each one of them.

And for this purpose the most convenient division will be the most ordinary one. Our vital energy finds issue in three great ranges and regions: those of thought, of word, of deed. In each one of these there is duty, and there is fault. In each of them there is the voice of God speaking in our consciences, there is the written law of God guiding, confirming, furthering, that inward voice: in each of them there is in us the constant disposition to set conscience and to set God aside, and to become our own guides, our own masters. Let us then take each one of these in turn, and shew in each, how manifold sin is, how deceitful.

Sins of THOUGHT. How best may we place ourselves aright to consider these? It is not easy to turn inward, and be faithful witnesses to what passes within us. Nothing is so deceitful, nothing so apt to become a delusion, as the taking account of our own thoughts and feelings. Memory cannot copy faithfully the picture which has faded away, but overlays and tricks it out with fresh and unreal colours. What, for example, so utterly empty and unprofitable as religious diaries, experience-records, chronicles of past states of mind, unless indeed traced by a master-hand, and laid down with rare and self-denying faithfulness? This very fact shews, how busy sin is in our thoughts: how it is ever waking and watching, and turning even the infirmities of our memory into occasions for itself. In this very matter, how deep is its deceit—how subtle its craft! Take a more special example. Often we find in such records, often we find in ourselves, a disposition to exaggerate our own sinfulness. All is put down as bad: nothing could be worse. Slight errors are magnified into great sins: real sins blackened into unpardonable enormities. O meekness, we may be disposed to say,—O humility! But pause a moment, and enquire, Is this really so? When self is both the accuser and the accused, both the prisoner and the prosecutor;—when again the crime charged is past, and the act of charging it is present;—when all the discredit is looked upon as belonging to a former and infirm self, and all the credit as accruing to a present better self,—O how strong is the temptation to get at the comfortable inference, I was worse then, but I am better now! How the treacherous self-gratulation mingles even with humility, even with thankfulness to God! How it lurks in and pervades all such recollections,—from the glorious confessions of the great African Augustine to the flattest memoirs of the most common-place religionist of our puny time!

But we must not stay talking about the difficulty of dealing fairly with our thoughts, though this very difficulty illustrates our subject: we must enter in, and grapple with the difficulty itself. There is no question that our real thoughts *can* be got at, and their liability to sin justly measured, if we will spend time and trouble over it. And it must be remembered, that here in public, and in dealing with the matter on a large scale, we are not beset by the difficulty in its full strength: we are not dealing with our individual selves, whom we love, alas, not wisely but too well; we are dealing with our public self, so to speak; with our whole species, of which we are at least somewhat fairer, though by no means infallible judges.

And, thus dealing, we may venture to say, that the

great burden of our sins of thought will be found to consist in this, in a want of honest, conscientious adoption and following of what we know to be real and true;—in Scripture language, "an evil heart of unbelief." We are *not* unbelievers: the bare idea is dreadful to us: we hold and we cling to the glorious doctrines of our redemption: if an hour of trial came, I do not suppose we should desert them; there would be found, as there have ever been found in Christ's Church, many ready to suffer, some even to die for them. But in spite of all this, it is too often certain that while the man, with his mind and his affections, thoroughly believes, the heart is, to a sad extent, an unbeliever. I mean that in the secret inmost chamber where ideas spring into life, where resolves are formed, and plans matured, the great truths which are believed are not given their due place, nor allotted their proper share. A man thoroughly believes that there will be a judgment of all things done in the flesh. But how often, in forming his plans and resolves, does he take this into serious account? How often, when called upon to decide on a course of conduct, does any one of us say within himself, How shall I give account of this to Him who is ready to judge the quick and the dead? Are not our determinations much more often principally brought about by considerations of a very different kind from this? Our own inclination, our worldly interest, the opinion of others, all these are first consulted, and first satisfied: if, when this is done, the path chosen happens to be that of duty and God's will, we are ready enough to take credit for it, and to flatter ourselves upon it: if it turns out to

c

be another path, we set to work, I am afraid, to invent some compromise wherewith conscience may be lulled into acquiescence. O for that clearness of inward vision, which shall ever see the great noonday sun of God's presence shining upon every thought, detecting its errors and prejudices and self-leanings! O for that singleness of purpose which shall be able to labour by that light alone, disregardful of how the work will appear under the dim and artificial candle of human estimation! There is no prayer of which we have more constant and urgent need than this,—" Unite my heart to fear thy name:"—make it to be in its life-thinking and energizing, what it is in its reasoning, what it is in its praying, what it is in its confessing, what it is in its teaching of others.

Again: a man firmly and without hypocrisy believes in the great sacrifice of Christ for him. He knows he is bought with the price of the precious blood of the Son of God; that he is a baptized member of Christ, and bound to live for Him and to Him. And yet, when we come to motives, when we come to resolves within him, where does this belief appear? Are our thoughts governed, are they penetrated, are they constrained, by any such considerations? When selfish views spread before us in all their attractiveness, the fertile plains of Sodom tempting us to dwell in them, does the course of self-denial to which we are pledged instantly assert its claim—does our eye at once rise to the thorny upward path, and to Him who bore his Cross, and dropped his Blood along it? When the temper is roused by insult, when the pride is stung by contumely, when the self-opinion is buffeted by designed slight, and the tyrant fiend of revenge springs to his feet in a moment,—do our eyes see, or do they refuse to see, the Spirit of the Lord lifting His standard against him? Do we hear, or do we refuse to hear, amidst the rising gusts of passion, the still small voice "Learn of me, for I am meek and lowly of heart?"

I have purposely dwelt on this particular class of sins of thought, because they are the most subtle, the least guarded against, the most seldom held up for warning: because they poison the very springs of life itself: because they are manifold and deceitful in every one of us: because they are ever undermining the building which we are raising on the one Foundation, robbing us of our full reward, tarnishing the brightness of our future spiritual crown. O that we might each of us have grace to wake and watch against them, and apply ourselves in earnest to their removal and cure!

I now come to sins of *word*. And here I shall not speak of bad and unholy and impure words,—not of evil speaking, lying, and slandering: these are open and manifest: if we fall into these, we know it, we repent of it; but I shall speak of sins of word more beneath the surface, into which when we fall, we do not know it, of which, when we have fallen into them, we are little accustomed to repent.

And I believe such sins will mainly be found, as regards our dealings with men, in stating or not stating the very truth of our sentiments and feelings and beliefs. I am not now speaking of hypocrisy, nor of any wilful and conscious disingenuousness, but of a general want of clear and fearless truthfulness, which pervades, it seems to me, the conversation of so many even good and religious persons. The motive for this frequently is, an over-cautious fear of the consequences of what may be said, or its effect upon those to whom it is said; a sense of the duty of *taking a side*, and fancying that this cannot be done without acting the partisan, and supporting that side at all hazards, even to the peril of truth and fairness itself. And thus in religious matters difficulties are glossed over, great questions which really agitate men's minds are kept out of sight, institutions merely human are held up as perfect, or their imperfections acknowledged indeed in the general, where no harm can be done, but denied in every particular when the pinch really comes. And so our holy Religion becomes a thing upheld merely because it is right and expedient that it should be, not because of its own claims to our allegiance: and the Bible is upheld, not with an humble and intelligent examination of its real meaning and undoubted difficulties, but with a blind dogmatic spirit, finding fault with honest investigation, breaking the bruised reed of incipient doubt, quenching the smoking flax of awakened enquiry. Now human nature cannot stand this, either in a man's self, or in others to or of whom he thus speaks. In himself, the consequences are deplorable. How many men uphold a rigid formal set of sentiments which in their hearts they do not believe! How many men are thus living at variance with their own reason and conscience, divided against themselves, and therefore, whatever may seem, of necessity falling into ruin and spiritual decay! How grievous it is, how sad it has been often in our own times, to see men from whose mouths has gone forth for years the pure language of religious truth, at last making wreck of faith and practice—proved to have been but counterfeits! And this, not in all cases, but I am persuaded in very many cases, because they never dealt ingenuously and fearlessly with their own hearts and with mankind about them: they professed to be fighting in armour which they had never proved, and so the enemy was too strong for them.

"What then?" I hear some one say: "are we never to take the side of God till we can understand Him? till we can penetrate the darkness in which He shrouds himself? Are we never to confess or to strive for a doctrine of religion, till we thoroughly and clearly see our way into it and round it?" Nay, my brethren, I said not any such thing. We never can by searching find out God: we must acknowledge many doctrines, which we do not understand. All I demand is that we freely and fearlessly confess these to be weaknesses. By all means let us stand on the side of God, on the side of the Bible, on the side of the Church, which we believe to be the best exponent of God as revealed in the Bible: but let this be done humbly, ingenuously, truthfully: not fearing to confess that there are matters regarding God which are as yet dark to us, that there are things in the Bible of which we cannot give an account, that there are infirmities and imperfections even in the best human setting forth of the Church on earth. When will we learn, that the consideration of the consequences of what we say is not to be entertained, when justice and right require of us to speak and fear not? When will men come to feel, that the blessed Gospel of Christ never was and never can be the gainer by any false statement, any equivocation, any shrinking from dangerous truth or unwelcome fact? Doubtless it is misery enough to be an unbeliever, even though honest in unbelief; but a dishonest believer is worse and more miserable than an honest unbeliever. And yet how many of the former, it is to be feared, have, in the history of God's Church, stood in high and holy places, and dictated, and persecuted: and how many of the latter might have been reclaimed and persuaded, had they been dealt with more in the spirit of Christ!

If again the effect of this timid untruthful religion be bad on a man's self, much more is it hurtful and fatal on others. The world outside, seeing the questions which it is ever too ready to press on Christians evaded, or insufficiently met, forms its own conclusion, unjust indeed, but hardly to be wondered at, as to the reasons why the Gospel of Christ is upheld by us; attributes it to the love of our position, care for our emoluments, or mere habit and use, and not liking to see the old faith decay: instead of that which is the real motive even in those who thus feebly advocate it, love to God and to man, and thorough persuasion of its truth.

And now let us advance to sins of *act* and *deed:* doing what we ought not to do, leaving undone what we ought to do. And here again, being anxious to speak of the manifoldness and deceitfulness of sin, I will not deal with known sins,—plain omissions or flagrant commissions,—but with those which we seldom think of or charge ourselves with. And this being so, it is plain that our attention will be almost entirely confined to sins of omission : as it is in course of these mainly that the attention is set to sleep, and the watchful guard is relaxed, and the standard of positive duty is lowered. One of the commonest omissions in the ordinary lives of Christian men is, *the neglect of the words of the Master of all Christian men :* the disuse of taking into account, as rules of conduct, the injunctions and precepts of Christ. Our lives are mainly spent in obedience to the common conventional rules set by the opinions and practices of those about us. Thanks to God, those about us form a community regulated in outward and plain matters by Christian rules : so that men's lives have become, by the leavening influence of Christianity, a decent approximation to the tenor of the precepts of Christ. Still there are many things yet left, in which public usage or opinion says one thing, and the Lord Christ says plainly another: many as to which the world's rule lays down nothing, but our divine Master lays down very much. It is in such matters, I believe, that we Christians are continually falling into sin. We think our actions good enough, if they will bear comparison with those of the society in which we move, and of the time in which we live : forgetful that our rule has been prescribed by One who speaks not on earth but from heaven: that our standard has been set for us in words which shall not have passed away when heaven and earth are no more.

O that there were in any of us the habit of referring our questioning thoughts at once to His verdict whom we profess to serve; of guiding our actions simply, humbly, fearlessly, by His precept and His example! And in order for this, there would be no occasion to run counter in ordinary things to the habits and feelings of those about us: if we were earnest like Him, humble like Him, wise like Him, at whatever distance from His perfect example, we should recommend and adorn our unflinching course of Christian duty by quietness, by unobtrusiveness, by consideration for others, by knowledge what to say, and when, and to whom. It is not the busy protester against what other men do, it is not the man who is ever found up in arms against the usages of society, who does the good; but he who is gifted with sound judgment enough to overlook things indifferent, to join in practices which he himself would perchance not have chosen, if by so doing he may cheer, and bless, and hallow, and leaven, the society in which God has cast his lot. Here again I conceive good Christian men are often led, in our time, into sin. For O it *is* sin, to misrepresent the profession of a disciple of Christ by a morose and unsocial and forbidding aspect; it is sin, always to be found in opposition, and never in hearty concurrence, when schemes are proposed which interest and please others. If a man's religion be so completely a matter of his own, of keeping himself so usually aloof from his brethren, all we can say is that it is not Christ's religion, who pleased not himself: it is not St. Paul's religion, who became all things to all men. An unsocial, uncomplying, individualizing life may be very flattering to pride: may serve as a salve to the conscience, and make a man fancy himself very good and pure; but there can be no doubt that such a course is a life-long sin, bringing dishonour on the blessed Gospel of Christ, and hardening men's hearts against its influence.

It is time to draw to a close; and the special object which I would recommend to you[1] to-day furnishes me with an eminent example of another branch of sins of omission on the part of Christian men. There are many things which Christ has expressly charged on His Church as positive and perpetual duties. The care of His poor, the instruction of His little ones, these are of this kind; and, not least among such, the evangelization of the whole world. Words cannot be more explicit than His parting command,—"Go ye into all the world: preach the Gospel to every creature." Whatever the time, whatever the appearance of things, whatever the state of the Church or the nations, whether hope or fear, exultation or dejection be our present attitude, these words change not: this holy command binds every Christian at every time. And remember the solemn words of Holy Writ—"To him that knoweth to do good and doeth it not, to him it is sin." You know, every one of you well knows, that each of us is bound to-day

[1] The Third Sunday in Advent is our Missionary Sunday at Canterbury.

to bring to God his contribution,—great or small matters not half so much,—to this His Society, by which this Church of England is fulfilling our Lord's behest. You know this. Are you going to *do* it? Because if, having this knowledge, you pass by and refuse to contribute, it is sin—a new stain on your own souls—a new mark against you in that book which shall be opened the next time we all stand together in God's presence.

Think of this: and God give you grace to act accordingly.

But, though my time has run out, and I have said what I had to say on my subject, none of you I am sure will to-day grudge me a few words more. I little knew, when I wrote of times of national dejection, what deep occasion we should have for it before that sentence was uttered here. A prince and a great man has this day fallen in Israel. At the very time when the vessel of the state requires most careful guidance, and none can tell what dangers are before her, one of those nearest the helm has been mysteriously snatched away. When none thought it—when it seemed as if unbroken prosperity were almost the heritage of our royal family, —in one night our princely house is fatherless, our Queen a widow. I pause not to-day to draw out the solemn lessons which such an event suggests. The blow is too fresh—the effect too numbing just now. All I say is this: First, pray, loyally, fervently, constantly, for her whose great grief is now uppermost in all our thoughts: and secondly, waken more than ever at this solemn moment to the claim of our national Christian duties. Let not the astonishment of your present grief supersede your zeal for God's work to which you are called; rather let the softened heart, the stricken spirit, acknowledge God as nearer, His voice as more plainly heard: and in this and all duties to which He summons you, make you more ready to say, Lord, what wouldst thou have us to do?

SERMON III.

(PREACHED ON THE FOURTH SUNDAY IN ADVENT, DEC. 22, 1861.)

THE GUILT AND CONSEQUENCE OF SIN.

EZEK. xviii. 4.

"The soul that sinneth, it shall die."

THE guilt and consequence of sin,—these form our subject to-day. May God give us grace to consider it aright. In order to this, we must bear firmly in mind one most important fact. Sin dwells in us,—works in us, —prevails too often over us: but sin is NOT OURSELVES. Sin is no more a man's self, than the disease is the patient. "It is *not I*," says St. Paul, "but sin that dwelleth in me." And this is closely connected with what I maintained in the first of these sermons; that the evil to which we are prone by the disease of our nature is not any thing necessary or natural to us, but something both hateful and hurtful. It is not our nature, but is destructive of our nature. And yet, at the same time, the tendency to evil which leads to sin is so universal, and our nature is so penetrated by it, that to separate man from sin is for man impossible. The taint is at our root, and every branch shares in it. It is not a mere act or set of acts; but a state, a condition of spiritual disease. The new-born babe, who never committed sin, is yet sinful, and it is certain to commit sin, as soon as its faculties begin to unfold themselves. Original or birth-sin is not merely a doctrine in religion; it is a fact in man's world, acknowledged by all, whether religious or not. Let a man be providing for an unborn child in case of distribution of worldly property; he will take care to bind him by conditions and covenants which shall guard against his fraudulently helping himself to that which he is to hold for or to apportion to another. He never saw that child: he does not know but that child may be the most pure and perfect of men : but he knows it will not be safe to put temptation in his way, because he knows he will be born in sin, and liable to sin, and sure to commit sin.

Now the GUILT of sin is a very important matter: and if you will give me your attention, you will at once see that the unbeliever, who denies the guilt of sin because it is a disease tainting our whole nature, has no ground to stand upon. If God had given us no means of resisting sin: if sin were identical with all our convictions and tendencies and desires, then sin would be equally destructive of our happiness and of our nature as it is now, but there would be *no guilt* in us personally : no one could find fault with us for falling victims to that which we should be powerless to withstand. We should be objects of pity, not of blame. But how different is this now. We have conscience, ever protesting against sin : the written law of God, guiding and enlightening the conscience: and more than all that, the great Redemption which is by Christ, providing a full and sufficient escape from and cure of the fatal disease.

Now you see, wherein consists the guilt of sin: why it is that though born in sin, and prone to sin, I yet am a guilty creature if I sin. It is because sin is not myself, but my enemy: because I *know* it to be my enemy. Wherever this knowledge is present,—and it is present in some degree in every son and daughter of Adam,—there is, speaking generally, no excuse for sin: it is known to be wrong, and he who falls into it is a guilty person. And observe, that in the just government of God, this guilt varies according to the degree of light and knowledge. The poor heathen, the very savage, has some light of conscience, however dim and insufficient. The Christian has the full light of God's revelation of Himself in the face of Jesus Christ. Between the savage who lives in sin, and the Christian who lives in sin, the difference of degree of guilt is immense. It will hereafter be made manifest in the case of many a Christian, that it would have been well for him if he had lived and died a poor ignorant heathen. It shall be more tolerable in the day of judgment for the lowest and most degraded of our race, than for us, the favoured of God, if we repent not, and serve Him with our hearts.

From guilt, we are naturally led on to PUNISHMENT. If the sinner is guilty, what will happen to him? Now to any of you who have intelligently followed me, it will be plain, that I have not put this question exactly in the form in which we must first answer it. It will be evident, that the punishment of sin will not be in proportion merely to personal guilt, but to the mischief which it works on our nature. Our whole nature is diseased and perishing: and if I encourage the disease, and give it opportunity, and way, and power over me, then my punishment will be, not only just retribution for that my undoubted and inexcusable guilt,—but also the consequence, whatever that may be, of the prevalence and history of the dread disease itself. And notice, that in the Christian man this also is a direct punishment for personal guilt. He knew the cure, and he did not apply it. He chose to perish, and he perishes accordingly.

But now, you see, two questions rise before us. What is the consequence of sin, unchecked, encouraged, prevailing, pervading a man's being? This is the first: and the second is, What have we reason to think will be God's punishment for one who has allowed sin thus to conquer him? Will it be simply the consequences of the malady, or will it be something else, over and above them?

Let us apply ourselves to the former question. We said in our first sermon, that sin was, entering into evil:—thinking, saying, doing that which is bad. We have simply to enquire then, what is the effect on us of thinking, saying, doing that which is bad? Let me ask any one of you, what do you suppose you were made for? I imagine the general answer will be, or will amount to this: "Our Maker must be good and beneficent, and must have made His creatures to be happy. And if He has given us powers and faculties above His other creatures, it must be because He wills that we should aim at, and reach, a higher degree of happiness than His other creatures." This reply which I have put into your mouths, is, as far as we are concerned, undoubtedly the right one. God made us to be happy, to strive after happiness to the highest reach of our faculties and powers. Well, now let me ask again; How do you suppose that happiness is to be attained? Is it to be a happiness gained by the pampering of the body, by giving scope to the lower appetites and passions? If so, why were we endowed with reason, and conscience, and desires after higher and better things? Go a step further:—Is it a happiness to be served by the indulgence of present temper and feeling,—by the lust of wealth and of power, by serving a man's own narrow interests, and earthly purposes? If so, again, how is it that such present indulgence constantly and proverbially does not bring with it happiness, does not bring satisfaction; but the man who gives way to it is ever casting it aside as worthless, ever seeking something beyond it; and the man who goes on for years giving way to it becomes at last a miserable disappointed creature, a burden to himself and all around him? Surely this cannot be the way to happiness. And if not, what is? Is it not this,—to flee from evil and seek good? Is not the man who does this as a principle, as a habit, is not this man every where and at all times the happy man? Has he not a happiness which the world with its varying circumstances cannot touch: which outward and seeming misery cannot deprive him of: which survives in the midst of desolation, of persecution, of sickness : which is not diminished but increased by that which to other men is the height of misery, the approach of death itself? And if this be so, if to depart from evil, if to fight with and overcome sin, be the way, and the only way, to real happiness, what do you suppose is the consequence of evil cherished, sin practised and followed, sin overcoming the man and leading the man captive, and triumphing over him? What can it be, but misery and ruin?

Look at its course; watch its progress. Let us try to enliven a dull but necessary argument by setting an example before you. Some matter is proposed to a man which he knows to be wrong—knows to be sinful. But it is very tempting; it will serve his interests; it will add to his means; it will increase his comforts; it will help his family after him. He stands at the parting of the two ways : duty, with toil and privation, with humble means for many a year; sin, with ease and competence, with worldly plenty and worldly consideration. One thought, nay not a thought, an intuition, a flash of irresistible light, tells him in a moment which path he ought to choose. But he hesitates, he parleys with the enemy, he looks twice and thrice, and he makes up his mind: he grasps the present advantage: he casts away the protest of conscience, and the dread verdict of the certain future, and he adopts the sinful course.

Now the question for us is, what has this man done? what has happened to him? First, he certainly is not a better man; he is, in our common language, a worse

D

man than he was before. And what meaning is there in these words, a WORSE MAN? O what is there not, that is miserable, that is deadly to all health, that is fatal to all happiness? His sin has put him further from good: he has descended a step from God and from happiness. And what is the consequence, I ask again? What further is in store for him? Can he rest where he is? Having made this compromise with evil, can he say "Just thus much I find necessary to my comfort, to my advantage, and here I will stop? I cannot have the full field of goodness for my course—I have barred myself out of part of it, but within the limits which remain I will be a good man?" Ah, my brethren, this may not be. Many and many a sinner tries it; jealously fencing round his reputation, taking credit for all that he does or says that looks like good, keenly resenting any charge on his fair name. But alas, he who lets in evil into his practice, is letting in a wild ocean to which no man may say "Hitherto and no further." He is a *worse man*. Not only part of his good is gone, but all his good is marred, is poisoned; his heart is no longer simple, it is divided; he is become a hypocrite, an actor of a part before men; he has a dark corner which he does not want the world to see into,—a locked closet at the door of which he keeps watch with fear and trembling, lest any discover its contents. And if this before men, O what before God? Ah, my brethren, when and as long as a man makes an agreement with evil, fosters evil, lives by evil, there is no more God for him; prayer, praise, the sacraments, God's word, God's house, God's ministers, God's people, these have all become for him nauseous things, unwelcome reminders whence he has fallen: for appearance sake he goes to church, he even presents himself, sad to say, at the Table of the Lord,—because if he did not, neighbours would question, friends would drop off, customers would forsake him; but he hates all such things; and he hesitates not, when he thinks himself safe, and worldly interests not at stake, to unburden his pent-up thoughts by shewing his hatred. The fact is, he has chosen that God shall be his enemy; and he cannot bear to face the terrible fact: and so he wants to forget Him, and not to have the thought of Him ever making him miserable.

And from this to the life of the scorner and blasphemer there is but a very short step, and one which few can resist taking. Almost all such characters among us, almost all those who are bold against God, questioning His word, despising His ordinances, are not men whose unbelief is their misfortune, an unhappy turn of mind, or a conscientious form of doubt: they are ever, it is true, ready enough to take refuge under this: but almost all of them are men whose unbelief has become a miserable necessity to them by reason of their choosing to live in and to live by sin: so that a professed unbeliever of correct life is a very rarity in nature. But whether in profession or not, in heart the sinner is an unbeliever and a hater of God.

And then further; how does this state proceed, supposing it unrepented of? Life is full of new temptations, ever arising: and in such a life, the enemy who has gained one victory is not likely to relax his assaults: he who consents to sin, draws on him sin, as Holy

D 2

Scripture has it, with a cart-rope: conscience, once overborne and silenced, speaks fainter next time, fainter still the time after, soon scarce audibly, after a while not at all. And so the sinner becomes hardened in his sins, more and more lost to true inward shame, less and less able to disentangle his feet from the net thrown round him: to conceal one sin, others have become necessary, and more again to varnish over those, until to stir without sinning has become well nigh impossible: he has to ask leave of evil, to let him speak or act at all. So life speeds on, and life's end stands before him, and the new and final state has to be entered. God, whom he has so long striven not to know, is unsought by repentance. He goes out of the world as he lived in the world; and what is his state then?

Remember we are confining ourselves at present to the mere *consequences* of his sinful life, irrespective of any actual infliction of divine wrath. What is his state, do we ask? what can it be, but what it was here, only with every deceit laid open, and every door of hope shut? God he hated and fled from; and the joy of that state is the shining of God's countenance: what has he to do with that? Good he deliberately refused: the delight of the blessed is to be purely good, to do nought but good, to bask in the beams of His light who is Good itself: what has he to do with this, or with them? What can the inward state of such a soul be but an enduring and living death?

Did we ever reflect on the terrible meaning of those words, ETERNAL DEATH? What is more dreadful to us here, than the process, the act, of bodily death? The great relief from our thoughts of it is, that it is short: it is the anguish of an hour, or of a few hours; or if it is prolonged to a day, or more than that, the announcement is terrible; "two days dying"—we shrink from the very mention of so distressing a fate. And why? Why, but because it is a time of sharp agony and fierce contention of hostile powers in man's expiring frame: life struggling to continue, decay holding its own, and increasing its domain; the soul in dire apprehension, or at least in unknown conflict? And if this be so, if the prolongation of bodily death even for a short time be dreadful, what must be the eternal death of the soul—all its marvellous powers, no longer dulled by the world and the flesh, at wild variance with one another; self-accusation and remorse for ever inwardly working, conscience no longer to be silenced, but speaking too late,—all the elements which should have contributed to happiness made, by the poisoning power of sin, ingredients in ineffable misery? And there is no reason to think that state on the other side to be a passing one, as this is, or to be a preparation for another; every thing tells us that it is final, prefaced and determined by this present condition of trial. Sin here, earns death there; not annihilation, not a change into some further state, but the never-ending break up, and confusion, and unspeakable terror, and dismay, and dejection, and despair, of the guilty and corrupted soul.

We have however yet another question to ask and answer. Such are the consequences of sin in a man: so destructive, so irreparable, so final. But is this all? Are these natural consequences of sin the whole punishment which it will bring? If it consisted merely in acts done against our own happiness, this might be so: but recollect a moment what sin is. We explained it, after the Apostle St. John, as being *transgression of God's law*. Now can we suppose that a just and almighty Lawgiver would make laws for His creatures which He knows to be for their welfare, promulgate them with all the sublime manifestations of His majesty, as of old on Sinai,—or with those of His infinite love, as by the mouth of Him who spake as never man spake,—can we suppose that He would do this, and then leave mankind, if they broke His laws, simply with the risk of the consequences upon them, as if those laws had never been thus made known? Is no penalty due to that God whom all sinners offend? Nor are we left to answer this question by our own speculations. God has again and again declared, that He will punish the sinner: that there are special punishments prepared for all who live and die in sin: punishments to which all the consequences of the sin itself, bad as they are, are as nothing in proportion. Holy Scripture exhausts the most terrible images in language and thought to make this clear to us.

But first, before them all, the plain words of our text demand our consideration, as announcing a punishment for sin, which is to be coextensive with its guilt: viz. that of DEATH. There can be no doubt that bodily death in its present form as existing in our race, is the punishment of our sin,—the consequence of our sinful state. Whether we have any right to carry this further, and to say that death would not have come into the world at all but for man's sin, is very doubtful: Scripture gives no authority for such an idea, and the appearances presented by nature are against it. But as now inflicted on all mankind, we are expressly told that death is the punishment of sin. There can indeed be little doubt that man, as he came from the hands of his Creator, was *liable* to death. This the Apostle Paul clearly shews us, when he declares that the first man was " of the earth, earthy:" this argument, and the propriety of the words " Dust thou art and unto dust thou shalt return," apply just as much to man before his sin as after it. But from a hint given in the third chapter of Genesis, it would appear, that had man remained pure and upright in Eden, the mysterious use of the tree of life would have wrought in him immortality and raised his body out of the power of decay. From this use however he was specially excluded on account of his sin. "Lest he put forth his hand and take of the tree of life and eat, and live for ever," a guard was placed which barred his access to that tree. So that death in us, with all its preceding evils, disease, weakness, pain, terror, and all its succeeding miseries, mourning, lamentation and woe, is the special punishment, by God's own declaration, of our sin. We are sinful: therefore we die. And from this portion of sin's punishment, no son or daughter of Adam is exempt. So entirely and of course is the whole of our nature subjected to it, that He who took that nature on him free from sinfulness either transmitted or personal, yet took it with this penalty attached to it, and became subject to all the approaches of death, and finally to death itself. It will come before us further on in our course to shew, how He by His death took the curse out of bodily death, and made it to us as nothing to them that believe in Him: it may be enough now to mention the blessed fact, and that by way of contrast: that we may be better able to declare that on them who live and die in sin, on the unbelievers in Christ, and the unworthy members of Christ, Death still retains all his hold and inflicts all his terrors. To them, death is not only the dissolution of the body, but the eternal misery of the soul: the state of the abiding wrath of God, from which there is for them no escape.

Thus much, my brethren, are we bound to believe, thus much to impress upon you, as to the consequence and punishment of sin. And all this is the *deserved* lot of every one among us; though by God's infinite mercy in Christ, which we have yet to unfold, it will be the actual lot only of those who refuse His offers of grace, and prefer the service of sin to His service. The progress of that wonderful Redemption which He has wrought out, will open before us in that which we have to say on the morning of the approaching great Christmas Festival.

Meantime let us earnestly lay to heart the deadly nature, and the grievous peril, of sin. Our Collect to-day teaches us to confess that "through our sins and wickedness we are sorely let and hindered in running the race that is set before us." May we not only say this to-day and during the week, but may we every one of us deeply feel it: by searching and knowing our own peculiar faults and infirmities, by watching and praying against them, by ever living closer to Him whose bountiful grace and mercy can alone help and deliver us.

SERMON IV.

(PREACHED ON CHRISTMAS DAY, 1861.)

GOD'S REMEDY FOR SIN.

Rom. iii. 3.

"What the law could not do, in that it was weak through the flesh, God sending His own Son in the likeness of sinful flesh, and for sin, condemned sin in the flesh."

WE have advanced thus far in our statement of Christian doctrine, or rather of the introduction and preliminaries to Christian doctrine. We have laid down the sinfulness of our whole nature: the manifoldness and deceitfulness of sin: the guilt and eternal consequences of sin. So far we have spoken of the disease: to-day we deal with the remedy.

Our text will furnish us in this matter with safe and sufficient guidance. It tells us of a way in which sin could not be cured: and of a way in which God has brought about its condemnation and cure.

Now remember how we have been treating sin throughout: as a taint, a disease in our nature, destructive to it, but pervading the whole of it, so that it is all sinful, all guilty, all perishing: so that it has absolutely no power to renew itself unto good or to cast out evil from itself. The witness of conscience it has: the help of God promised, and vouchsafed, we believe, even in ignorance and degradation: but this is not of itself: this depends entirely upon and flows from that Redemption of which we are to speak to-day.

Behold then man, guilty, helpless, lost. And what do we now hear of? How first does God manifest himself to him? We now first hear of a *law* being revealed to him. But it might be said, of what use can a law be to one who has no power to obey it? The answer is very simple: *to teach him that he has no power to obey it.* This was the use of the law given on Sinai. We have already seen, that one of the most fatal symptoms of the disease of sin is, a man's unconsciousness of its presence. The sinner goes on imagining all is well; saying peace, when there is no peace. And in this ignorance he would live and die, were there not something to bring out and detect sin within him. This office the Law performed: by the Law is the knowledge of sin. But the Law had, and could have, no power whatever to overcome sin, nor to enable any man to contend with sin; any more than a command to rise up and walk could have on the man laid helpless on a bed of sickness. And this is what is meant in our text, when it is said, that the law was weak through the flesh. Its only organ of acting was, the weak, powerless, helpless flesh of man: that flesh which is infected and penetrated by the taint of sin. And let us stop as we pass by, to remark, that this same must be the case with all human systems of morality, all rules for good conduct, all discipline and codes of law: they have not, and cannot have, any power whatever to renew human nature, or to help it to overcome sin. Sin reigns in spite of them: nay sin has reigned most, and most fatally, where they have been best known, and most deeply studied, and most implicitly trusted to. All of them are just what their far greater example, God's revealed law, was; and that is, merely a means whereby sin might be brought to light and known: means whereby the sinner might be rendered inexcusable, the proud heart might be crushed down, the dry and tearless eye might be filled with tears of repentance, and the sinner, hardened and careless before, driven to fly to God for mercy and pardon.

But here comes in a question which requires an answer, and to answer which will materially further our enquiry. "You tell us," it may be said to me, "that the law on Sinai, that every moral law, whether in the conscience, or in man's writings and declarations, was given just to prove man guilty, and to drive him for mercy to God. But you know, and we know, and this Christmas Day reminds us, that it was not till four thousand years after man's fall, that God's grace and mercy was revealed to mankind by the Redemption which is in Christ. Do you mean to tell us, that the great God of compassion and goodness, who alone knew the way in which this dread disease of sin could be healed, allowed men to go on in their disease all this time without that cure, contenting Himself with making provision that they might know their guilt, and, knowing it, perish in it?" No, my brethren, nothing of the kind was the case. This Redemption by Christ, which first began its real course on the stage of this world about four thousand years after the creation, was no mere worldly course of events then first brought about,—no happy discovery then first made: it had been fixed in the divine counsels, and its glorious effects anticipated in God's infinite loving-kindness, before the world began, before man's sin was ever committed. Nay, all creation, the whole of this visible universe, is but a part, but a trifling portion, of this great divine scheme of Redemption. Every thing ever created, every thing that ever happened or shall happen, all these are simply elements in, contributions to, the glorious issue of the mediatorship of our Blessed Lord. All things are by Him and for Him: by him the universe holds together. And accordingly, we believe that there never was a time, in the history of man's sin and of God's dealing with it, when there was not opened to man a way of pardon and peace with God, through a Redeemer to come, or present, or having come. The antediluvian church, the Patriarchal church, the Jewish church,—these were in the direct track of that ray of light from above, which was to shine ever more and more unto the perfect day. By sacrifices, by types, by prophecies, the great Redeemer to come was made known to them as God saw fit for them, as they could bear and profit by the knowledge: at no time was access to God, and reconcilement, and pardon, denied to the sinner. Before the flood, Enoch walked with God, Noah was perfect in his generations, and preached righteousness: before the law, Abraham's faith was counted to him for righteousness,

Jacob wrestled with God and prevailed, and, dying, waited for His salvation: before the Gospel, Joshua determined that as for him and his household they would serve the Lord: David, amidst grievous weakness and sin, sought pardon and found it, and was the man after God's own heart: Hezekiah walked in all the ways of the Lord, turning not to the right nor to the left: Simeon waited, in the light of the promise of the Holy Ghost, for the consolation of Israel. And if we turn to the other nations of the earth, though the picture of man's delinquency is dark and gloomy enough, though our knowledge of their state and opportunities is but scanty and surrounded by difficulties, yet the argument of the Apostle in the first chapter of the Epistle to the Romans, and other expressions here and there dropped in Holy Scripture, enable us safely to affirm, that God left not himself without witness even amongst them: and that no where and at no time has it been true, that man has been abandoned by God to live and die in his sins.

This reply has prepared the way for entering on the further portion of my text, which indeed forms our proper subject to-day. The Law,—any law,—could not save man from sin. But God has done what the law could not do. He has sent One into the world, whose express object, as testified by the very Name given him, is, to save his people from their sins. He sent One into the world:—and who was this? That it was no mere son of man, must be evident at first sight: any and every such person would be born with the taint of sin on him, powerless to save himself, to say nothing of others. Every such person would be a mere unit in manhood, bounded by the limits of his own responsibilities, and unable to transfer any thing or pass it on to another: so that even suppose he could save himself, that would be all. The same objection would apply to any created being whatever: and this besides, that the combining our nature with any other nature, however exalted and angelic, would not do for us that which was required to be done: no angelic being has, or can have, righteousness of his own: every such one stands by divine grace imparted, may fall by grace rejected. No such Saviour could suffice for us, or could save us from our sins. Then what did God? The language of our text is very important and explicit on this point: "HE SENT HIS OWN SON." There is here a peculiar and intended emphasis on the words HIS OWN. *Angels* are sons of God: *we* are said to be sons of God: but neither angels nor men are God's *own* sons; for that imports, of His very nature and essence, very God begotten of very God,—eternal as Himself,—equal to Himself. There is but One, there never was but One, of whom this term can be used. That One was in the beginning: before creation existed: in union with God, and himself God.

But the particular respecting Him with which we are now more immediately concerned is, that God SENT HIM INTO THE WORLD. The question, *when?* is readily answered: as on this day. The event was one which happened, and was recorded, like any other in the history of our earth. In Bethlehem, a town of Judæa, a place which may even now be visited and seen, a child was born, whom we and all Christians believe to have been, and to be now, this Son of God,—God's own Son,—the Saviour of mankind. Important as the fact is, it requires little dwelling upon by me: because it is so plain, so well understood, so universally known. But the question, HOW He was sent into the world, is one which does require dwelling upon: because on the rightly answering it depends our soundness in the Christian faith;—depends the fulness of our joy in believing, depends the firmness of our trust, and the acceptableness of our obedience, and the progress of our sanctification, and the measure of our heavenly glory. According as a man does or does not apprehend rightly the Christian doctrine of our Blessed Lord's Incarnation, depends it, whether his belief will yield him full consolation in his daily want of pardon and grace, in his daily struggles with sin, in the solemn hour of death, and in the decisive day of judgment. So let us endeavour earnestly to lay hold on the truth revealed to us in this all-important matter.

God sent His own Son into our world: HOW? Our text tells us one most essential particular. It was IN THE LIKENESS OF SINFUL FLESH: of THE FLESH OF SIN. The form in which He appeared in this world was this form of ours. He was MADE MAN. That flesh of ours, which had become tainted with sin, prone to sin, sure to commit sin,—did He take that on Him? Now observe the words of our text, and remember well what has been before said in these sermons. Remember how earnest we have been to impress upon you, that sin is NOT OURSELVES: is not our nature, but is something fatal and hostile to our nature. The Son of God took on Him OUR NATURE; became VERY MAN. He therefore took on Him our FLESH; for this tabernacle of flesh and blood is necessary to the nature of man, and none is full and very man, but those who bear it about with them. But sin is not man: sin is not necessary to our nature: sin is destructive of our nature: sin is the very negative of our nature. And for this reason, and by a reason also inherent in Himself, on account of His absolute and perfect holiness and purity, the Son of God did not, when he took our nature, take sin with it: did not, when he entered into our flesh, enter into sinful flesh. His flesh was our very flesh: it had the same attributes, the same necessities, the same pains, the same liability to death, even as had Adam before his sin: but SIN it HAD NOT. He looked like sinful men: was of the same shape and form: mingled in their crowds, conversed with them, felt for them, wept when they wept, suffered as they suffer, died even as they die: but He was not sinful man, nor was His flesh sinful flesh. In Him was NO SIN.

But our text tells us, that besides sending Him in the likeness of sinful flesh, of that flesh which had become pervaded by sin, God sent Him into the world FOR SIN. Sin was the reason why He came; the errand on which he was sent had regard to sin: "He was sent," says St. John, "to take away our sins:" "He himself," said the Prophet Isaiah, "bore our sins:" "He who knew no sin," says St. Paul, "became sin for us."

Now this taking away our sins He accomplished by two great things which He did: by His life, and by

E

His death. The Apostle Paul puts this very plainly and clearly before us: "If," he says, "when we were enemies, we were reconciled to God by the Death of His Son, much more being reconciled we shall be saved through His Life." The whole process of this wonderful matter—how His Death reconciled us, how His Life saves us, will come before us, please God, hereafter: to-day we are concerned with the first step, leading on to both: His Incarnation—His being born into our world.

What then do we see in the event of this day; in that event which fills every Christian heart with joy, in spite of adverse circumstances,—in spite of national mourning? We see this eternal and holy Son of God, becoming man. Let us take care that we get a right apprehension of this. That clear and most valuable confession of our faith which we have used this morning, will guide us aright. "The right faith is that we believe and confess, that our Lord Jesus Christ, the Son of God, is God and man: God, of the substance of the Father, begotten before the worlds: and man, of the substance of His mother, born in the world: perfect God and perfect man: of a reasonable soul and human flesh subsisting: equal to the Father, as touching His Godhead: and inferior to the Father, as touching His manhood. Who although he be God and Man: yet He is not two, but one Christ (i. e. not two persons, not two Christs, but veritably and only one Person and one Christ): one, not by conversion of the Godhead into flesh: but by taking of the Manhood into God"—that is, when he united the Godhead and the Manhood in

Himself, becoming God and man and still remaining one Person, He did it, not by sinking, as it were, the Son of God into the Son of Man, becoming a human Person and ceasing to be a divine Person: but by the very opposite: by continuing to be the divine Person which He was from all eternity, and into that divine Personality taking the nature of Man. And then the Creed in its next verse further explains the same by saying, "One altogether: not by confusion of substance"—not by mingling together in a confused manner that which constituted the Godhead and that which constituted the Manhood: "but," it goes on, "by unity of Person:" by the divine Son of God entering, with all His Divinity entire, into our nature: taking it on Him, as St. Augustine excellently says, "from the very highest boundary of the rational soul down to the very lowest boundary of the animal body."

Now, my dear brethren, let not these considerations seem to you dry refinements of technical theology. They are, I assure you, far otherwise. They are statements of great doctrines, on which rest the very foundations of our Christian life: and I could not make to you this year what I am very anxious to make, a full and clear statement of the doctrines which form the faith of the Church of Christ, if I did not thus try to lay them out and explain them.

It is only left for us now to shew, how thus the foundation is laid for the Redemption of our race and its restoration to righteousness. The Son of God has become Man: our nature is united to the Godhead. A new and righteous seed is implanted in it: a second and perfect Head is granted. The first Adam was tried and fell: but this new Adam shall be tried and shall gloriously conquer. The first Adam, being created liable to Death, lost by sin the means of escaping death, and bound it as a lasting curse on himself and his posterity: the second Adam, also born liable to death, was pleased to become obedient even unto death for our sakes; thus condemning sin, the cause of death, in our flesh. The first Adam brought the penalty of his sin on us, the Head on the members: the second Adam suffered the penalty of our sin for us, the Head for the members. Whosoever believeth in Him shall not perish, but shall have everlasting life : for to believe on Him is to be united to Him, and to do as He has done, and to go where He is: and He did not perish, but rose up out of death, and was glorified, and when He had by Himself purged our sins, sat down at the right hand of God.

It is His Birth into our world which we celebrate to-day. It is the day which the church has set apart as the Birthday of Christ. It is for us a day of joy, as it ought to be. Shall we not rejoice, that our deadly wound is healed—that there is pardon and peace provided for the guilty sons of men? And it need not be surprising to any, that this our joy is not confined to devotional exercises of prayer and praise, but spreads itself over our social life, and is, even by faithful Christian men, celebrated outwardly and visibly, in mirth and gladness peculiar to the season. To forbid such manifestations, would be surely to forget that He who took our whole nature upon Him, came to bless it not in one part only, but altogether : came to make our desert rejoice and blossom as the rose : and to hallow even those bodily recreations and enjoyments which sin has polluted and marred. To keep Christmas by excess and licentiousness, is to profane it, and to insult Him whose birth we profess to honour : to shew ourselves to have no part nor lot in Him who was manifested that He might destroy the works of the devil. But to keep it in peace and good-will and hearty thankfulness, gathering our families about us, and making what cheer we may, to keep an English Christmas, open-hearted and open-hearthed, this is not to dishonour Him, but to do as He would have us, who rose as our day-star, that we might walk in His light; who left us His words and triumphed for us, that our joy might be full : at whose birth angels from heaven sung peace on earth among men of good-will.

With such joy as this no deep religious feeling need be inconsistent, no time of prayer need be incongruous, no note of praise discordant : with such joy as this not even times of national grief need interfere. For is it not this day's birth which has taken the sting from death ? is there not to-day, even for the bereaved and weeping, the joyous cry, "Unto us a child is born, unto us a son is given?" is not this the day above all others which calls back again, and places by our sides those who have gone before us ? which fills up the gaps in families, and brings round us our long-parted friends? the day which carries our thoughts onward to that great second birth, when He who sitteth on the Throne shall make all things new ?

SERMON V.

(PREACHED ON SUNDAY, JAN. 5, 1862.)

THE RIGHTEOUSNESS OF ONE MAN.

Rom. v. 18, 19.

"As by the offence of one, judgment came upon all men to condemnation: even so by the righteousness of one the free gift came upon all men unto justification of life. For as by one man's disobedience many were made sinners, so by the obedience of one shall many be made righteous."

Two things are to be noticed in this text, before we proceed to consider the subject of it. First you will observe that in our bibles the words "judgment came" and "the free gift came" are in italics, that is, are put in by the translators to fill up the sense, but do not form any part of the sacred Word. The verse more simply stands, "As through one trespass, the issue (or effect) was unto all men to condemnation, even so through one righteous act the issue (or effect) was unto all men unto justification of life." And secondly, that the "*many*" spoken of in the latter portion of it are clearly the same as the "all men" in the former, the word being used only by way of contrast with the word "*one*," and not as meaning a different set of persons from that spoken of before.

We may now ask, what it is that the text tells us. Here we have two things set over against one another; trespass, righteous act: one man's disobedience, one man's obedience: all men made sinners, all men made righteous: an effect upon all unto condemnation, an effect upon all unto justification of life.

Now that which we have to treat to-day, CHRIST'S OBEDIENCE, AND ITS EFFECTS, is a very important subject: important to our soundness in the faith, and to our answering the unbeliever, and to our own purity and our own comfort in believing. May God guide us to consider it aright.

We address God in our Collect as having made His blessed Son to be circumcised and obedient to the law for man. We take that undergoing of the ordinance of circumcision as an example, as the first and chief example, of our Lord's becoming obedient to the law. And rightly: for though it was not originally of the law, as we shall see further on, yet it was the law's first command when a man came into the world; and without obeying it, the whole life would have been an act of disobedience to the law. He entered on his course of obedience to the law by this act. So that we need not to-day fix our thoughts on that ordinance any further than as it brought the Lord into the state of being under the law and obedient to the law.

But first, WHAT law? Not, the universal moral law of conscience: this He had as Man, had in its highest and purest form as Man without sin: in unclouded certainty, in undeviating equity, in uninterrupted action. When He was made man, He was rendered subject to this law, and needed no outward rite to introduce him into its dominion and obedience. Again then, what law? The answer is plain. A certain code of laws given on Mount Sinai to the children of Israel. But why should the Son of God humiliate himself for us in this peculiar manner, so as to become subject to that law and not to any other? In order to answer this, remember to whom and for what purpose, that law was given. It was given to a nation chosen out from among the other nations of the earth by God, that they might be a people of his own—the selected vehicle of his revelation of Himself to mankind. And the purpose of its being given was, we are expressly told, to bring about the knowledge of sin; to detect, as we heard in a previous sermon of this course, and make men aware of, their guiltiness and helplessness in God's sight. Mind,—and this is a most essential point for us to-day, as you will presently see,—this law was not given to bring any man to salvation: as I then tried to make plain to you, no law could do this: much less could this one, which was but an imperfect manifestation of God's holy will,—holy, just, and true as far as it went, but going only a little way: not helping man's weakness, not revealing God's law, not shedding abroad God's Spirit.

Now all this which I am saying is not meant by way of going over old ground again, to prove that by the works of the law shall no flesh be saved in God's sight: this we know: but it is in order that we may the better and the more clearly see, what it was that our Saviour did, when He became obedient to, when He fulfilled that law for man. Now look at it in this way. This law was not, could not be, for salvation to any man. Did then, could then, our Blessed Lord work out salvation for us by keeping this law? Most clearly not. We sometimes hear it said, that His perfect righteousness was found in his fulfilment of this law of Moses, and that His righteousness, as thus formed and wrought out, is imputed unto us. But I cannot find such a doctrine either in Scripture or in the belief of God's church. There is a doctrine which sounds something like it, and might be mistaken for it, and on which I shall have a good deal to say by and by: but which is not, and is very far from being, the same.

But let us for a moment imagine that the matter were so: that Christ's fulfilling of all the Mosaic law in all its requirements constituted His perfect righteousness before God, and is made ours by being imputed to us. Well—what follows? Why, two most unsatisfactory results. First, the righteousness thus obtained is *formally* not of the kind we want. We, all mankind, we Gentiles, were never bound under the law of Moses: Gentiles were never invited to put themselves under it, nay they were expressly excluded from its obligations and its benefits. So that, according to this view, Christ did for us what we were never bound to do for ourselves: and more: Christ justified Jews only. And secondly, this righteousness is not, *essentially* and in itself, of the kind we want. We want something far above and beyond the ordinances and provisions of the law of Moses. That law crept in, was introduced by the side, as the Apostle says in the verses following my text, for a lower and a special purpose, to persuade of their guilt that people to whom the Redeemer was to be sent, and by its types to keep their minds fixed on Him and His future work: but we want what it could never give, even had a man obeyed it to the utmost; transformation into God's image; new creation in the power of purity and love; the inspiration and indwelling of God's Holy Spirit. The righteousness in which our Redeemer must be perfect, and which by his Death and Resurrection and circumcision and gift of his Spirit He must make ours, is something infinitely above and more glorious and heavenly than this law of carnal ordinances, this law given by Moses. It was not by fulfilling the law of Moses that our Blessed Lord became our righteousness. He did fulfil it indeed: not one jot or tittle of it was neglected or passed uncared for, because every part of it was given by divine command, and by the mediation of angels, and men appointed by God: He did fulfil it: and He fulfilled it for man. But His fulfilling it was not our righteousness.

What was it then? How does Holy Scripture ever speak of it? Why simply thus; as a taking out of the way—cancelling, annulling, of that law. He fulfilled it, and made an end of it. He was the end of the law with a view to righteousness. It has lost its power as regards us who are in Him. And it did thus lose its power, the day that our Blessed Lord was fastened to his Cross; He blotted out the handwriting of ordinances that was against us, and took it out of the way, nailing it to his Cross. This marvellous completion of the work does not form our subject to-day: it will come before us, God willing, hereafter; but the great preparation for that completion does come before us to-day and thus early in our course. And we shall be led to speak of it in several of its forms and manifestations; among which one is, this keeping of the limited, special, Mosaic law of ordinances and precepts. Let us then now look at this observance a little more closely. What was it, in itself? and what was it, for us? In what consisted its necessity, its fitness, its usefulness for mankind?

What was it IN ITSELF? It was careful, precise, undeviating, complete. From his eight days old circumcision to the Passover the night before his Sacrifice, our Lord made a point of not falling short in any thing, but walked in all the commandments and ordinances of his Father blameless. Then, it was necessary for us. In the course of God's arrangements for the salvation of man, the Redeemer could not and must not be born a Gentile. The Jews were the people set in the bright line of the revelation of God to man. To them belonged the law: this is much to our purpose: but, which is much more to our purpose, to them belonged the promises and the covenant of faith with Abraham, in fulfilment of which promises, and in the discharge and line of which covenant, this very Redeemer was to come. The terms and matter of these promises and covenant absolutely required that our Lord should be a Jew. And what was a Jew? One born under the law of Moses. As a Jew, condescending to take our nature in that particular form and under those special circumstances, our Lord became personally bound to the observance of this law. Had He not observed it, He would not have been the spotless One in all the will of God: He would not have Himself stood accepted with our nature perfect and acquitted in the sight of the Father: and we should not have been accepted in Him.

So that thus He kept the law for man: not that man might get righteousness by that kept law, which righteousness it could not give, whether Christ kept it, or any one else kept it: but that He who was to be the righteous Head of our nature, might fulfil all righteousness. And so, when He came to be baptized by John His forerunner and His inferior, and John was preventing him, He replied, Suffer it to be so now; for thus it becometh us to fulfil all righteousness.

And I entreat you, in fixing in your minds the verities of the Christian faith, to remember this clearly and well; that it was not on our Blessed Lord's fulfilment of the law that our justification in God's sight by His righteousness depends, as some would try to persuade you. This is only in one, and that a partial sense, true: that law indeed *lay in the course of* His own personal work: in the course of working out that perfect Righteousness which when complete in Him is reckoned for ours, and wrought in us by the Holy Ghost.

Now to-day's subject, the Circumcision, will carry us a step further yet in the direction of the great doctrine given out in our text. The ordinance of circumcision, as stated just now, was not first given when the law was given. It was not of Moses, but of the fathers, declares our Lord Himself. And St. Paul teaches us, in a passage read for the Epistle to-day, that Abraham received it as a seal of the righteousness of the faith which he had being yet uncircumcised. So that our Lord not only obeyed the law for us, and entered on that His obedience, in this the first ordinance of the law, but by it He also entered into and complied with the terms of that covenant of faith which God made with Abraham centuries before the law was given. Now this covenant was of a far higher order than the law: for remember how St. Paul compares the two in the third chapter of the Epistle to the Galatians, and proves the promise and the covenant greater than the law. It is of that promise that we are the inheritors, and by that covenant that we look for God's heavenly kingdom, and not by the law at all. And now just consider what that covenant is, and what were its promises. It was universal—" In thy seed shall all nations of the earth be blessed:" *faith* was its very entrance and condition—" Abraham believed God:" justification was its firstfruit: " it was counted to him for righteousness:" sanctification and renewal in holiness were its conditions also—" God said to Abraham, I am Almighty God—walk thou before me and be thou perfect." And into this covenant and condition did our Blessed Lord enter for us by this ordinance, and all his life through He continued to fulfil it: He walked by faith in his heavenly Father: He walked before Him and was perfect: not in the law only, with which we have no immediate concern: but in God's higher and better covenant of faith, which is our covenant and condition also.

But there is more than this yet behind: nor have we yet reached the wide stretch and universality of the assertion in our text. The law of Moses, which our Blessed Lord fulfilled, was, so to speak, a narrow and prescribed path or groove of obedience: and even the covenant made with Abraham was in a special line of descent and with limited ordinances of obedience, however much in character, and duration, and ultimate extent, superior to the law. But the obedience of the One Man must reach beyond either of these: it must be as wide in its extent and effect as the disobedience of the one man had been in former times which had brought death on all our race. By means of that, death spread through unto all men, for that all were sinners. There was, as our text says, a consequence resulting to all men from that one offence, Adam's disobedience. And so is there, as it also says, a consequence resulting to all men from that righteous act, Christ's obedience. What, even to those who are not in the covenant of faith, not in the line of Christian ordinances, not in the fold of Christ's church? Yes, my brethren, even to them: or else God's word in our text cannot be true. As all men are partakers of the detriment occasioned by Adam's sin, so all men are partakers of the benefit occasioned by Christ's righteousness.

First WHY? and secondly, How? And to the first I answer, Because Christ is the righteous Head of our whole race: because His obedience was not limited to the law, nor to the covenant with Abraham, but was perfect, entire, universal: because that obedience of His was carried infinitely further than any code of precepts could order, than any conditions of a covenant could prescribe. What does St. Paul say? "Being found in fashion as a man, He humbled himself and became obedient even as far as unto death." OBEDIENT, EVEN UP TO DEATH. Why this is no mere obeying of law. No law ever ordered a man to die, as one of its duties. We shall say more of this another time; but you see even now how infinitely the bounds of the Lord's obedience for us transcend those of law and covenant. He came TO DO GOD'S WILL: not His revealed will merely, but His entire and perfect will: not His will as a Jew only, but His will as Man. Standing in the centre and stem of our Humanity; with all its duties, all its dignity, all its blessedness upon Him, He carried out all that the Almighty Father ever intended it to do and be: He brought it through trial and temptation and suffering, spotless, blameless, perfect: He, being not a single individual man self-contained and limited, but being God, the Son of God in man, the second and righteous Head of our nature, undid in it what Adam did, planted righteousness in it which it had not without Him, and finally carried it up through Death and out of the grave to God's own throne, where He at this moment is reigning as Man, in your nature and mine, having obtained eternal redemption for us.

And, my beloved brethren, now come we to our second enquiry about this matter of the effect of one man's obedience on all men. *How* does it affect all men? You may say to me, "Do you mean to tell us that a poor heathen who has never heard of Christ, that a hard-hearted sinner in Christendom who will not have Christ for his master, that such as these are affected by the righteousness of which you have been telling us?" I can only answer that my text tells it you; and it is not for me to question what Christ's Apostle says, but to endeavour to understand it for myself and to explain it to you. There certainly is an effect produced on every man living, by Christ's finished work of righteousness. Let me make this plain to you in one, or two ways. We all believe in the certainty of a Resurrection of the dead: that all men with their bodies will one day come up out of their graves: the just to the resurrection of life: the unjust to the resurrection of judgment. Well: why is this? why shall this be? Go to one of the most solemn chapters of the Bible, and read the reason. Hear how St. Paul proves it. It is, and shall be, just simply as a consequence of this obedience of the man Christ Jesus of which we are speaking. His death was the crown of that obedience: His resurrection followed on that obedience, because on Him personally death, the consequence of disobedience, had no lasting power: and because He rose, all shall rise. Here then is one such effect upon all men, good and bad, Christians and heathens, believers and unbelievers.

But I will tell you another and a more notable effect of the obedience of this one man: even your existence and mine; the fact, that we are in the world at all. If it had not been for this obedience of Christ, foreseen and graciously reckoned as belonging to our nature, the race of man must have come to an end at the time when Adam sinned. "In the day thou eatest thereof, thou shalt surely die," was the word to him of God who cannot lie nor repent. And why did he not die? why did he not cease to be? why did the holy and pure One who cannot abide iniquity, tolerate him any longer? Simply because of the Blood of Jesus Christ which taketh away the sin of the world: because of that Lamb, slain from before the foundation of the world in God's gracious purposes. And the power of the same blood,—the atoning virtue of that obedience, crowned by the propitiatory sacrifice of His death,—is the simple reason why you and I are alive before God at this moment. The blessed and glorious Son of God has reconciled God and man; and by His obedience this effect has come upon all men; that, though sinners, they live and move and have being in the presence of a God who hates sin, just because Christ is the Head of their nature; because Christ in that nature obeyed God to the utmost; because Christ died and rose again and is at God's right hand in heaven.

And there is yet another effect which this obedience of Christ has had upon all men. It has brought them all within the blessed range of the promises which are in Christ; so that there is now no longer any distinction in this matter between one nation and another, or one man and another, but "Christ among you, the hope of glory," is preached to all the world,—to learned and unlearned, bond and free, Jew and Gentile. But this part of my subject will more properly come before us next Sunday, when we shall have entered the season beginning to-morrow with the Epiphany, or Manifestation of Christ to the Gentiles.

I must not however conclude my present sermon without reminding you that there is a meaning for us in the circumcision of our Lord, touched on in the Collect, and deserving our serious attention. What He did and submitted to for us, not only had its own value as a part of His working out of our redemption, but also in every case was our example, by some sense which it bore, having a reference to our spiritual state and duties. And this ordinance was one typifying the cleansing of the faithful soul from all uncleanness. "Grant us," we pray in the Collect, "the true circumcision of the Spirit, that our hearts and all our members being mortified from all worldly and carnal lusts, we may in all things obey thy blessed will." Just as this ordinance was the first and necessary step in our Lord's obeying of the law for us, so is that which it signified, the cleansing of our hearts and bodies from all impurity, the necessary condition of our serving God and obeying His holy will. Only the pure in heart shall see God. Though the effect of Christ's obedience passed upon all men, and brought all men near to God, only those who, turning to Him with their hearts, perfect holiness in His fear, are made partakers of the divine nature, and inherit the blessedness of justification unto life. Let us, now we are beginning the duties and the faith of another year, cleanse our hands and purify our hearts: let us prove ourselves God's peculiar people, by being zealous of good works, and enemies of all impurity, all untruthfulness, all serving of Him deceitfully and in a worldly spirit: that so our obedience may be, if not up to the measure of, at least after the pattern of Christ's obedience: simple, earnest, pure, self-denying and self-forgetting: the blessed and acceptable fruit of faith working by love.

SERMON VI.

(PREACHED ON THE FIRST SUNDAY AFTER EPIPHANY, JAN. 12, 1862.)

THE UNIVERSALITY OF THE GOSPEL.

GAL. iii. 28.

" There is neither Jew nor Greek, there is neither bond nor free, there is neither male nor female: for ye are all one in Christ Jesus."

WE have advanced thus far in our statements of Christian doctrine. Our race is universally tainted with the disease of sin, and guilty in God's sight. But it has pleased Him, of His infinite mercy, to provide a remedy as wide and universal as the disease. The eternal Son of God has taken our nature upon him, and in it wrought out on our behalf a perfect obedience, even up to the point of suffering the penalty of the sin of mankind. On this His work, anticipated as complete in the divine counsels, we asserted that the very existence of this our world depended, and that He does at the present moment, and ever, uphold all things in the sight of the Father by virtue of the eternal redemption which He has wrought for man.

Now our subject to-day, naturally suggested by the

Epiphany, or Manifestation of Christ to the Gentiles, is a very simple, but a very instructive and edifying one: the fact that, in the offer made to us of the acceptance for ourselves of this redemption and all its manifold blessings, there is absolutely no difference between one man and another, but all have a right to it alike, all are alike invited to share it, all have common capacity for receiving it.

Who, you may say to me, does not know this? Why preach us a sermon about so plain and acknowledged a fact? I answer, because it was one of the most wonderful revelations of God to man when it was first made, however plain it may seem now: and also, because, however plain it may seem now, thousands of those who think it so plain, do not understand it, do not feel it, do not act upon it.

First, it was a most wonderful thing, when God revealed it to mankind. All the ages which had passed since the Creation had been putting wider and wider difference between man and man,—between nation and nation, between men's bodies, and between men's souls. One nation was God's people, worshipping they knew what, in communion with the Father of Spirits, walking in the light of conscience and of revelation: another was building altars to the unknown God, bowing down to images graven by art and man's device, but at the same time acute and trained and instructed to the highest power of the human intellect: a third had almost cast off all religion, but had taken for its acts the governing of the world and the humbling the haughty, and ruled far and wide with its laws and its arms. Then again, one man was much more different from another than we know any thing of under the more equalizing influences of modern times; the conqueror and the vanquished, the master and the slave, the learned and the unlearned,—there was a far wider gap between these than there ever can be under the power of enlightened Christian public opinion, by which all have rights, all have instruction,—and injustice, and cruelty, and grossness, can hardly abound among us. But that a remedy for the evil of the world should be proposed which would suit equally all and each of these,—which could be taken alike, and taken in the same form, by the despot and his bondsman, by the master and his slave, by the learned and ignorant, by the Jew and Gentile,—this was the wonderful thing which had never been revealed to man before; and much trouble and time it cost, before man could receive it.

First came the difficulty about Jew and Gentile. The conflict about it raged long even in the apostolic church itself. It required a heart as fervid, and a spiritual sight as keen and single as that of St. Paul, to see the truth at once, and unflinchingly to maintain it, even against Apostles, when they wavered and dissimulated. How difficult must it have been for one born and bred a Jew, ever to take in the truth that he was to have one Lord, one faith, one baptism, with a man that was born and bred and remained a Gentile! How almost impossible to make such an one ever to bring himself to allow, that the Gentile, without fulfilling any one requirement of the law, was yet to be an heir of God's covenant promises in their highest sense, just as much and as completely as he himself, a circumcised Jew, an Hebrew by descent inheriting from Abraham! We can little imagine the widening of the view, and enlarging of the heart, and breaking down of prejudices, necessary before such a truth could be taught to a man. We cannot even devise an example in modern times which should teach us this. Every thing about us tends to widen our view, to open our hearts, to diminish our prejudices: but every thing around them tended to shut up their hearts, to narrow their view, and to fortify them in every adverse feeling. One week, they saw the Gentile taking part in his abominable idol rites; the next they might be called on to pass to him the kiss of peace as a Christian brother. It was the first great trouble in the infant church: a trouble which divided even holy Apostles asunder, and which some think was ultimately the cause of the persecution to death even of St. Paul himself.

And the difficulty, though it began here, did not by any means end here. It is natural to us to build up barriers of division between bodies of men and between individuals. The selfish heart is ever insulating itself, and its set, from other persons and other societies. If there were no more proof than this that Christianity came from God, the very fact of such an announcement being made as that in my text, would shew that some influence was at work in it which was not from man alone; some Spirit which was wider than man's thoughts, deeper than man's sympathies; which overleapt all distinctions raised by time and place and descent and circumstance, and referred men's practice for its rule to the primal truth, that God had made of one blood all nations on the earth.

And let me notice before I come to, and in coming to, the treatment of this great truth for our own times, what a fundamental and all-important principle it has ever furnished for the working and influence of the Church of Christ in all ages. What has been the one thing which has ever made the Christian Church the benefactor of mankind,—the advocate of justice and of mercy,—the enemy of the oppressor, the friend of light and the upholder of freedom? Why is it, that wherever she has not been this, she has decayed and corrupted;— wherever she has taken up the part and done its work, she has energized and prospered? Is it not simply for this reason, that the sacred doctrine, that all mankind are one in Christ Jesus, lies at the very corner of the foundation of her fabric wherever she is built up? that without it her message of mercy falls powerless, her proclamation of truth is a delusion, the God whom she preaches is not the Father of our Lord Jesus Christ? Her errand can only prosper in the broad sunshine:— she requires for her healthy breathing the whole wide atmosphere of the world:—limit her, and she becomes paralyzed: set bounds to her, and her voice sinks to a whisper: confine her to a privileged set, to a national form, to the habits of one or another age of men, and she ceases to be the Spouse of Him who is the Head and Husband of our entire humanity: put Roman before Catholic, put Eastern before Catholic, put Anglican before Catholic, and you contradict your own words as you speak, and nullify your own deeds as you act. The Church of Christ is catholic, is universal: over all, in all, belonging to all, fitted for all: all things to all men, as was he who wrote of her in our text: taking into herself, hallowing by her influence, transforming for good, all men's temperaments, all men's sympathies, all men's energies: not too narrow for the mightiest of human powers to work in, not too vast and stately for the meanest to find place and honour: limiting none, despising none, degrading none, excluding none. Round her course, through the ages, have sprung up all the blessings of civilization: her path has ever been marked by the soft verdure of the kindnesses of home, the fresh shade of the courtesies of society, the fair trophies of science, the bright blossoms of art. When she has awoke to the purity and holiness of her mission, with her have awoke the exploring eye of discovery, the searching effort of invention: when she has made an onward step, with her have advanced the powers of mind over matter, and love over hatred, of peace over contention: it was she who knit up at first, it is she who has healed when threatened with severance, the bonds of intercourse among nations; and all because of this, that she is the fulness of Him that filleth all:—because she is founded on Him in whom there is neither Jew nor Gentile, there is neither bond nor free, there is neither male nor female: but all are one in Christ Jesus, the Head and Saviour of all.

But though all this is so, and though we thank God for it, and many of us live in the strength and hope of it, how little it has been understood in ages past—how little is it understood even now! What a record of the forgetfulness of this great principle has ever been the history of Christ's Church! How its blessed effects have broken forth and spread, not because of, but in spite of, that which men purposed and intended!

Let man set up a principle, and work according to a rule of his own making, and the great tide of God's providence rolls on, and the barriers which are thought so strong are swept down and carried away before it: but let God set up a principle of His, and let men counter-work it as they will, it shall prevail; working under the surface, till the surface heaves with it, and it comes uppermost, and asserts itself in spite of us all.

And so it has ever been in the history of Christ's Church. Men have attempted to change its character— to profess conformity to it without acknowledging its principles—to get gain out of it while it should lie dormant and be merely a decent outside; to crush down the truths they daily confessed in their creeds, and hinder the efforts which they prayed for in their prayers; but blessed be God, notwithstanding their efforts, and by the very means of their efforts, the holy cause went on and the Truth prevailed: the sowers sowed evil seed, but God transformed it to good; and while they thought they were doing their work of effective repression, He was doing His work of surer and safer advance.

And how stand we now, my brethren, with regard to this foundation principle of the Gospel and Church of Christ? Have we thoroughly made it our own? Is it one of those things which we take most completely for granted in our thoughts of ourselves and others—of our Christian state and work in the world? Are we satisfied, after all these centuries, and all these conflicts, and all these proofs which God has given, that there is neither Jew nor Greek, bond nor free, male nor female: but that all are one in Christ Jesus?

Alas, would that we were! Let us try the matter by some of its plainest consequences, and judge of ourselves accordingly.

First, if the Gospel is wide enough for all humanity, and embraces it all indiscriminately, then does it not at once seem to follow, that it should take up into itself, and hallow, the whole, and not a mere part of the being of each of us? Now in connexion with such a result as this, what think we of Christ and His salvation? Is it not notorious, that most of us, that Christians in general, regard their religious life and their ordinary life as two distinct things—say in fact in an impossible sense the saying, "Give to the world the things that are the world's, and (not therefore but separately) to God the things that are God's"—as if all things were not God's—as if our whole lives, our whole being, body, soul, and spirit, were not bought with the blood of Christ, and His of right by that purchase? The error runs through the thoughts and actions of modern Christians to an extent which we hardly suspect. Our lives are divided into two inconsistent and incompatible portions: we try to be two persons—religious on our Sundays, at our times of devotion, on our sick beds,—and worldly all the rest of the week, and of the day, and of our ordinary time. Many and many a man, who would be offended not to be thought a good Christian, never dreams of acting, in his common resolves and determinations, from simply Christian motives,—because Christ has commanded, or has forbidden, this or that.

Now He who came to fill our whole nature with Himself and His grace, will not submit to be thus limited to a small share of it. He must have it all or none. "Whether ye eat or drink, or whatsoever ye do, do all to the glory of God." It is as much a sin against the universal spirit and power of the Gospel, to limit it to one part of our own lives, and exclude the remainder, as it is to limit it to one part of mankind and shut out the rest. We know nothing of its transforming power, or of its efficacy to supply all the wants of humanity, until our own lives with their energies and interests are carried on in that power, and draw, according to their daily need, out of that efficacy.

But again: all are one in Christ Jesus. The most ignorant, the most degraded, the most remote from the abodes of that grace which the Gospel gives, are just as capable of receiving and growing by it, as we who have been born and brought up under its outpouring. Where then is the hindrance to their doing so? Why have they not long ago heard of this universal Saviour and been informed of their privilege and claim to be His? Who is in fault? Not God's Providence, which has cast our lot on days of such wonderful discovery and facility of intercourse with distant nations, that a messenger may go to the ends of the earth now in less time and with less risk than we once could visit the distant parts of our native land: not God's lovingkindness, which so wonderfully preserves to us the blessings of peace, that His work may not be hindered; which from year to year showers His bounties on us, filling our hearts with food and gladness. No, neither of these,—but our own worldliness, and want of zeal and self-denial; our fear of the scorn of the idle and foolish world about us, which laughs at Missionary enterprise, and questions Missionary success, and so tries to keep the Gospel of Christ from asserting and carrying out its universal kingdom among men. If we really believed this universality, this oneness in Christ, as we profess to do, we should not be content, as we now are, with a list of religious Societies for home and foreign missions, every one of them struggling for existence from year to year; the poorer among us would not be content to let the wealthier do all the work of the Church, but would cheerfully claim their share of it: the wealthy would not let a few do the work of the whole body, but would eagerly vie with one another in hastening on the glad result. We do not, my brethren, present to God or to the world the aspect of a nation which believes in this universality of Christ's church and kingdom. Compare any one of our great public commercial enterprises with the whole of our puny efforts for Christian missions, and we painfully gather what I much fear is the truth in general, that this people is thoroughly convinced of the nature of the things of this world, but has no such conviction of the reality of its faith. On the one side we see enthusiastic eagerness, active competition, thousands and millions poured along almost any proposed channel, with or without prospect of large remuneration: on the other all is dead as winter, silent as the grave; interest barely kept up by meetings too often without any life in them, leaving for the most part on the heart a painful sense of unreality and hypocrisy: parades of names in subscription-lists, all cramped with the dreary uniformity of the conventional pound or guinea; in too many cases names of persons without heart for the enterprise, without interest, without love, without expectation of result. We serve the world by stirring personal energy, by unbounded hope, by endless contrivance: we excuse ourselves from serving Christ's Kingdom by delegating our blessed part in it to a lifeless mechanism, from which our persons and our sympathies are alike absent. O beloved, these things would not be so, did we know each for himself, did we know, as a church and nation, the fulness of the power of that Salvation which the Saviour of all men brought into the world for all men.

But one more lesson springs from the truth in my text—and that is a lesson of kindliness, of charitable feeling, of allowance for one another. If Christ's Gospel is this wide and universal remedy for our sins and miseries, it is so not by crushing all men's characters into one prescribed form, but by adapting itself to, and taking into itself, every variety of human character, with its defects, its weaknesses, its points which are unwelcome to society, and contemptible in the sight of man. It has been said, and not untruly, that the most accomplished man of the world is he who has best learned to hate and to despise. Directly opposite to this is the character of the accomplished disciple of Christ. He is the man who has best unlearned how to hate and despise his fellow-man. And I know of no consideration so effectual to this end, as those which spring from this great doctrine of the universal sufficiency of Christ's Gospel. Only let it present itself in this light to us. The weakness which you see in your neighbour's character, which makes you estimate him so cheaply, and regard him as so worthless in the world, is perhaps the very holding-ground for the anchor of a faith which keeps him firm in the truth, and which you yourself do not possess. And again, the very eagerness to seize on faults and to take the unpleasant view of things, which makes your neighbour so disagreeable to you, may be but the rough outer shell of a precious centre and heart of a character which loves righteousness and hates iniquity. The surface may be ruffled and irregular, but it may be only a broken and imperfect representation of the great ground-swell of truth and holiness, stirring the depths of the character. O who that knows himself, will not rather rejoice that others are not as he is? It is, my brethren, because we do not know how wide and large and all-embracing Christ's Spirit is, that we are always tying it down to rules and frameworks, and one or another form of human character, when we ought to be thankful for its manifold operations, glad that it lays hold of and fills and sanctifies every anxiety, every want, every special tendency of our common humanity. We need a large infusion of this Spirit of Christ which wrought in His holy Apostle, before we can properly teach, properly hear, properly feel, on such a subject as this of our text to-day. We need it in our Church life, we need it in our social life, we need it in our individual life: for unless a man be penetrated through and through by it, he has it not worthily at all.

Finally—if this Gospel be thus adapted for all, offered to all, sufficient for all, then is that person inexcusable who, when it is offered, has not accepted it in its power. My brother—my sister—you are sinful, guilty, perishing. You have that in you and about you which will ruin you for this life and for eternity: you have not that in you, or within your grasp, which will rescue you from this ruin. But here is a remedy. Here is a divine and all-sufficing Saviour;—yours, thank God, by right of your humanity which He took upon him, and in which He has satisfied God for you;—nay more, yours by the profession of your baptism, and your membership of His Church. If you will not believe in Him with heart and practice;—if you will not have Him to reign over you;—if you will not come to Him that you may have life, O where can the blame lie but with yourselves? God has done His part: the Father sent the Son; the Son obeyed, and died, and pleads in heaven for you; the Holy Spirit is ever striving with you in your consciences, and in the ordinances of the Church, and by my voice here: the Church has done her part; she brought you near to Christ, and washed you in the font of the new birth; she taught you all that a Christian ought to believe and know for his soul's health; she offers you the rich Feast of her Lord's Body and Blood, and holy ordinances without number. All has been done, all is ever being done, except your own part.

O delay no longer : but accept in the depths of your heart, and in the fountains of your life, this universal and all-sufficing Saviour : take up and fulfil the holy challenge of the Apostle in our Epistle this day, chosen by the Church as a fit conclusion from the rich blessings of the Christmas season—from God's loving-kindness in having spared us yet another year :—

"I conjure you, brethren, by the mercies of God, that ye present your bodies a living sacrifice, holy, acceptable to God, which is your reasonable service."

SERMON VII.

(PREACHED ON THE SECOND SUNDAY AFTER EPIPHANY, JAN. 19, 1862.)

MIRACLES: WATER MADE WINE.

JOHN ii. 11.

"This beginning of miracles did Jesus in Cana of Galilee, and manifested forth his glory."

IT is very instructive, particularly when any course of teaching like our present one is undertaken, to notice the way in which the Church has chosen the passages of Scripture which are to be read on the different Sundays. I told you, that in our series of doctrinal sermons I should follow the great events of our Lord's life as brought before us by the Church. Now let us observe what she has done for us about this time of the year. We have passed the nativity of Christ: His circumcision: His manifestation to the Gentiles. Last Sunday the Gospel contained the narrative of the only event recorded as having happened during His youth. On that I did not preach to you: both because I had once treated it fully before, and because I had already said so much on the perfect manhood of our Lord, which that wondrous story most concerns.

But now let us observe the six following Sundays, beginning with this one, the second after Epiphany. To-day we have for our Gospel the miracle of the water turned into wine: next Sunday, the healing of the leper and of the centurion's servant, which occur together in Matt. viii.: the Sunday after, the three miracles of the stilling the storm, the casting out the devils at Gadara, and the destruction of the swine, which also occur together in the same chapter. Then on the next Sunday, the fifth after Epiphany, we have the parable of the tares of the field: and missing the sixth, which occurs but seldom, and has a peculiar subject of its own, on Septuagesima Sunday we have another parable, that of the labourers in the vineyard: and on the next, Sexagesima, that of the Sower: the next Sunday to that introducing the solemn season of Lent with a Gospel pointedly announcing our Lord's sufferings for our sins.

Thus we have before us, as there are this year five Sundays after Epiphany, three Sundays of miracles, and three of parables. And this circumstance will guide me in choosing our subjects for those Sundays.

Our Blessed Lord's Person is the great centre of all Christian doctrines. According as you do, or do not, see clearly who He is, and what was and is His work, you will or will not be sound in the faith, and led on to true and blessed belief in the other great verities of His religion. I shall need therefore no apology for devoting these six Sundays to the subjects thus pointed out to us; three to our Lord's miracles,—three to His parables and discourses. May God guide me to speak, and you to hear, that which is according to His will, and the mind of His Spirit.

We are then to speak of CHRIST'S MIRACLES.

And first, WHAT IS A MIRACLE? This is a most important question: for on the right answer to it depends, whether we understand or not of what use Christ's miracles were when they were wrought, and what purpose they are intended to serve for us now, and for the Church to the end of time. A miracle is *an interference with the common course of nature by some power above nature*. Thus an earthquake or a volcanic eruption is not a miracle, because it is a result, though an unusual result, of natural causes: a comet is not a miracle, because it is, though a rare thing in nature, yet brought about by no divine interference, but occurring in the course of nature herself. Divine interference might exalt either of these into miracles, by specially announcing them as sent for a purpose: as the prophetic voice of Samuel did thus exalt into a miracle the thunderstorm in the wheat harvest, when he foretold it as a sign of God's anger for Israel's sin. The healing of a disease is not a miracle, if brought about by ordinary means, although we know that God's blessing must be given on those means; but it is a miracle, if it is produced by a word, or a touch, and would at once shew that he who did it possessed some power greater than that of nature, and of man, nature's servant. *Some power greater*, I said: and I said it purposely: for all miracles do not come from God: some come from God's enemy and ours, the devil, and from his agents and subordinate powers. The magicians of Egypt were able to perform the same miracles as Moses, up to a certain point: and we have it from the lips of our Lord himself, that the Antichrist of the latter days, when he shall appear, shall shew signs and wonders, so as to deceive, if it were possible, even the elect of God. St. Paul also speaks of the same Antichrist as "him whose coming is after the working of Satan with all power and might and lying wonders." Mere miracles then are no proof of a divine mission, but only of some power from heaven or hell superior to that of man, and of nature in her ordinary working.

I shall have occasion to return to this point again by and by, and to say a good deal upon it. Meantime one general remark must be made here in the outset. It will be plain to you that any one who believes in a personal Author and Governor of nature, will have no difficulty in believing in miracles. The same Almighty Being who made and upholds nature, can interfere, whenever it pleases Him, with the ordinary course of nature, which He has Himself prescribed. To say that He cannot do this, is to deny His almightiness, and consequently His existence. To say that He never will be pleased thus to interfere, is manifestly foolish and presumptuous in the extreme: we cannot set bounds to His purposes, nor tell beforehand how He may be pleased to accomplish them. It does not follow, because we have never witnessed an unusual exertion of His power, that such never take place. By the same argument we might refuse to believe any wonderful thing which we have not ourselves seen. Then again, every one who believes in the existence of spirits and powers of evil must allow that they exist and act only by permission of God, and for mysterious purposes of His. And the trial of our faith and obedience is certainly one of those purposes. There is then no antecedent difficulty in believing that miraculous powers are granted, or have been at certain times granted, to these evil spirits, to exercise the faith of men: and Scripture positively assures us that such is the case. Whenever a man refuses to believe in miracles, one of two things must be the case: either, believing the possibility of miracles, he does not think the evidence enough on which the miracle is sought to be established; or, disbelieving their possibility, and thinking no evidence sufficient to establish them, he must, if he be consistent, also disbelieve the existence of,—or the continued government of the world by,—an Almighty Creator and Upholder. We, while we believe the evidence of the Scripture miracles to be sufficient to prove them to be facts, take the former course, with regard to the recorded miracles of the Saints of the Church of Rome, and to those which she from time to time reports in our own days: we believe well-attested miracles, but we do not believe these, which we find will not bear the test of a searching examination into their facts. The unbeliever takes the latter course, when he refuses to receive the miracles related in Holy Scripture, on the ground of its being impossible or improbable that they should have happened. I say, the unbeliever; meaning he who rejects Christ and Christianity: for it is clearly impossible to receive Christ as the Saviour, and not to credit those very works to which He constantly appealed for the truth of His mission.

But now it is time to return to the more interesting matter which we just now left. If there are good and bad miracles,—miracles of divine goodness, and miracles of lying spirits,—one thing must be very plain to us: viz. that by *miracles alone* no man can be proved to be sent from God. He may be proved to be sent either from God, or from God's and man's enemy: but miracles alone will not determine which.

And now we have come to the point as regards our blessed Lord Himself. Our enquiry to-day, on which we wish to gain some information for ourselves, is, What were our Lord's miracles, as regards their place in His great work? They held a very important place, but they did not hold the chief place, in the evidences of His mission. He often appeals to them in proof that He came from God: but He does so in a peculiar manner, and one very instructive to us. He himself actually at one time had to reply to the charge that he wrought them by Satanic influence. " This man casteth out devils by Beelzebub the prince of the devils." And the way in which He answered the accusation is most instructive. He did it, not by appealing to the greatness, or even to the beneficence of his miracles alone, but by asserting that if it were so, Satan would be divided against himself. Our Lord was his well-known opponent,—the man of truth, the man of purity, the man of God; whose meat and drink it was to do God's will; and the idea of Satan working by means of this man would imply that Satan was *his own* enemy, and therefore could not stand, but must have an end. And this is just the course which our Lord ever took with regard to His miracles. You will find it in St. John's Gospel most plainly set forth. There the Evangelist's purpose evidently is, not merely to relate the events as they happened, and the discourses as they were delivered; but so to collect and group them together that they may best illustrate our blessed Lord's purpose and method of manifesting himself to men. And you will ever find Him in that Gospel insisting on this point in all His conflicts and controversies with the Jews,—that His life was holy and blameless; that He was a good man, and spoke good, and did good, and shewed them good. This was the great and firm basis on which Jesus rested for the acceptation of his ministry and mission; that none could convict him of sin; that He was like God, and of God. And *now* came in His miracles; not as chief proofs, but as proofs in aid, of this pure and holy life and mission. They were wonderful works; they were suspensions of the course of nature: this shewed Him to be one endowed with supernatural power. He turned water into wine :—He spoke and the winds were silent :—He commanded diseases with a word. So far the power might be from above or from beneath. But, coupled with his holy and blameless life, and his love for God, and obedience to God, these works of power took another character, and became *signs*, St. John's usual word for them; signs whence He came: they could have but one source,— they could not be from Satan; He could not be a magician, in league with the powers of evil:—they were proofs that He was what he asserted himself to be,—from God, and the Son of God:—they became, when viewed together with the consistent and unvarying character of his teaching and life, most valuable and decisive evidences to his Messiahship. "No man can do these miracles that thou doest, except God be with him," said the Jewish Rabbi to Him: "the works which the Father hath given me to finish, the same works that I do, bear witness of me that the Father hath sent me."

But besides that our Lord's miracles came in aid of His spotless and holy life to prove Him the Son of God, they have a distinct and most important meaning and teaching of their own. This will be best introduced by for a moment comparing them with the thousands of reported heathen and middle-age miracles which have been reported in history and legend. What was the meaning and import of all these? What good did they do? What result came of them? Can any instruction be got from them, or is any meaning for men's souls concealed beneath them? But with every one of our Lord's miracles, this is otherwise. They are full of goodness to the bodies and souls of men. Each of them has its own fitness as adapted to His great work, and to the will of the Father which He came to accomplish. Each one tends, in its place, as St. John says of this one in our Gospel, to manifest forth His glory: shews forth some gracious attribute, some deep sympathy: testifies to Him as the light, or life, or consolation, or sustenance, of man and man's world. Let us take general instances, which we shall be able afterwards to follow out into particulars, in the miracles which are brought before us in the Gospels for these three Sundays.

Sin is, as we have seen, the great disease of our nature, which this divine Saviour came to heal. Bodily disease is not only a type, it is the consequence of sin. So that when our Lord puts forth His hand to heal, or speaks the words which are followed by healing, He is forwarding, at the same time that He is prefiguring and illustrating, His healing power for the whole world, for men's bodies and souls alike: when He raises the dead, He is conquering Death, the result of sin, and He is giving a foretaste of the day when all that are in the grave, shall hear His voice: when He feeds the five thousand or the four thousand in the wilderness, He himself teaches us that He is not only doing a beneficent act to men's bodies, but is teaching them that He is the Bread of life for their souls: when He casts out devils in relief of the peculiar spiritual affliction of that time, He is teaching us that He came to destroy the works of the devil. Some of the miracles are *acted parables:* similar lessons of instruction are conveyed by them to those which at other times He expressed in his teaching. We have a notable example of this in the miracle of the withering fig-tree, in which He sets forth to us, in connexion with his well-known parable, the barrenness, and the punishment, of unfruitful Israel.

So that our Lord's miracles form a precious and most important body of proofs of his holy mission and his

Sonship of God: and not only this, but they come powerfully in aid of his discourses, in setting before us the truth of his divine Person and Work. We know his Power by them; we are assured of his Wisdom and his Love. The faithful soul, in its wants and its weaknesses, finds these testimonies to his loving-kindness a rich treasure-house of personal comfort.

I will devote the rest of my sermon to considering how this is so with regard to the class of miracles to which that in our Gospel to-day belongs.

That class is a very remarkable one. And it is especially worthy of note, that our Lord should choose a miracle of such a character with which to open his whole course of supernatural working. For it is one in which we have not the healing of disease, not the abolition of death, not the freeing men from any of the plainer and more obvious consequences of sin, but the supply of a want which was not a need, the ministering to mere festive joy, not to destitution and distress. It may at first sight appear strange that such a miracle should be selected by our Lord as one especially calculated to manifest forth his glory, and to cause his disciples to believe on him. There is then all reason why we should closely examine it and try to discern its worthiness for such a place and office.

Our first observation shall be this: that whereas other of our Lord's miracles concern some particular portion of human infirmity, or divine power and mercy, we might well expect this one, which was to begin and head them, to convey a lesson of a more general nature respecting both ourselves and Him who wrought it.

And such indeed it does convey. We see Him here as the true source of all joy and happiness: we see Him in his highest and most blessed influence on man and that which belongs to man. For He came, as we insisted last Sunday in preaching to you on the universality of His Gospel, to heal and elevate and bless our whole nature, in all its wants, all its employments, all its joys.

And what is it that we find Him here doing? The holy estate of marriage was instituted of God in the time of man's innocency. It is an institution still in full force among us, and dating from before the time of the first ravages of sin. Sin indeed has abused it, and counterfeited it, and interfered with its blessedness: but for all that, its own holiness and purity, and capability for blessing and elevating humanity, still remain for those who use it aright, in the faith and fear of God, and in holy forbearance and love. What occasion then so fitting for the Son of God to shew his divine power of blessing and hallowing humanity, as that of a marriage? He might have entered the abode of sickness and healed with a word, as often afterwards: He might have stood over the bed of death and called back the parted spirit: each of these miracles would have had, as each ever has, its own deep and blessed significance: but we may venture to say, that neither of them would have spread so wide, or risen so high, in its manifestation of the Redeemer's glory, as did this one. Those would regard more the means whereby the great work of Redemption was to be accomplished,—the healing of sin, the overcoming of death:

but this shews us the blessed work completed, and in its most glorious result. "These things speak I to you that your joy may be full." This was the tendency of his discourses, and of the writings of his apostles:— and thus, in ministering to the fulness of human joy, He is going further, and shewing more completely the glory of his Incarnation in our nature, than if He had ministered to human sorrow,—because under Him and in His Kingdom, all sorrow is but a means to joy,—all sorrow ends in joy. "Ye now therefore have sorrow," He says to His disciples of their orphan state in the world : "but I will come and see you again, and ye shall rejoice, and your joy no man taketh from you."

Take yet another view of this miracle. The gift which our Lord bestowed in it is ever used in Scripture, however it has been perverted by man's evil and sinful lusts, as setting forth to us the invigorating and cheering effects of the Spirit of God on man's heart. "The Lord will make a feast of wines on the lees well refined:"—"Come ye, buy wine and milk without money and without price:"—these are the prophetic representations of the rich blessings of the Christian covenant. And so our Lord, in opening His treasure of these rich blessings, does so by imparting the lower gift, the type of His better and more lasting bestowal. And St. John has thought it worth while to record, that the wine which He bestowed was the best of its kind, as all His gifts are better than any other gifts: as His works of nature and His works of grace are ever the best and the noblest, marvels of skill and mercy:—for He doeth all things well.

All this was manifesting forth His glory, and the character of His work on earth: and so it was, when He turned water into wine, the baser element into the nobler, the weaker into the stronger. For thus He ever does with all that is merely ours, when He comes with His transforming power and His heavenly grace. By that power the weak becomes strong, the earthly becomes heavenly, the transitory becomes abiding añd eternal. It is He alone who can turn the mere flashes of human joy into a holy and steady flame which even the grave shall not extinguish: He alone, who can change the sorrow of the world, which worketh death, into godly sorrow, which bringeth forth the peaceable fruits of righteousness:—who bestows the oil of joy for mourning, the garment of praise for the spirit of heaviness.

But more manifestations of His glory yet remain behind. He did all this simply by His own creative power. And the process was hidden from human view. In the vessels, or in pouring from vessel to vessel, did His power in a moment work that wondrous change, which is yearly during a whole season wrought by Him in nature, when the moisture of the earth is taken up by the vine, circulates as sap in the branch and the bud and the bloom, becomes ripened into the juice of the grape,—and yet more, being by man's labour gathered, pressed, fermented, put by, after years mellows into the good wine. He, who commonly creates by means and secondary causes, can do without them when He will; will do without them, when it pleases Him, in the bringing about of His great purposes.

Yet again. There is something in the very order of His course here which is instructive to us. "Thou hast kept the good wine until now," says the ruler of the feast. Ever His best, last:—not even His best first, as the world, anxious for present shew, present effect, careless about the distant future. It is not His way to be very gracious at first, and then to cool towards His people: to invite them to Him, and then fall back from them: His mercies are new every morning: He giveth more grace,—grace for grace: and evermore those who have loved Him longest love Him best, those who have served Him longest can tell most of His loving-kindness. He keeps His best until last. Never, till we sit down in the Kingdom of God, shall we know the fulness of joy which is in His presence, and the pleasures which are at His right hand. There none will be disappointed: every one will know and confess that He has kept His best bestowal, till body and soul and spirit were ready to be filled full with it.

But lastly, all this He will do, not at our time, but at His own. See how His blessed Mother urged him forward, being convinced in her own believing heart that He could and would do, what He eventually really did. But mark the reproof which even she earned from Him—"Woman, what have I to do with thee? mine hour is not yet come." And so do many of us, my brethren, without half her faith and clearness of insight into His purposes, often urge Him forward for our own ease or consolation, or as we fancy, for His greater and speedier glorification: but the same answer awaits us,—if not from His lips, yet from His Providence: we shall be thrust back, and kept standing without and disappointed of our earnest wish, till His time is come: and then, but not till then, will He help us, and clear us, and justify us, and save us, and glorify us:—then when we are fittest,—then when His will is ripest,—then, when it is best.

Such, my beloved, are some of the lessons to be learned, some of the rich consolations to be drawn, from this one miracle of our Blessed Lord. Notice the effect in our text:—His disciples believed on Him. O may this same result be produced on every one of you. You have heard in these sermons of your deep need of Him,—of His eternal Godhead,—His grace in becoming man for you,—and now to-day of His glory as manifested by His miracles generally, and by this one in particular. And to what purpose shall I have spoken and you have heard these things, unless some hearts here be brought to receive Him for their Saviour and Lord: to trust in His power and mercy, to thirst for a share in His glory?

Go and think of Him, and pray to Him, and serve Him: strive by prayer, by obedience, by patience and hope in believing, for more of His spirit and His likeness, that one day your vile body may be changed, by a far more wonderful miracle, to be as His glorious body, according to the mighty working whereby He is able even to subdue all things unto Himself.

SERMON VIII.

(PREACHED ON THE THIRD SUNDAY AFTER EPIPHANY, JAN. 26, 1862.)

MIRACLES OF HEALING.

MATT. viii. 13.

"And Jesus said unto the centurion, Go thy way; and as thou hast believed, so be it done unto thee. And his servant was healed in the selfsame hour."

From the consideration of the nature and use of our Blessed Lord's miracles in general, and the example of that first great miracle of turning water into wine, we now come to speak of those which have a more particular character. And the Gospel to-day brings before us two of these, the cleansing of the leper and the recovering of the centurion's servant, both belonging to the same class: that of the healing of disease.

In order to understand the bearing of these on Christian doctrine, let us first enquire, *what disease is:* what place it holds with reference to the office and work of the Redeemer. That it does hold some important place, is evident, from the great number of His wonderful works which had respect to the healing and removing of it. Disease, then, is simply the beginning of death. It is, in its various forms, that part of the dark procession of miseries consequent on sin, which ushers in the dread executioner of the primitive sentence, "Thou shalt surely die." So that He who came to abolish death, and to bring life and immortality to light through the Gospel, might well be expected, among his wonderful works performed in confirmation of this his mission, to heal diseases. For He would thus be shewing the great restoration which He came to effect in our whole nature: the health, and life, and vigour, which accompany His presence, and His touch, and His word. And He was not content with healing every sickness and disease among the people: He even exerted his power over the king of terrors himself, and His voice was heard by the spirit of man in the realms of the departed, and He was obeyed.

All these miracles form one great class, and that by far the largest, of those which our Lord wrought on earth. And the lessons taught by them are manifold.

There is first the plain fact, that the Son of man came not to destroy men's lives, but to save them. How familiar this is on our tongues, but how little do we really think of it in our secret hearts! Many are the works related of him: why should by far the greater number of them be miracles of healing? Was there nothing more important to do in the world? One of the bitterest enemies of Christianity in ancient times, Julian the apostate, denied that our Lord ever did any really wonderful works: "He only cured a few sick people in villages like Bethsaida and Bethany." Why, if our Lord had been pleased, He could have done works which would have struck with terror every caviller at His Gospel. But He mainly confined himself to these, wrought on obscure persons, and in obscure places, because He wanted, not to be glorified of men, but to teach and bless and console His people to the end of time. And when we see Him thus laying out the precious days of his ministry, and inspiring his Evangelists to write these accounts of his works of healing, and providentially preserving the books in which they are related down to these latter days, we ought to feel thankfully convinced that He came, and wrought his works, and had his Gospels written, to help us, to heal us, to make us sound and happy, and to prolong and cheer our lives, not to bring misery and fear and weakness of purpose and terror of death among us, as some would have us believe. What a comfort, my brethren, this might be to us, if we would but think ever of Him thus; as of one waiting to heal and to bless! How would pain be lightened and sickness patiently borne and death lose its terrors, if we always saw His hand stretched forth to heal us, His form standing by the sick bed, or walking on the waves of affliction, and saying to us " It is I, be not afraid!"

It may however be said, But He does not do this now: we are left to bear our pains and troubles without Him. Not indeed without Him, for He is ever thinking of every one of us: but in part, the remark is most true. He did not come into our world to work miracles, to heal diseases, or to raise the dead. There were thousands of sick in Judæa and Galilee during His ministry, who never saw His face nor partook of His healing power:

of all that died in those three years, He raised but three, that we are told of. He came into the world to do that far greater work of which these were but the signs and tokens;—to put out and abolish for ever the great disease of our nature;—to take away the sin of the world. And this He has done once for all, and is ever applying the blessed fruits of His work to the members of His Church. It was to shew you His gracious mind in doing this, not to lead you to expect bodily healing or raising from the dead, or to murmur, because such blessings are now withdrawn, that I dwelt on the consolation which these His miracles may afford us.

Another lesson which His wonderful works teach us, and which we deeply need, is, the importance of these our *bodies*, in the great process of Redemption. It is a very common mistake to imagine that the *saving of the soul* is to be the great object of religion. Nay, religion itself is called the interest of the soul: and by many Christians the body is as little regarded as having any share in it, as if it were to be left behind in the grave, and a blessed eternity would be passed without it. Yet nothing can be more contrary to the teaching of Holy Scripture, than such a way of viewing the subject. In Scripture Christ is called the Saviour, not of the soul, but of the *body:* that for which St. Paul tells us the whole Church of God is waiting, is, the redemption of the *body:* when the same Apostle has finished the great argument concerning salvation by grace through faith in the Epistle to the Romans, he beseeches us by the mercies of God to yield, not our souls, but our *bodies*, a living sacrifice to God: when he warns the Corinthians against sins of uncleanness, he says, "Know ye not that," not your souls, but "your *bodies* are temples of the Holy Ghost?" And the one distinctive doctrine of Christianity, by which it was different from every other religion in the world, was, not the future life of the soul: this was known to Jew and to heathen long before: but it was, the resurrection of the *body*: that all men should come out of their graves with their bodies; and that the entire man, body, soul, and spirit, should live for ever in bliss, or endure for ever in woe, without separation or diminution.

Our modern religion is become far too spiritual—far too much a matter of thought, and opinion, and inward feelings and experiences, and this has led men to unite it so little with their common lives, and make it a matter of such convenient secrecy and mystery, that they may do and say just what they please in the body, without their religious profession being affected by it. And another result of this so-called spiritual view of religion is, that in treating of the heathen abroad, or the far worse heathen at home, those who hold it will almost forbid, or at any rate depreciate, the attempt to better their bodily state by civilization, by sanitary improvements, by elevating arts and kindlier habits; and tell us we must care for their souls first, if not only. To all such views I conceive our blessed Lord's own practice is our best as it is our most decisive answer. He preached the Gospel of the kingdom: but while He did it, He went about doing good:—healing the sick, giving sight to the blind, making the lame to walk, the deaf to hear, restoring the withered limb, and the uprightness of the bowed-down frame. These were the ways in which He prepared men for His Gospel, and in which He has taught us to prepare them: not by putting it in contrast to all our blessings, but by making it the crown and topstone to all our blessings: not by giving out that health, and spirits, and the use of our senses, and the information of our minds, and the decencies and courtesies of life, are all bad, and religion only is good; but by ourselves feeling, and telling others, that all these are good, very good,—rich gifts of our merciful Father,—but that faith in Christ, obedience to Christ, is better than all of them, best of all of them;—and Christ Himself the gift of gifts,—God's unspeakable gift.

The next remark which I have to make on this class of our Lord's works will of necessity introduce us to the particular character and features of the former of those related in our Gospel to-day. The remark is, on the *typical import* of these healing miracles, as pointing to the Lord's power over the diseases of our souls and spirits: and the miracle which best illustrates this is the cleansing of the leper, with which our gospel begins. It can be no new thing to you to hear, that this disease of leprosy was chosen for notice in the ancient law, and a special set of enactments made concerning it, not for any sanitary reasons, but purely because it was taken as a type of man's great disease of sin. Although one of the most loathsome and terrible of bodily plagues, it was not contagious:—there was no fear of its spreading from man to man. This would be plain, by merely observing that in cases when it could not be helped, the leper was employed in high offices: in cases which were perfectly hopeless, he was, even by the law, relieved from many of the restrictions laid on his fellow-sufferers, and was allowed to mingle in the haunts of men. The whole treatment of the leper, his separation, the multitude of precautions taken concerning his examination and his cleansing, appear to have been imposed by the law to set forth the impurity and loathsomeness in God's sight, and the difficulty of removal, of the deeper and more fatal spiritual disease of man. It was fitting then that the Lord should exercise His power of healing prominently on the leper, and should leave us an express record of his grace and power in dealing with this disease. It was just as He had ended that great discourse known to us as the Sermon on the Mount,—that discourse in which He describes himself as come not to destroy the law but to fulfil it. Having exhibited this character in his teaching, He descended from the mountain, great multitudes following him. As He was entering a certain city a man met him full of leprosy. With a wonderful simplicity combined with strength of faith, falling down before him he cried, "Lord, if thou wilt, thou canst make me clean." We may observe that long before this Jesus had made circuits in Galilee, teaching and healing. So that it was no new thing that the leper was announcing;—no new thing that the Lord did. But this Evangelist, who loves to set forth the kingly office and majesty of Christ, was directed to put this miracle in the very forefront of those recorded by him, doubtless because it was so direct an appeal to our Lord's will and power, and because that appeal was so plainly and undoubtingly answered by Him. For

He does not say, "Go pray to God who alone can heal thee:" He does not reply, as Joseph did, "It is not in me: God shall give Pharaoh an answer of peace;" nor as Peter did to Cornelius, "Stand up, for I also am a man:" but He at once claimed and proved what the leper asserted him to possess, by the open and immediate exercise of it. He put forth his hand, and touched him: thus Himself by imputation partaking of our uncleannesses,—for whosoever touched a leper became himself unclean. Moreover He said "I will: be thou clean."

My brethren, what an assertion of power, what an exertion of it is here! He WILL: of His own authority and of His own good pleasure He doeth that which is done. And the same mighty will which in our miracle last Sunday had silently and without expression changed the element of water into the juice of the grape, and had superseded the slow work of human manufacture and the ripening processes of time, now by a spoken word purified the tainted juices of the body, annihilated the loathsome traces of disease and decay, and recreated that frame which His power had originally made. "Immediately his leprosy departed from him."

And, if we come to consider the miracle in its deeper import, O what is leprosy of the body, loathsome and fatal as it was, to the ruin and decay of man's soul by sin? We hear indeed, that the wretched persons who were thus afflicted carried about with them a living death; that the body under its influence lost its sensation part by part, and dropped into decay and dissolution: but does not all this happen more dreadfully and more hopelessly to the victim of sin? When the heart hardens, the pure affections become polluted, the will enfeebled, the judgment impaired, personal freedom of action lost owing to the bondage of long prevalent evil habit, what is it but a leprosy of the soul,—the sign and the precursor of eternal death? Yet if out of this depth of misery the sinner turn to Him who healed the leper, not doubting, but receiving with simple faith His power and will to cleanse him, then has the Lord taught us by this miracle, that He can and will heal and cleanse: not indeed now by a touch, nor in a moment: this kind cometh not out thus: but as surely, as graciously, as completely: by the gradual means of grace, by His word and His ordinances, and the purifying influences of His blessed Spirit, renovating him as the flesh of a little child in the new life unto God.

Let us now turn to the lesson prominently taught us by the latter of these miracles, in our gospel of this day. I say nothing at present of the secondary instruction to be derived from the remarkable faith of the centurion, who was a Roman and a heathen: I am in these sermons more concerned with that which has respect to our Lord Himself, as testimony to us of the doctrines regarding His Sacred Person. Looking then at this only, our lesson is, the absolute command which He has over all diseases as His servants, going and coming at his bidding. The faithful centurion compares Him to the captain of a great army, having soldiers under him and at his beck. He himself knew something of this, being one whose position required him both to obey and to command. That obedience which he yielded to his tribune or his general, that obedience which his subordinates yielded to him, the same obedience the painful disease of his favourite servant, the same obedience all diseases, would yield to Christ. And this again is not treated as a fond and superstitious view of the matter: our Lord does not take him up and explain to him how the fact really stands by depreciating His own power or limiting it. But he turns and says to those around him, "Verily I say unto you, I have not found so great faith, no not in Israel." And then to the centurion, "Go thy way, and as thou hast believed, so be it done unto thee." "And his servant was made whole," we read, "in the selfsame hour."

Now doubtless this narrative does not relate to us the same fact as that occurring at the end of John iv., and there stated to be our Lord's second miracle after He was come from Judæa into Galilee: any one may become convinced of this by carefully reading and comparing the two. But it is remarkable, that the two, the healing of the nobleman's son and this of the centurion's servant, have one particular in common, lying at the very root of the character of the miracles. In both, the healing is wrought without any contact, without our Lord even being on the spot: in one, in the same town, but far from the centurion's house: in the other, at the distance of Cana in Galilee from Capernaum, about twenty-five of our miles. In the cleansing of the leper, as in so many of His works of healing, He establishes a communication between Himself and the person healed,—"He put forth his hand, and touched him:" there is a lesson for us in that:—the life and health which come from union with Him. In this miracle, He speaks at a distance and the effect follows: and we may learn from that too: He is absolutely master of all:—near or far, present or apparently absent, on earth or in heaven, by his word or by his look or by his will, or entirely as He pleases, He can and He will cleanse and purify and save. It is that we may rest on Him, wait for Him, lie content in His hands, that these miracles, these signs of His power and love, are given us: that we may imitate the faith which He praised, and the earnestness of supplication to which He was pleased to yield: that we may bring all our diseases to Him, all our troubles, all our cares. "If thou wilt," is no longer needed now: the manger at Bethlehem, the subjection at Nazareth, the temptation in the wilderness, the agony in Gethsemane, the cross on Calvary, the ascension from Bethany, all these declare "I will." He triumphs to help us: He reigns, that we may reign with Him: He intercedes, that our faith may not fail. What more can invite us? What more can assure us?

SERMON IX.

(PREACHED ON THE FOURTH SUNDAY AFTER EPIPHANY, FEB. 2, 1862.)

MIRACLES OF POWER.

MATT. viii. 27.
"What manner of man is this, that even the winds and the sea obey him?"

THIS is our third sermon on our Lord's miracles as illustrating the doctrines of His sacred Person and office. And we have to notice in it another class of those wonderful works, not indeed wholly distinct from those which have already come before us, but distinct in their leading features and character. The two miracles in our Gospel to-day are emphatically instances of His POWER. Not that the power shewn in turning water into wine, in cleansing the leper, in healing the centurion's servant, was one whit less than that exerted in the stilling of the storm, and in the casting out the legion of devils at Gergesa: but that in the former miracles, Love and Mercy seem to stand out as the prominent features, whereas here, above all other things, the sense of almighty Power is carried irresistibly into our minds as we read. And such seems to have been the impression made on the beholders in each case. The men in the ship exclaimed, "What manner of man is this, that even the winds and the sea obey Him?" The Gergesenes besought Him to depart out of their coasts;—fearing the presence of one so mighty, and whose might had been shewn in a manner working them worldly loss.

We will then treat these miracles to-day mainly in this light—as proofs of His POWER: but not only so— we will also take up and turn to account such other incidental lessons from them as occur by the way while we proceed.

Our Lord had been all day speaking that great series of parables, opening with the parable of the Sower, which we find in Matt. xiii., five chapters after this in which our narrative occurs. It would appear, that St. Matthew does not relate these events in their order. For we are positively told by St. Mark that this miracle took place on the evening of the day when all those parables were spoken. Our Lord was wearied out with the long day's teaching, probably in the heat and glare of the beach of the lake. We see from the minute and beautiful touches in St. Mark's narrative, how the multitudes had been for some days pursuing Him about, eager for His teaching and healing, till that frame which, though it bore the Divinity, was itself limited and liable to exhaustion, was well nigh crushed with toil: till his near relations, seeing His unsparing exertions, came out to lay hold on Him, thinking that He was beside himself, carried away by self-sacrificing enthusiasm. "Let us cross," He said to his disciples, "to the other side of the lake." They embarked in the boat, probably Simon Peter's, which He commonly used, other small boats also accompanying them. St. Mark adds, "they took Him with them in the boat *as He was,*" without any preparation, perhaps even too weary to take refreshment. They spread for Him in the stern the cushions commonly used on the rowers' benches, and, exhausted as He was, He laid him down, and slept the sleep of the weary. I have enlarged on this scene, that we may have the whole blessed truth of the matter vividly before us. Behold him in his humanity;—handle him in your thoughts, and see that it is He himself. This is indeed no pretended man; no god in disguise, as the heathens sometimes fabled of in their legends. Nay this is a veritable human frame, worn out with toil: not a form assumed for an apparition of thirty years on earth, but the form, as indissolubly united to the Person of him who bore it, as this of mine, and these of yours, are united to each of us. And observe, that in its union, it is very man: not, except at special times when He pleased, lifted up to superhuman capacity by the indwelling Godhead, not ordinarily able to endure without fatigue, to subsist without food, to renovate itself without sleep: but as was necessary for the Bearer of man's infirmities, for the Sympathizer with man's troubles, for the great Consoler of all who need consolation, like his brethren in all things, with one only most necessary and most teaching exception.

And so He sleeps on: and the oars plash regularly

in the falling twilight, till at length one quarter of the sky gathers darker than is wont, and suddenly there bursts down on the inland sea from its bordering valleys one of those squalls of wind, well known as the chief perils of all lake navigation. The tempest quickly, in those confined spaces, lashes the water into fury: the little vessel labours among the breakers, which begin dashing over her sides, and she is soon rapidly filling. Still, the weary passenger sleeps. So, and yet not so, did Jonah sleep in the sides of the ship, when he was fleeing from the face of God: for there may be deep sleep of different kinds. One may be calm in danger from apathy or unbelief, and another from blessed faith and reliance. Shall we not say of this Sleeper, that his slumber was deep and undisturbed, because it never had been broken by the start of guilt, or the working thoughts of terror? Shall we not feel that the beautiful words of our Poet are true of Him only,—

"He feared no danger, for He knew no sin?"

Such was the manhood of the Lord in its infirmity and in its perfection: in its weakness, and in its strength.

But meanwhile the disciples are filled with terror. Their boat is beginning to sink: and He, who they knew could save them, is all unconscious of their common danger. They awake him with something of reproach: "Master, Master, carest thou not that we perish?" It is not as it was to Jonah, "Awake, thou sleeper, and call upon thy God:" they know thus much, that He has power to save them: but they wonder that that power should not have been exerted before it came to this. Their call to Him is variously given by the Evangelists; as above,—or as in the gospel for this Sunday, "Lord, save us: we perish;" or as by St. Luke, "Master, master, we perish." "The sense is the same in all," says St. Augustine; "in all, they wake the Lord, and beseech Him to save them; nor is it worth our while to enquire, which of these contains the actual words said to Christ rather than the others. For whether they used any one of these three expressions, or some other words which none of the Evangelists has related, but amounting to the same verity of meaning, what has it to do with the matter in hand?" It had been well, if these remarks had always been borne in mind by those who compare the gospels one with another; they would have ensured its being done more in the freedom of the spirit, and not so much in the bondage of the letter.

The Lord is not slow to answer to their cry, though He reproaches them as being of little faith. They who had seen so many of His wonderful works, and who knew the love which He had for them, should have known also that He was not one whose power could be in this manner taken at a disadvantage, or whose care for His own could be thus defeated. But none of us, my brethren, can say that their conduct was not natural. I fear we all are of little faith: for I am sure we should all have done likewise. In the account in St. Matthew's gospel, this rebuke of His comes before the act of power: in St. Mark and St. Luke, it follows it. Whether it went before or followed, the certainty that it was given, and the lesson in it for us, are the same.

But now let us fix our attention on that which was done: for surely we are reading a narrative which stands alone in the history of our world. This man who, but a moment since, was fast asleep from weariness, rose and rebuked the wind, and said to the sea, "Peace, be still." We all know the effect of a sudden lull in the raving of the storm: the perfect peace which seems to take the place of the war of the elements: the sense of thankfulness and surprise with which we look abroad into the stillness. What then must this have been, when it was the instantaneous effect of the command of a human voice? "There was a great calm." No ordinary calm: not as usual after the cessation of a tempest, the waves still tossing with their disquiet, but half-appeased; but the lake became as in the calm of the breathless noon,—it instantaneously put on the glassy surface of the misty morn, or the long level lines of the solemn twilight. As before, in the Lord's first miracle, nature was silently endowed with powers not her own,—her slow processes anticipated,— her ordinary requirements superseded: so now, at His spoken word, her own powers are suspended, and their exercise forbidden. And as in that case imagination fails to trace the procedure of the creative act, so here of the repressive. We hear the wind, and cannot tell whence it cometh and whither it goeth: but He knows: the necessity that there is for the air to rush hither

I

and thither, filling up its void places,—where this exists, and why, He has it all in his thoughts: and what He commands, He works also. It was not in sober reality, as the wondering shipmen expressed it: the winds and the sea were not animated beings, who heard and obeyed, so that He should have no part in that which was done, but to command it;—far otherwise: it was all His doing. He who spoke was present in the far-off mountain passes whence the winds issued forth: He made the gathering eddies stand still, and stanched the pouring mist. The result was seen, the workmanship was hidden. He worked as God ever works: His ways were in the vast deep, and His path in the trackless air; the great calm, the accomplishment of that which was done, was the least thing that was wrought;—was but the token, that God had passed by, and nature was silent.

And so, my brethren, we have our blessed Lord in His weakness and in His strength: in His weariness as man, and His unwearyingness as God: in His tired sleep, and in His unslumbering watchfulness. "What manner of man is this, that even the winds and the sea obey Him?"

Turn we now to another aspect of His glorious Person and office. "They came to the other side, into the land of the Gergesenes." It was a land of limestone cliffs, pierced, as not uncommonly, into hollow caves, which were used in that country for the burying-places of the dead. Dwelling in those tombs, disputing possession with the wild beasts of the wilderness, were two creatures scarcely human, though bearing the forms of men. On one of these wretched ones is our attention specially concentrated. Terrible indeed is the description of him by the Evangelists: "When He was come out of the ship, immediately there met Him out of the tombs a man with an unclean spirit, who had his dwelling among the tombs, and no man could tame him, no not with chains; because that he had been often bound with fetters and chains, and the chains had been plucked asunder by him and the fetters broken in pieces: neither could any man tame him. And he wore no clothes; but always night and day he was in the mountains, and in the tombs, crying, and cutting himself with stones, exceeding fierce, so that no man might pass by that way." Was ever description more wild and fearful?

And as it is the most dreadful of its whole class, so let us take it as a type of the whole class, and ask ourselves, what was this which is here spoken of—this possession by evil spirits? And observe, that I am not now going into the general enquiry, which is a very wide one; but am asking the question with a view to our Lord Himself—His truth, His mercy, and His power. I may simply then and in a word say that whoever believes in Him at all, must also believe in the existence and agency of both good and evil spirits. For it is again and again certified to us both by His words and by His actions. There is no getting over this, or explaining it away. If such men as these, and the rest on whom his miracles were wrought, were not possessed by devils at all, but were only madmen,— and if He, in what He said and did, was only countenancing a popular delusion, why then I say, all trust in Him and in His words, is gone: He was no true Teacher, no pure and sinless Saviour: for He must have acted and spoken dangerous and blasphemous falsehoods. I speak thus strongly, to shew you how vain is the attempt to separate these cases from Himself and his teaching. Reject them, if you like: but you reject Him with them. Doubt and disbelieve, if you will, the existence of an unseen spiritual world about us and in us; but in doing so you doubt and disbelieve Him by whose holy Name you are called, and to whom you owe all you have both here and hereafter.

Well then, with this caution, we will speak as we believe, and simply assume the fact as certain, that these men were, or rather this man,—seeing that the second bears no prominent part,—was the wretched victim of possession by devils, the peculiar disease and burden of that age of the world. Evil spirits had entered into and taken possession of him. They used his voice, his thoughts, his limbs, for their unholy purposes. He was not his own master, but their slave. And this miserable state gave rise to a sort of double personality, not altogether unknown, be it observed, to those even now who study the more desperate forms of insanity. In this condition, while the man sometimes besought for deliverance, the demon broke in with his superhuman confessions that Jesus was the Son of God. We have this latter feature in the history before us. The evil spirits know the Son of God: and through the voice of their victim they pray Him not to torment them before the time. They know His lordship over them—they know that a day is coming, when He will adjudge their everlasting doom. Among the doctrines regarding His Person, notice this well. He is Lord of heaven and earth and hell:—of the evil spirits, as well as of His holy angels:—and He is their judge, and will pronounce their sentence in the end.

And now, for I deny it not, we come to matters of detail, strange, and passing our comprehension. The request on the part of the devils that they might not be sent out of the country,—or not into the deep,—but into the swine,—the permission given,—the destruction of the herd,—all this has time out of mind furnished ground of cavil to the unbeliever, and of reverent question to the enquiring Christian. But what wonder if we find ourselves out of our depth, when introduced but for a moment into the spirit world, of which we know absolutely nothing by any research or experience of our own? Rather should we receive such notices as these as each lifting some portion of the veil which hides that world from us, and teaching us by analogy how to think and judge of it. For instance, we are at least informed by this narrative, that certain evil spirits were then suffered to abide, tempting men, in certain portions of the earth; we see that the grosser animal nature, as well as that of men, is able to receive their attacks and incursions:—and we gather that it pleased our Lord, for reasons no doubt understood and sufficient at the time, to permit this to take place, and to destroy the swine in the waters. Among such reasons at once occurs to us this;—that the fact may have furnished more perfect assurance to the restored man himself, and to the neighbourhood around, of his complete deliverance: and as it has well been said, what wonder that He who ordains that myriads of animals should daily be slaughtered for the sustenance of men's bodies, should on this occasion have permitted the destruction of a few, for the better health of their souls?

But let us now turn to another and a very different spectacle, to him that had had the legion, sitting at the feet of Jesus, clothed, and in his right mind. O blessed result! blessed, in the fact itself; blessed, in the lesson which it echoes onwards through the ages of Time. Yes, my brethren, even thus it is that every one of us must fare at His hands, if we would be healed and live. We, thank God, have fallen in other times than those. His blessed Gospel, next to His holy Presence, has won its way on earth. He subdued the enemy for us—He saw him as lightning fall from heaven; and the softening and humanizing influences of his descended Spirit have followed. But there is a Satanic possession of which the world is not rid, and never will be, till He comes to judge it. We were all born in sin, and children of wrath; and though in Christ's church we have become the children of grace, yet is the old Adam not thoroughly driven out; yet is the law of sin still found active in our members, and furnishing material for our spiritual enemy to work on:—yet are we in that divided state, that the good which we would do, that we cannot: and the evil which we would not, that we do: even yet is the best of us in that condition which forced from the great Apostle that exceeding bitter cry, "O wretched man that I am, who shall deliver me from the body of this death?" Who, but He that rebuked the winds and the waves, and there was a great calm,—who but He that changed the fierce demoniac into a humble disciple,—He of whom the Apostle spoke, when he replied to his "who shall deliver," with "I thank God, through Jesus Christ our Lord?"

O Thou Stiller of the tempest, Thou Conqueror of the enemy for us, hear us, and save! In all time of our tribulation: in all time of our wealth: in the hour of death and in the day of judgment, good Lord, deliver us.

SERMON X.

(PREACHED ON THE FIFTH SUNDAY AFTER EPIPHANY, FEB. 9, 1862.)

PARABLES: THE TARES OF THE FIELD.

MATT. xiii. 3.

"He spake many things unto them in parables."

IN considering and applying the sacred Doctrines relating to our blessed Lord's Person and office, one of the chief sources of our knowledge must of necessity be found in His own discourses. He Himself said to the Jews, "I am, that which I speak unto you." He is His own best expositor.

Now in studying His discourses, one peculiarity cannot fail to strike us, which they have even amongst the sayings of inspiration itself. All these sayings are equally true, but they are not all equally deep and manifold in their meaning. Some sayings, for example, of the Apostles, are very simple and plain, and clearly have but one reference, which every body can perceive. Then again, if the Apostles' sayings are difficult to understand, it is very often a difficulty of this kind: do they mean this, or do they mean that? or, out of three or four possible meanings, which shall we take? And one man understands them in one way, another man in another way; or perhaps in the course of time some laborious student hits upon a meaning which all agree upon afterwards, and so the difficulty is solved. I do not mean to say that such is always the case with the sayings of the Apostles: but it is beyond doubt their general character. If we now turn to the sayings of our Lord, here again we meet with many which are very plain and simple, and with many also which seem difficult to understand: but, easy or difficult, they all have *this* about them, that they are inexhaustible in their depths of wisdom, and in their applications to man and to man's world. In the one case, the divine treasure was in earthen vessels: in the other, in a heavenly. In the one case, the Holy Spirit spoke by those who were limited in their powers and knowledge, and He adapted His divine inspiration to their human characteristics, and styles, of thinking and writing: in the other He spoke by One to whom the Spirit was not given by measure: who knew all things from the beginning; and to whom, even in the emptying of His glory, to which He submitted Himself in his humiliation, all the realities of things lay open. And hence too it is that, while we speak, and truly, of the peculiar style of writing of St. Paul or of St. John or of St. Peter, no one ever thought of attributing a *style* of speaking to our Lord. Our very feelings shrink from such an expression; which is no mean test of its being an improper one. The reason is, that His sayings are the very expressions of endless and fathomless truth; in human form indeed,—spoken with the tongue and written with the pen,—but spoken as man never spoke before,—written, when written down, as faithful remembrances of what He said, and unmodified by the individual style and character of those who recorded them. And pursuing the same thought, it is interesting and instructive to note, how the holy Evangelists have been guided to follow their individual bent, not in composing, but in choosing among, the discourses of our Lord: St. Matthew, who loves to write of Him as the King, and of His Gospel as the Kingdom of the heavens, giving us more those discourses which set forth his glory and majesty;—St. Luke, who presents Him to us as the gracious and immortal Saviour, giving us mostly discourses full of his rich mercy and loving-kindness;—while St. John, whose object it is to set Him before us as the fulness of light and sustenance and life to man, as coming to his own and rejected by them, but as loving and loved by his disciples, follows his great scheme regularly onwards, by recording for us those discourses in which all these points are one after another brought forward.

After what has been said, another matter regarding our Lord's sayings naturally comes to our thoughts. He who knew all truth in its purest and holiest forms, —*what was His method* of teaching? Let us first ask, *whom had He* to teach? And the answer is, He had various classes of persons, very differently affected towards Him, and very differently endowed with power to understand Him. First, there would be his own disciples, willing indeed to listen to and appreciate what He said, but mistaken in their view of that which He came to do, and quite unable as yet to take in any explanation of it. Then there were the common people, variously disposed;—for the most part hearing Him gladly, but dull of comprehension, and ready to be influenced by his enemies. Then there were these last, the Scribes and Pharisees, learned in the outward science of the law, eager for his halting, ready to catch hold of and press to the utmost against Him any thing falling from his lips which should at all violate their formal and superstitious maxims of interpretation and practice.

How should the Allwise one, in his humiliation, and condescending to be as man among men, proceed in one way of teaching for all these so widely differing hearers? Should He lay before them naked spiritual truth, such as in the unfathomable depths of his own divine Being He contemplated? Alas, to say nothing of what those hearers were,—what human ear could hear, what human soul could bear it? Should He anticipate the teaching of the Spirit who was to come upon the Church, and set forth the mighty doctrines of atonement for sin, of justification by faith in Him, of sanctification by the indwelling of the Holy Ghost? Again, should He declare himself the fulfiller of the types of the law—the Lamb of God that taketh away the sin of the world? Who among them could receive these things? When we hear, late on in his course on earth, that His very disciples questioned among themselves what the resurrection from the dead should mean, we may well imagine how hopeless, in the ordinary human methods of teaching, it would have been to introduce topics of this kind among his audience, before He had been lifted up on the Cross,—had risen from the tomb, or had sent down His Spirit from the Father. Once more;—should He become the stern and lofty moralist, and lay down to them the eternal limits of purity and of vice? Doubtless this was his office in a sense; and this He has done as none other ever has; but if it chiefly moulded the form of his discourse, how were they to be gained to this teaching? He came to teach all, as He came to bless all, and to die for all. How many, think you, among those He addressed would have gathered round him to listen to the purest and truest of moral disquisitions? He, remember, was not one set to teach by institution of man's device: one sure of an audience, and privileged to be dull: He came with a mission higher than that from men, to seek and to save: He was to draw men with the words of interest and sympathy;—to attach them, so that they would rise up from their occupation, leave their fishing and their tax-gathering, and go after Him.

Again then, what method of teaching did He choose? How did He produce the wonderful effects of which we read? Before we fully answer, let us take into account one more circumstance very essential to be remembered. Never man spake like this man. Doubtless it was a spirit-penetrating and heart-stirring thing, to sit and hear that Teacher speak. O what it must have been to look but for once on that brow, calm as the evening sky; to hear but one saying uttered in that voice, whose every tone sunk with gentle persuasion into the very depths of the being! Well might the Lord Himself say to His disciples, "Blessed are the eyes that see the things that ye see, and the ears that hear the things that ye hear." Still we know how variously even excellencies of speech and manner are interpreted, according to the feeling towards the speaker. What one enjoys and feels in his heart as simple earnestness, another turns away from and loathes as affectation: what one finds attractive, is repulsive to another. And doubtless so it was also in the case of our blessed Lord himself: His enemies, in order to remain his enemies, must have had their minds poisoned against him; and even his divine benignity, and his loving wisdom, can only have exasperated them more from time to time in their predetermined enmity to him. It was when this spirit of implacable hatred first began to manifest itself, when the Scribes and Pharisees began to ascribe to the influence of Satan our Lord's gracious miracles, that He saw fit, in his wisdom, to adopt that peculiar method of teaching of which my text speaks. "He began to speak to them many things in parables."

And what is a parable? I am not going to lay down all the distinctions which separate it from the fable, or the proverb, or the allegory: this has been excellently done by those who have written on the subject: but I will only say, bearing these distinctions in mind, that a parable is a fictitious story intended to convey spiritual truth, and is of a nature such that it is always taken from what might be actual life among men. Its form is grave, as its purpose is serious. It enters into the relations of life,—father and son, husband and wife, master and servant, king and people; into the operations of agriculture and commerce, the pursuits and ways of living among men, their differences, and their affections. In the highest sense of the word, but One Person could ever have worthily taught in parables, and that One was the Creator Himself. For it is required in such a story, that it should enter into the deep spiritual meanings which lie under all the relations and employments of life: and who knows these but God only? A mere man might make the parable fit the truth here and there: his applications of his tale might be doubted, might be criticised: he is commonly obliged to take a lower form for his instruction, and to put it into the mouths of unreasoning beings, as in the fable; thus leaving the region of reality, and missing all the deeper purposes of the other. But when our Lord spoke the parables in the Gospels, He himself tells us that He did it with the view of their carrying various shades of meaning, according as men's hearts were or were not disposed to receive, or capable of apprehending them. They were in fact in this respect just what that world of beauty and truth is from which they were taken. The child rejoices in the flower that he has plucked: its gay colours delight him, its sweet scent is pleasing to him: the botanist makes the same flower a study, and classifies it, and examines its structure: the moralist, and the poet, and the painter, also claim it for the uses of instruction and of art. And so it may be with the parable. First there is the simple story, which may interest even the heart of an intelligent child. Which of us is there that does not remember his fresh interest when a father's or a mother's voice first told him of the sower going forth to sow, or of the lost sheep, or of the prodigal son, or of the wise and foolish virgins? Nor is this the case only with the young at one time of their lives: it is so with the simple and half-educated all their lives:—with often this exception, which will lead us on to the next step in those that hear,—that ever and anon some real event in their own lives, some joy or sorrow,—some overflowing of mercy, or some bitter drop of anguish in their cup,— seems to bring out new meaning from that which they fancied they knew before. As with the Æolian harp that has long sounded one chord only in the gentle breezes of ordinary life, at times like these the strong wind of God's Spirit rushes over the strings and awakens new and higher harmonics, unheard before. And if this is so with them, what is it with those who love to think, and to weigh, and to delve into the deeper senses of those wonderful revelations of truth? Evermore by them are the Lord's parables seen in many and shifting lights, evermore are they heard speaking to them new and rich counsel as their need requires. None have ever exhausted their depth, none have ever so discovered their reference and connexion, that there are not new references and new connexions left for others to discover. Not unfrequently, as for instance in the parables of the unforgiving servant who had himself been forgiven, and of the good Samaritan, great Christian doctrines lie beneath the surface of their tale: sometimes, as in those of the wicked husbandmen and of the barren fig-tree, they are pregnant with prophetic meaning which time shall bring out: sometimes again, as in those of the lost sheep, and of the rich man and Lazarus, they open to us glimpses into the unseen and unknown world: still more frequently, as in the great first parable of the sower, and in that of our gospel to-day, they describe to us the state of the Church of God, in the world, and at the end of the world. And as we study each of these, and place it in new lights and connexions, more and richer meanings continually open to us, and will do so as long as we are in this realm of imperfect and still to be completed knowledge.

With these remarks before us, let us spend the remainder of our time in considering the parable which is contained in our gospel to-day; that of the TARES OF THE FIELD. It forms, as we well know, one of the most important of our Lord's parables. Of itself it would take this rank, owing to the great and world-wide interest of its subject: and its importance is increased by its being one of those of which the great Teacher Himself has vouchsafed to give us a full and minute interpretation.

First let us notice what the parable is about. It is a likeness setting forth to us the kingdom of the heavens :—by which name the Christian dispensation, or the state of the Church of Christ on earth, is generally known in St. Matthew. It represents to us a field, which is explained to mean the world;—and a man who has sown good seed in it, who is said to be the Son of man, i. e. Jesus Christ, the incarnate Saviour. This exactly agrees with what our Lord Himself tells us of

His gospel;—that it should be preached before the end, in all nations. This preaching He himself began; and in His strength, and by His commission, His Apostles and those who have followed them have carried on, and still are carrying on. And that which is sown, the good seed, is the word of God;—the good news of the Holy Gospel. No one need be surprised, that this very seed should be said in the explanation to be the children of the kingdom, i. e. the true servants of Christ. For it is here, as in the parable of the sower: when the seed has fallen into the soil, and taken root, it becomes the plant, transforming the soil into itself: so that they into whose hearts the seed is dropped, when the seed grows, become themselves the plants which that seed produces. The main principle of life and action which we follow, is not *part of us*: we are *part of it*; and it is the root and centre of our being. Thus then, and with this purpose, the good seed is every where dropped by the Great Sower and His servants.

But this is not the only sowing that takes place. The sower of the good seed has an enemy. His enemy came while men slept, and sowed the seed of noxious weeds over the field. This wicked act is an exercise of malice not without example even in our own times. I have myself known such a thing wilfully done, and made the subject of legal damages.

Now notice the doctrine herein contained. This enemy, our Lord expressly tells us, is the devil. While men slept,—not, while the Son of man slept,— while, not the Great Head of the Church, who never slumbers, but they who were His infirm and imperfect

K

ministers, slept,—came this enemy, this arch-enemy of God and man, and sowed his evil seed. I told you last Sunday that if you believed in Christ at all, you must also be prepared to believe in a spiritual world;—in good and evil spirits, both employed in us, and around us. And observe here His own distinct assertion of this:—of the good by and by;—of the evil here. These children of the wicked one,—these tares that spring up in the field of the Church, are the sowing of God's enemy, the devil:—of him who is ever counterworking the blessed work of the Son of man and His agents. Nothing can be more plainly declared as a truth for us by our Lord, than this.

But we proceed. When the wheat came up, and put forth its fruit, then appeared the tares also. And now comes the difficulty felt by the servants of the owner of the field; "Didst thou not sow good seed? Whence then came the tares?" And so it ever is and will be in the Church. The Gospel is good; its preaching is good; the ordinances and sacraments are good; good seed is sown, and Christ sows it. And yet how is it, that evermore in the Church there are multitudes of bad men, unholy men, unbelieving men, growing among good men, looking like good men, partaking of all the rich privileges of membership of Christ? How, and whence, came they? Hear the Lord's answer: "An ENEMY hath done this." "They are the children of THE WICKED ONE:" none of Christ's sowing: no growth out of the sacraments and means of grace: no result of men trying to be righteous overmuch: nothing of the kind: but distinctly, and as matter of fact, the result of the devil's work counteracting Christ's work. And yet silly shallow men, with all this taught and forewarned them, stand and look on upon the Church, and in the spirit of an unbelief they have not the courage to profess, whisper about, "What is the use of all this stir about the Church,—all this praying and preaching and sacraments and ordinances? We don't see that men are made much better by it: we can point out as bad men among Churchmen, even among ministers, as any that are found in the world outside." And suppose you can. Did He who founded the Church, and who saw all her course before Him, ever lead you to expect otherwise? Nay, has He not here expressly told us it would always be so? That this is no excuse for the sins of Churchmen, we see by the awful end of the parable; but it is an accounting for what will ever be found in the Church,—the mixture of good and bad men.

But we now come to another feature. The servants are not only surprised, but offended, by this state of things: scandalized, that their lord's field should grow evil weeds with the wheat: "Wilt thou then that we leave our work and go and gather them up?" Now this question represents the mind of a very large party in Christ's Church in all ages. Its acts are stamped on her history: and not only so, but they are among us in our own time also. Make the Church pure, say they: count those only the Church, who are converted to God, and live by faith in Christ: let us have a close communion; none at our Table, who answer not to our test. O how prevalent is this spirit; not among one party only, but among all parties: and how busy it ever is in men's hearts and practices.

But let us hear the answer. He said unto them, "Nay: lest while ye gather together the tares ye root up with them the wheat also." Memorable and blessed words! How do we know, how does any man on earth know, the good from the bad, so as to be able to say, as between two men of outwardly correct life, which is, and which is not, a servant of God? What folly it is, as well as sin, to make the use of certain religious words and phrases, or the use of certain devotional practices or postures of outward reverence, the test of inward spiritual good in a man! What hypocrite cannot put on either of these, as much as may be required of him? And is not every age full of sad examples of hypocrites who do, and end by bringing open disgrace on the party which adopts them?

But look on the other side. "Lest ye root up the wheat with them." How many genuine servants of God have been discouraged, dejected, robbed of their hope, and perhaps of their faith too, by this narrow and unchristian zeal! "He is not one of *us:* his words and gestures and religious practices are not *ours:* therefore he does not belong to Christ." This is what our religious leaders and writers on either side think and say every day. And what is the effect? Discouragement, coldness of hearts, deadness to Christ's work, general distrust of one another. But what does our Lord command? "Leave both to grow together till the harvest." Feed both, love both, anathematize none, exclude none: make tares into wheat if you will, but destroy not God's wheat by making it into tares. For there is not the slightest fear that any tares will ever be gathered into God's barn at His harvest. Vex not and fret not yourselves. He knows His own; He knows those who are not. At the season of the harvest, He will say to his reapers, "Collect first the tares and bind them in bundles in order to burn them." "So," our Lord tells us, "will the holy angels go forth at the end, and will collect out of His kingdom all the causes of offence, and will cast them into the furnace of fire: there shall be the great weeping and gnashing of teeth."

Let not us then anticipate that final separation, but rather take care above all things that at that time He find us bringing, or having brought forth, good fruit to His praise. Blessed are they who shall be thus found at His coming. For He who is all mercy and grace, and who spoke this parable, not to denounce judgment, but that place for repentance would be given to all, ends it with gracious and joyous words: "Then shall the righteous shine forth as the sun in the kingdom of their Father."

SERMON XI.

(PREACHED ON SEPTUAGESIMA SUNDAY, FEB. 16, 1862.)

PARABLES: THE LABOURERS IN THE VINEYARD.

MATT. xx. 16.

" So the last shall be first, and the first last."

THESE words occur both at the beginning and at the end of the parable which forms our gospel to-day. They are as it were the burden, or refrain, of it, carrying with them its point and its moral.

The parable is one of those which convey to us important lessons of Christian doctrine. It, like our last, that of the Tares of the Field, gives us a representation of the whole course of the divine dealings with mankind. And also like that last, it brings out one particular point in those dealings for our instruction. In this case that point is the one expressed in our text:—the independence, in God's judgment of men, of all our human estimates of priority of claim or superiority of deserving. He is not accountable to us for His bestowals of His sovereign grace: He does what He wills with his own; whether nations or individuals, we are the clay and He is the potter, to make one vessel to honour and another to dishonour: God putteth down one and setteth up another: He hath mercy on whom He will have mercy, and none may call Him to a reckoning.

Now these may be difficult doctrines; they may be even to some disagreeable doctrines; they may be doctrines not safe in every one's hands, nor desirable for any of us to be always thinking about: but they are Christian doctrines, constantly and solemnly urged upon us in Holy Scripture, and therefore not to be missed out in any statement of Christian doctrines, such as that in my present course of sermons,—destined as they certainly are by Him who has revealed them, to exercise, when soberly stated and humbly thought on, a salutary effect on our hearts and lives.

With these introductory remarks, let us approach the parable itself. Now perhaps of all parables, this one depends the most for its being rightly understood, on a full knowledge of the circumstances which led to its being spoken. For it forms a direct commentary on a question asked of our Lord, and on His own answer to that question. The circumstances then were these. A rich young man, who had enquired of our Lord what good thing he should do to obtain eternal life, had gone away disappointed, on hearing of the sacrifice of his worldly substance which was required of him. Our Lord hence took occasion to speak of the difficulty of a rich man entering the kingdom of heaven: adding, in reply to a question of the Apostles,

"Who then can be saved?" that with God all things were possible. Then came the enquiry which led to our parable being delivered. Peter, who was ever the forward spokesman, framing in words, and boldly uttering, the thought which was doubtless on the minds of the rest, rejoined, "Behold, we have left all things, and followed thee: what shall we have therefore?" And then our Lord, with that simple truthfulness which ever presents both sides of a matter, without fear or bias, first announces to them the pre-eminent greatness of their own reward—their sitting on twelve thrones in the new state of things, judging the twelve tribes of Israel;—and not only this, but He also proclaims the general law of his heavenly kingdom, that every one who shall for His sake leave brothers or sisters or father or mother or children or lands, shall receive many fold as much, and shall inherit eternal life. So much for the positive promise; which, remember, no opposite doctrine can ever modify or explain away; and which nothing in the following parable must be understood as contradicting.

Now however we come to the other side of the divine dealings. "But," our Lord adds, "many first shall be last, and last first." Let us see how we should have understood this saying, if the parable, with its connecting words, "For the kingdom of heaven is like," had not followed upon them. I suppose we should have understood them somewhat after this manner. We could not have imagined them for a moment to mean that God's dealings would be uncertain and capricious, or that any who were really first, in sacrifice or in service, should be by Him accounted last in His final apportionment of reward: but we should have so interpreted the word "*first*," as to secure for it a meaning of this kind,—that these persons, many of whom would turn out to be last in the end, imply those who *think themselves* first, or whom *men think* first, or who on account of any seeming advantage appear to have prior and greater claim than others,—who really are first, at a certain time, and for certain reasons, but are not first on the whole, and at the end. Many of these, our Lord says, will discover in the end that their claim is nothing;—or that it has been marred by some fatal set-off against them; and they will have to take their place among the last: will be least in the kingdom of heaven, or even excluded from it:—among the last of all, whose lot will be then adjudged. And on the other hand, in interpreting the other clause, "and the last shall be first," we should take the word "last" with the same caution,—and understand it to mean, those who think themselves last, or whom men account last, or who from any apparent shortcoming, of time, or birth, or place, or circumstance, appear to have served God at a disadvantage as compared with those others. Many of these again, our Lord tells us, will find at last that their place is not where they humbly placed themselves, nor where men placed them, nor in proportion to their manifold disadvantages, but far better than so:—among the first, and most honoured, and most richly rewarded.

Such, I suppose, would have been our understanding of these important words, if the parable had not been spoken. Now this understanding of them the parable is intended to make surer and deeper and clearer: while at the same time it opens to us,—as does every illustration spoken by our divine Teacher,—other and new truths as to God's dealings, which we could not have known without it.

It begins with the small but most important word "for," rendering a reason for that which has just been said. It shall be so, because God's kingdom,—His way of proceeding with men—His bestowal of grace and work, with a view to a great final award, and that award itself,—is like the following account of what might be human, every-day transactions. And the account is this; taken, as we shall afterwards see, not for example of what is right, but to illustrate the great truth just spoken in this case.

A householder,—a man, that is, occupying an estate or farm,—goes forth in the early dawn to hire labourers into his vineyard: the vineyards, in that country, being the principal portion of cultivated land, as the cornfield or the hop-garden might be with ourselves. And the supposition is, that he does not employ a certain staff of labourers in permanence, but goes out into the market or public place to seek them from day to day. On this particular day, he wants as many as he can find; and he seeks them, and finds them, at several different times, answering to the quarters of the day, with one remarkable exception presently to be noticed. With the first lot of men engaged, he makes a special agreement. He hires them at what is called in our version *a penny*, but what really is a denarius, about eightpence, for the day: which, according to the practice of the time, was a liberal day's wages. With the second lot, hired at the third hour,—say nine in the morning,—and with the two following lots, hired at noon and at three P.M., he makes no such agreement: he only tells them that whatever was just, he would give them. But he pays one more visit to the public square, and that at the eleventh hour,—one hour before sunset: when the shadows are beginning to lengthen, and the men in the vineyard are thinking, in their weariness, on the near approach of their dismissal. This may seem a strange proceeding, but none have a right to find fault with it. The work of the day in his vineyard is not accomplished, and he wishes for more hands to bring it to completion. To these, after remonstrating with them on their standing all the day idle, and receiving for answer that no one had hired them, he simply gives an order to go also into his vineyard, without exciting in them any expectations, further than would necessarily arise from the very fact of hiring at all;—the confidence of fair remuneration, which underlies every commercial contract between man and man. It may be well now to pause, before we come to the next incident in the parable, and to make sure of our interpretation thus far. Clearly, for here there is no doubt, in the householder or landholder here, we have set before us Almighty God,—the owner of all and the employer of all;—the great Taskmaster, to whom our time and labour is due. His vineyard again is His work in the world, or in the Church, or rather in the world by the Church:—

that work to which He calls whom He will, and when He will:—which He is pleased to carry on by employing His creatures as His instruments and fellow-workers. As to the rest of the machinery of the parable, it is evident it admits of many interpretations. The *day* here spoken of,—we may take it, if we will, for the whole lifetime of the world,—the whole day of time; and then the labourers first called will be the Jews, whom God summoned to His work under a special covenant; and those who succeeded will represent the Gentiles, with whom as yet, when our Lord spoke the parable, there was no special covenant entered into; and these coming in one after another, even to the nation, whatever it be, which shall receive the Gospel just before the end shall come:—or we may, if we will, take the day as representing the lifetime of the Christian Church, and the first labourers as the Apostles, with whom our Lord, by his reply to their question, had just entered into a covenant, and a definite promise of reward;—and then those called afterwards will represent us of later times, who have followed, with no such high mission and no such special promise, trusting in His faithfulness who hath called us:—or again we may take the day to represent the day of human life, and the first called labourers those who have in the morning of life entered the service and begun the work of God, taking up and making their own the covenant obligations of their baptism, serving on certain and known conditions: and then those hired at the following hours will answer to men who have obeyed the call of God at various periods of their lives, in high youth, or when the work of life is at its busiest, or when life's sun is beginning to decline, or even when the light and strength of life is well nigh over,—at the eleventh hour of old age.

All these various meanings have been given, and all I believe are right. The parable is manifold in its applications; it has in fact many more than these; any circumstances whatever, which can constitute a difference in *time* of God's calling of men, or in *advantage* of using their powers for him, in the *amount*, or the *kind*, of work done, of sacrifice made, of apparent claim for ultimate reward,—to any of these will the parable fit, and in any of them so far find a lawful application to the distinctions between man and man as labourers in the vineyard of God.

But now let us advance in our consideration of the Parable itself. At length the evening arrives, and the labourers come in to be paid. The lord of the vineyard says to his steward, "Call the workmen and give them their wages, beginning from the last even to the first." This prescribed order does not in itself seem to mean any thing, but as you will observe, it is necessary for the working out of the parable : it must be previously seen what the last were to have, in order for the first to find ground of murmuring.

First then among the workmen appear those who were called at the eleventh hour. They receive every man the denarius, the sum agreed upon for the full day's wages. This was more than they had a right to expect, bestowed out of the free bounty and good will of the owner of the vineyard. And so the payment goes on, each receiving the same, until the steward arrives at those who had been hired earliest in the morning. They thought they should have received more: their amount of work had been more, they had borne the burden and heat of the day. And here we cannot help thinking on the Apostles' question and its ground: "Lo we have left all and followed thee: what shall we have therefore?" But observe:—they also received each the same denarius; the fair day's wages for the fair day's work; and further than that,—the very sum covenanted at the beginning when they were hired. Now those who would rightly interpret the parable must not shrink from acknowledging, that there does seem, if we look merely at the human side of the story, and judge by those expectations which all men form of proportionate amount of remuneration for work done,—that, I say, there does seem some reasonable ground why these first hired labourers should be dissatisfied. It would be vain to deny it: nor does our Lord mean, I believe, that such treatment would be always just and right in human dealings: but that, for certain other reasons, which do not apply to our human dealings, the way in which men will be dealt with in the kingdom of heaven resembles the conduct of this householder, which, as I said before, is not proposed as an example for us, but only as something by which the great truth may be illustrated. The words which the householder uses in reply to the murmurers, undoubtedly would not satisfy a fair-dealing judgment as between man and man: we should certainly say, that though he had a right to do what he would with his own, he was hardly acting fairly in the disproportionate favour which he shewed to those who had been standing all day idle, and had only worked one hour, and in the neglect and scanty measure with which he treated those who had spent the long weary day in his service.

Now it is very important to bear all this in mind; and it has been far too little thought of by those who have dealt with this interpretation. For this parable is like that of the unjust steward, or that of the unrighteous judge, in this respect, that our Lord takes the worldly dealings of worldly men, not for us to imitate as they are, but for us to learn heavenly things by, and to become as wise in our state as children of light, as they are in theirs as children of this world.

Let us then go on to say, in order that we may make this instruction clear, that the answer which these first labourers got was, in the mere human meaning of the parable, rather hard measure. A man who is liberal, should also be just. We can scarcely suppose that all the early-hired labourers were bad, and all the late-hired good: they were the same kind of men: but the owner of the vineyard chose, in doing what he would with his own, to favour the one set, and to disfavour the other. And this, judging hardly and literally, according to the strict technical rule of his covenant, he had a right to do. He gave the first what he had agreed to give them: he gave the last what he pleased. With the first there was a covenant, which he fulfilled to the letter; with the last, there was none, and he was to them very liberal. And when one of those first murmured at what he received, the householder had a perfect right, in strict hard justice, to say what he did: "Friend, I do thee no wrong: didst not thou agree with me for a penny? Take that thine is and go thy way: I will give unto this last even as unto thee. May I not do what I will with mine own? Is thine eye evil, because I am good?"

I say this was strictly and barely *just*: it was not what we call *fair*, using a wider word, which takes in not only agreements and covenants, but also tacit and unwritten expectations. But such expectations themselves, let us remember, are grounded on a certain state of things, found in men's mutual intercourse with one another: on the value of one man's work to another,—on the right which we have to look for an equivalent for pains bestowed:—all, thoughts and hopes dependent entirely on the equality of rights and merits as between man and man.

And now let us endeavour to translate the parable into the realities of spiritual things, remembering well what has been said concerning it. First let us see what it cannot mean, and clear it from one or two misunderstandings. Well then, we are sure that the Judge of all the earth will do right; and that whatever there appears of wrong or hardship in the parable, belongs to its mere human machinery, and not to its interpretation as applied to the divine treatment of us all. Now let us return and ask, what is it that makes the appearance of hardship here? Is it not,—to follow out what has been already hinted at,—the fact that we all regard wages for work done as bearing a certain proportion to that work, so that the more work, the more wages? And consequently we cannot help feeling that if the eleventh hour men were, for whatever reason, paid by the penny, the men who had worked all day ought to have had more? Now this, I think, clears up very much the spiritual interpretation. Between man and man, there is a debtor and creditor account of obligation incurred and payment due; even when not absolutely stipulated, men take this for granted, and expect accordingly. *Between man and God, there is no such relation.* No man ever made God his debtor, or laid Him under obligation to him. Every covenant between God and man is an act of free undeserved grace on God's part. We have forfeited by sin all claim to God's favour; and even had we never sinned, all we have and are is His, and we can earn nothing from Him. The man who has served Him during a long life has no more claim on Him than he who was converted to Him yesterday; and the question "What shall we have therefore?" was one deserving the rebuke given to it by this Parable, as founded in ignorance of the true position of man in the service of God. It is entirely of God's free grace that we can do works well pleasing to Him at all: and this doing what He will with his own, which was the somewhat harsh measure dealt out by the earthly master, is, as applied to God, His absolute right, founded in eternal Justice, and exercised by infinite Love.

But again;—another error to be avoided is this, which persons very commonly fall into in interpreting the parable. All got their denarius,—their penny. All, in the story, were paid the same. Therefore, say some, all will get the same, who are saved and rewarded in the

L

end. To which I answer, Impossible. Scripture is against it,—every declaration of divine love, every consideration of common justice is against it. Let us consider the interpretation with a view to make it clear that it is not so. *What is* this reward of the Christian? Eternal life, you will rightly answer. But what is eternal life? I reply, the enjoyment of God:—the knowing Him, loving Him, seeing Him, as He is. This is life eternal. Take one hundred men, and give this gift to all of them: I say that no two of them will have received the same. The greatness and the richness of the Christian reward are measured by the man's capacity for knowing and seeing God. Take for example these murmurers at the owner of the vineyard: do we suppose that such a spirit as that was likely to enhance the value of the denarius which they got? Would it not be absolutely worthless to them? Would not the heavenly inheritance be to such men without a charm, even if they entered on it?

And so it is and will be with God's unspeakable gift of Himself, and His heavenly kingdom. On His part it is the same to all His people. All who are saved have life eternal; all who are saved have Himself to enjoy. But very different will be the enjoyment of Him in those who have loved much, and sought Him early, and served Him long, and in those who have but a short time of their lives turned to Him: at least such will be the case generally, and as a rule: the more love, the more obedience: the more obedience, the more knowledge of Him; the more knowledge of Him here, the brighter revelation of Him hereafter: the brighter the revelation, the richer the joy. But all this will be marred and blighted, all this will be reversed, if pride suggests, and presumption puts forward, the question "What shall we have therefore?" Such a thought will reduce the first to last: the creeping in of spiritual pride will poison a thousand Christian virtues; will spoil the final reward, by dimming the sight of God and cooling the love of Him.

And to every man of us, to each in his place, to each with his advantages, to each with his causes for thankfulness, come these words like a solemn knell of constant remembrance:—"THERE ARE FIRST THAT SHALL BE LAST." Let us take them to ourselves before we end this subject.

In how many things, my brethren, may we be said to be first, or among the first! Born in this happy land of light and freedom: dwelling under the vine and fig-tree of spiritual abundance,—ever drawing water out of the very wells of salvation;—such are we of this realm and of this Church of England;—first in the world in the knowledge of God, in the acquaintance with,—and, notwithstanding our many faults, in the practice too of His holy will. And then to come nearer; what are we in this place, we worshipping day by day in this glorious temple, we summoned week by week to the Table of our Lord, we who dwell in a city of which, if she disgraced her Christianity, the very stones would cry out? Truly, my brethren, we are first among the first; most privileged in a privileged land: longest at work in the vineyard, bound to God by the most ancient and the most explicit covenant. "But there are first that shall be last." We of England—we of Canterbury—we of this church,—do we mean thus to fall through from our high estate, and be cast away after all? Are we resting in our own superiority, pluming ourselves on our pure belief, and our apostolic Church, and our burning and shining line of Christian worthies? and are we looking down on others who have not had our advantages—others who in our esteem are last,— and hardly to be counted at all? Ah, my brethren, there may be many of those who will be preferred before us, in that day when we shall stand before God. And there assuredly *will* be,—if we do not, each in his place, give ourselves up to the humble and zealous service of our heavenly Master.

But there is consolation in the words, as well as warning: and with that I will end. "THE LAST SHALL BE FIRST." Be of good cheer then, humble and unknown Christians, whom no man has placed among the busy outward religious,—whose tongues are silent, it may be, on holy things, and with whose hearts' secrets the stranger intermeddleth not. Men may despise you, but God knows you: men may slight you, but Christ loves you: the sheep may not know one another, but the Shepherd knows them all; the Church's brightest lights often shine heavenwards, and she never sees them, because she does not live enough in heaven.

At the same time, let us remember what has been already said. Though reward is not of merit but of grace, yet as God is true, REWARD THERE IS, rich reward there shall be, when He cometh in his kingdom: reward not for pretension, not for spiritual pride, not for priority of calling, not for accumulation of claims before God, — but for humble earnest self-denial, for meek submission, for cheerful resignation, for love that spends and is spent.

May you and I by God's grace thus sow our seed in this time of tears and of toil, that we may stand laden with the golden harvest-sheaves of His rich approval, in the day of His appearing.

SERMON XII.

(PREACHED ON SEXAGESIMA SUNDAY, FEB. 23, 1862.)

PARABLES: THE SOWER.

LUKE viii. 15.

"That on the good ground are they, which in an honest and good heart, having heard the word, keep it, and bring forth fruit with patience."

THERE is hardly any of the parables fuller of instruction than this of the Sower. The two which have come before us on the two last Sundays, those of the tares of the field, and the labourers in the vineyard, have been rather concerned with the great outward course of God's church and government: but this has to do with the effects of the gospel, when preached, on men's hearts and lives. Its character is more spiritual and inward than that of those others. At the same time it, like those others, bears its testimony to great Christian doctrines: and the two which stand most prominent in it are, the power of the word of God, and the power of the heart of man to receive or to reject it. The word of God is likened to seed: the heart of man to soil, on which the seed is cast.

The power which lies wrapt up in seed is wonderful. It contains the germ of the future plant: and not only that, but a faculty, granted by the Creator, to develope that hidden form and become itself the plant, and in time to bring forth new seeds, like what itself once was. But the exercise of this power is altogether dependent on its being deposited in soil favourable for it.

The soil, on the other hand, has certain powers imparted to it by the Great Creator, of acting on the seed: and without these being called out, the seed remains barren and unfruitful.

Even so it is, my brethren, with the word of God, and the heart of man. The word of God is quick and powerful, containing in it all the germs of spiritual life, able to make wise unto salvation, able to multiply itself indefinitely by the living plants which spring from its deposition up and down the world. But it again is altogether dependent on its being deposited in the soil of the human heart, and on that soil being favourable for its reception. And that soil, the heart of man, has certain powers imparted to it by Him who made it, powers of acting on and vivifying the seed of the word dropped upon it, or of excluding it from entering into its inward parts, and rendering it unfruitful. These are the lessons given us in the main by the parable. Let us deal with them separately, and then go briefly through the various classes of hearers which it brings before us.

The word then is SEED: sown, as our first great parable told us, by Christ, Himself or his agents: sown every where: sown at all times. Principally perhaps in preaching: but in plenty of ways, besides preaching. The sower is ever sowing. The word of God is cast upon us in our private thoughts, in our converse with others, in our hearing or reading of daily events, of mercies, of judgments: in our education, and in our business: in our sicknesses, our bereavements, our hopes, our fears: day by day and hour by hour, as well as in solemn places and times.

And O what wondrous power this seed has, if it do but penetrate a man's heart and grow there! First of all, it is quite unlike any word of man, any mere piece of human wisdom or human information. Drop that into a man, and if he receives and understands it, it becomes part of his mental or practical store, he becomes so much the wiser, so much the better informed: but drop the very least word of God into a man, and it does not become part of him, but he becomes part of it: it springs up in him, and does not cease growing, till it has taken up and overshadowed his whole being. It changes him into itself: in its light he sees light: deeper and deeper, higher and higher, reach its root below, its branches above; and it, which was once less than all seeds, has become a great tree, in which all his thoughts and feelings and desires find shelter and abode. A man may come to know that Cæsar invaded Britain, and he has an addition to his knowledge, remaining the man he was: but a man cannot come to know that Jesus Christ died for sinners, and remain the man he was before he knew it: it enters his heart, and constrains him by love, and penitence, and gratitude, even till he loses his former life, and lives by faith of the Son of

God, who loved him and gave Himself for him. I say this will be so, when a man *knows* this for a fact: not merely when he hears it, reads it, speaks of it, preaches of it :—for thousands do all these, without ever KNOWING it :—thousands do all these, and go on in the service of sin, in the pursuit of pleasure, being in and of this present world, thinking they have only to perform their moral and social duties, and all will be right in the end :—but let only the fact, "JESUS DIED FOR ME A SINNER," sink down into the caves and springs and deep soil of a man's heart, and he cannot live in sin,—he cannot follow the world's fashions,—he is discontented with and loathes his own best performances of duty :— he sees God in another light, he sees himself in another light, he sees the world in another light : in a word, "if any man be in Christ he is a new creature : old things are passed away, behold all things are become new." Such is the wondrous power of the divine seed : such the transforming energy of the word of God, received and understood.

But now let us pass to the other great truth—the preparation of the heart in man. This immense result of which we have been just speaking, it is not in man's power to bring about, any more than it is in man's power to make a plant out of a seed. It is God's doing : and all the means and ways to it are of God's providing. But though this is so, yet here, as with the seed, God is pleased to make men his fellow-workers. He provides the inherent power both in seed and soil. But He does not put the seed into the soil : He does not, except by larger and more general influences than those of which we are at present speaking, prepare the soil for the seed. Both these he leaves to be done by man. It is true, that even these are from Him: it is expressly written that the preparation of the heart in man is from the Lord : but this clearly means that it cannot be carried on without His gracious help and continual blessing ; not that He does it, and leaves man to sit still. The Christian doctrine is this : not that divine grace comes down upon us, carrying us out of ourselves, overbearing and superseding our own natural will: rather does it affirm that it is of God's unspeakable grace that we have a will to seek to Him,—that the power of exercising that will is granted and is continued to us by the same free and undeserved grace : but that it is WE who must use that grace, it is we who must exercise that will, it is we who can exclude His word and His grace from working in our hearts, it is we who can seek His promised help simply and earnestly, and by it can open our hearts to His word, so that the seed shall drop in and work by its own wonderful inherent power.

Now in what we have to say about the various classes of hearers in the parable, we shall see various degrees of this preparation or of the neglect of it, and corresponding various degrees of the failure or success of the deposited seed of God's word.

In considering the first class of hearers, we must form to ourselves some idea of the spot where the sowing takes place. Imagine a field, extending over portions of soil brought under various degrees of cultivation, by and by to be described. Through this field there runs a beaten path. Such a field is represented by the rude but vigorous hand of the ancient glass-painter in one of the larger windows of this north aisle of our choir: and it is interesting to remember, that that representation of the parable, which has stood there with its silent testimony for nearly 700 years, was made for the worshippers here when there were no printed Bibles, and when in fact those illustrations were the great Bible for the people. How much better ought we, who have the written word in every room in our houses, to understand its teaching:—how much more deeply to feel it! But this only by the way. Imagine then such a field, —and such a path across it. The sower casts his seed every where. So God casts all His bounties. "Why this waste?" is not Christ's question, but Judas's. "What is the *use* of doing this and that good, kindly, liberal act?" is not a wise man's enquiry, but a fool's. And the seed being cast every where,—some of it, much of it, falls beside this beaten path: on ground partly trodden, full of footmarks and hard spots. What is likely to become of this seed? There is doubtless a chance of its coming up, and even prospering. The ground is not all hard: softening showers may fall,—or, as it lies there on the surface, the foot of the passer-by may tread it in, instead of crushing it:—when the crop comes up, the path may be reduced more within bounds, and it may become a portion of the crop itself. But it has other enemies, besides the passing feet and the half-beaten soil. It lies exposed—it has not sunk in. The birds of the air came and devoured it up. And so, our Lord tells in the explanation, it is with a whole class of hearers of His word, who when they hear, do not understand: do not *take in* what they hear. It passes over the outward ear: it lies for a time on the surface of the memory. There are soft places in the heart, into which it might sink if it had a chance: even the most frivolous and least earnest are not past feeling;—they have their hopes, and their loves, and their little interests, through which the good word might find a chink of access, however unpromising it may seem: and now and then God's heavy hand descends on the brittle fabric of their trifling pleasures, and the softening hour of sorrow might let the good seed into what soil there is in them. But this is all too good to be true in their case. The enemy of souls is too quick for such triflers. Those who will not take care of their own souls are wards of his, and he takes care of them for them. "*Immediately*," our Lord tells us, he "comes," losing no time, "and takes away the word which has been sown in their hearts, lest they should believe and be saved." Takes it away; how? Has he then access to our hearts and can he remove thoughts and facts out of them? Perhaps we should be wrong in saying that the parable asserts so much as this. There may be many methods of taking away the good seed. It has merely lain on the outer surface, and has never in reality become the thought of the heart. And so any bird of the air, any passing thought, any trifling or flitting concern,—a coming entertainment, or a past one,—or an idle jest on coming out from the place of hearing,—or a thousand things even less marked and assignable than these, may prove the breath of the

Tempter, and the descent of the evil bird,—and the good seed shall be gone, and its place shall know it no more.

Multitudes of every congregation, multitudes of you, my brethren, belong to this class of hearers: people who sit and listen, without any real interest or earnestness: on whose minds there remain perhaps a few things that have been said, for a little while: but the Tempter, whom you see not—and perhaps only half believe in, so far has he deluded you,—is ever busy about you; and before the Sunday is over, or perhaps before you are out of these precincts, he will put in his thought, his fact remembered, his prospect looked forward to,—and what you heard is gone for ever.

And yet—*gone for ever?* was this true? Ah no, my brethren: nothing ever goes for ever. The seeds were sown in the wind, and it blew them away: but you will reap them in the whirlwind: not in blessed fruit, but in bitter ashes of remorse, in the day of desperate sorrow.

And what class comes next? Truly, a very different one. Some portions of the field are very near upon the native rock:—stony places, where there is not much depth of earth. The moisture lies confined here; the sun's rays act with power on the rock, and its scanty covering: the seed falls as on a hot-bed: long before the rest of the field, this plot is clothed with beautiful green blades: it is a speedy and a wonderful promise,— and the inexperienced husbandman passes by and rejoices. But alas for all his hopes:—let the sun rise high,—or, as we should rather say in our less tropical and less certain climate, let dry weather set in; there is no depth of soil holding store of moisture: there is no root sent down into places where the hot sun, or the drought, has no power: the same beam which once heated into life, now scorches to death:—all the blades wither away,—all the fair hope is disappointed:—and when the field is golden with rich corn, that corner is a rustling mass of shrunken straws.

Now who are these? Who, but those hearers who are ever impulsive, ever ready to run after the sound of preaching, receiving the word with joy? With them, all seems done in a moment. O blessed sound of God's word! O quick and ready effect! What a warmth of heart, what a softness of feeling must be there:—what a blessing, if all were like these:—what an encouragement to a preacher; what a present reward for his toil! But wait awhile, and the more experienced pastor will wish all were like any but these. Track them into life: watch them in what ought to be their growth in grace. Where is the blessedness they spoke of? Where is all that gushing forth of earnestness which seemed ready to lead to any amount of fruit? Where are these, when the hard eye of the man of the world lights upon them:—when scorn and derision encounter them? Before we answer the questions, let us look at these hearers a little more closely. This warmth and openness of heart, what is it—how deep does it go? What is there beneath it? The hard impenetrable rock. They are even more hopeless, as to any lasting effect, than the former. In them the surface was hard, but there was good soil beneath, if it could be got at. And so it very commonly is with the rash and impulsive, with the ready praiser and the soon-moved: he is even harder beneath than the trifler and the light-minded. In this latter the hindrance is on the surface: you never got down into his real self; but you may some day, and you may find a good sterling character after all. In this second case, the *advantage* is all on the surface, and the hindrance is *beneath*. When you look for depth in the character, and for root to the plant, you find there is none. All is stir, show, earnest feeling: but the whole character is not an inch deep; there is no sub-soil, for any thing worth having to grow in. And so these hearers cannot stand even the least amount of trial from without. At the first contact with tribulation, persecution, ridicule, the heavenly shoot that was so promising is all withered up and gone. They are offended. The joy at hearing the word cannot last for ever: the word, if rightly heard, brings sorrow as well as joy; and when that comes, they fall away. These are not so common as the former; but they are by no means uncommon. They constitute a great portion of the audiences of popular preachers; running about at the call of "Lo here," and "Lo there," but shewing no solid fruits of grace and obedience in their lives. They are more to be found perhaps in great cities, where all is intelligence and stir, and there is abundance of choice what people will hear, than in retired country places like our own, where the current of thought moves slow, and the area is but limited: and every where they are more to be found among the softer sex and the young, than among those who are habituated to the real business of life.

The mention of these last brings us to the next great division in the parable. In the field there is also a portion of soil to all appearance good and well prepared and deep, but not well cleared from the roots of noxious thorns, which at the growing season will be sure to send up their shoots and cover the soil. There the seed falls in, and for a time all goes well. It sends down its root, and pushes its blade upward: but with the blade come up also the rank vigorous runners from the unclean weeds. And the result is as may be supposed. The weed is ever stronger than the wholesome plant: that which is indigenous, than that which is brought from afar. And so the tender blade is choked, and draws up weak and yellow and sickly, and its ear just appears, but there is no fruit in it, and so it dies away.

Ask we what class of hearers we are now dealing with? Let us listen to the great Teacher Himself: "That which fell among thorns are they which when they have heard, go forth, and are choked with cares and riches and pleasures of this life, and lusts of other things, and bring no fruit to perfection." Observe, that here all goes well at first. There is not the inattentive ear of the first set, nor the easy and shallow susceptibility of the second. The soil is good and deep. These men hear and understand. They go their way, and remember what they have heard, and resolve well; but their hearts are preoccupied with other things: they have no room for good thoughts in them: no time for doing good and obeying Christ. Now such hearers are very common indeed: far more so than would at first sight appear: far more so among us, than those of the last class. And one large detachment of them consists of persons in whose hearts the good seed was sown by Christian parents in welltended childhood, and who have always been leading moral and correct lives, and imagine on that account that the heavenly plant is prospering in them: forgetting that the good seed is not the only thing that has been growing there; that evil propensities, fleshly appetites, selfish ambition, and other evil weeds, have been growing too, and will assuredly, unless they be rooted out, choke the divine plant and render it unfruitful. "Render it unfruitful:" for they will not quite destroy it: there will be the form of godliness; the coming to church, and it may be to Holy Communion: the correct belief, the carefulness about all proprieties: but NO FRUIT: no real self-denying living zeal for Christ or His work. O how often do we see this—a sickly dwindled religion, dragging on in men a miserable contemptible existence; known by all but themselves, and sometimes known by themselves too, to be an empty farce; upheld on fitting occasions: defended with indignant assertion when their credit is at stake or their worldly advantage,—but forming no part of their belief, and being a matter on which they never so much as waste a thought in private, or a prayer by their bedsides, unless some one else sees them. And even what appears to be fruit, in such persons is not fruit. They give it may be for charitable ends; but it is because it is expected of them, or to get rid of importunity, or that they may not appear less liberal than such or such a neighbour; but never because they love the Lord Jesus Christ,—because they would obey what He has commanded;—which is the only motive that bears fruit towards God. And many of this class too belong to those who really intend to be Christian men, but the world is ever coming in and preventing them: Sunday's resolves melt away before Monday's business,—are replaced next Sunday, again to disappear in like manner.

But is there no class in whom the seed really does change their nature and find fit soil to grow in? O yes, brethren: "Some fell on good ground, and sprung up, and bore some thirty, some sixty, some one hundred."

And who are these in the interpretation? "They who in an honest and good heart, having heard the word keep it, and bring forth fruit in patience." Observe first here, the *honest and good heart*. This is the very first condition of hearing the word profitably. The intent must be clear and simple. *Clear:* a man must not come to church he knows not why, but with a view of getting good and becoming better; and *simple:* this view must not be only one among many, but must be the ruling and the only one. Look at the difference from the other classes. In the first, the wayside hearers, there was no intent at all: they were shut up and hardened by carelessness and indifference. In the second, the joy with which they heard was no settled purpose: it merely rustled on the surface, and was not felt beneath at all. In the third, the intent was neither clear nor simple: it was complicated, uncertain, disunited: there were side-purposes, worldly regards, present and prevailing. But in this last class, there is the requisite; an honest and good heart. And therefore the holy seed comes to maturity, and bears according to their capacity,—in which one man is made different from another. Having heard the word, they keep it; hold it fast, clasp it to them: the little tendrils, so to speak, of their thoughts and affections twining round that which they have heard, so that it is the stay and stem of life to them. There is in these what there was not in any of the others, inward disposition of heart acting on life. "It yielded fruit springing up and increasing," says St. Mark: it sprung up, for there was no hardness of surface: it increased, for there was both depth of root, and clearness of space for its growth.

And notice, that the fruit borne is the man himself, not something outside him: not an assignable quantity of good deeds which may be laid to his account,— but HIMSELF, body, soul, and spirit, made into a tree of righteousness which the Lord hath planted.

Notice also the various proportions of fruit-bearing which are mentioned. Here indeed in St. Luke we have but one : "they bare fruit an hundredfold." But in the other two Gospels we have three degrees introduced:—some thirty, some sixty, some an hundredfold. It is remarkable, that here none merely gives back what he received. There is no "Lo here is thy talent which I have kept wrapped up." The *least* in the kingdom of heaven brings forth fruit *thirtyfold* what he received as seed. And what wonderful power again this shews us in the heavenly seed itself. That which lay light on the surface of the trifler's heart, and was swept away by the whisper of another trifler when church was over, has sunk into the honest and good heart, and reappears thirty, sixty, an hundredfold increased in the life and actions of a good Christian man, or a good Christian woman,—bringing glory to God, and blessing to mankind.

And once more notice these degrees for another reason. See how they are calculated. It is not, which ear stood highest, grew rankest, furnished the better sample; but, which produced MOST FRUIT. It is not birth, nor acquired station, nor personal influence, nor wealth, nor intellect, which will tell in the great harvest : it is, how much fruit was brought forth for God and for good.

And remember as we separate, that we have been speaking to-day not of a matter of choice, not of something which may or may not take place in us; not of a growth which if it goes on may make us somewhat better, and if it is checked may leave us somewhat the worse: but we have been dealing with a matter of life and death. We MUST receive the seed, we MUST spring up, we MUST bring forth fruit to God, or we are LOST MEN. If we come here merely to listen, and remain as we are; if we come here merely to receive the word with joy, as we would the sound of an instrument, and in time of temptation to fall away; if we come here to hear and understand, and then let the miserable world choke the seed and make it unfruitful, —we are not better, but worse, for coming here; and what we hear shall appear against us in the great day.

O may God deliver us from hearing with the hardened heart, from hearing with shallow and unabiding excitement, from hearing amidst worldly thoughts and choking cares: and may He give us (for it is His gift alone) the honest and good heart, that having heard the word we may keep it, and bring forth fruit with patience.

SERMON XIII.

(PREACHED ON QUINQUAGESIMA SUNDAY, MARCH 2, 1862.)

WHY CHRIST SUFFERED.

LUKE xviii. 31.

"Then Jesus took unto him the twelve, and said unto them, Behold, we go up to Jerusalem, and all things that are written by the prophets concerning the Son of man shall be accomplished."

WE are close upon the season which the Church sets apart for meditation on the sufferings of our Lord, and on our own sins, which were the occasion of those sufferings. And this gives at once an opportunity to one preaching a course of sermons on Christian doctrines, to employ this Sunday in enquiring, for our profit, HOW CHRIST'S SUFFERINGS AND OUR SINS WERE CONNECTED. Further on in the season, we shall be employed more with the details of both sides of the subject—with the necessity of our repentance and sorrow for sin, and with the whole procedure of our blessed Lord's death and self-sacrifice. So that it will be better for us now at the entrance of Lent to follow the guiding of the

Church, and put and answer this question—WHY DID CHRIST SUFFER?

Now bear in mind what was said in the very beginning of this course. "All have sinned:" this was our first subject. We tried to shew you the truth of this, as opposed to modern unbelief: to bring out the fact that there is in us a continual protest against wrong, testifying that we were made for better things: but at the same time a continual doing of wrong, testifying that we are fallen to worse things. Then, after, in our second sermon, shewing the deceitfulness of sin, as accounting for the many treacherous forms of mental and practical unbelief, we insisted, in our third, on the solemn and just sentence, "The soul that sinneth, it shall die:" shewing to you that death, bodily and spiritual, flows from and is the consequence of the sin of our nature. Then on Christmas day came before us the great leading truth of redemption;—that God, sending His Son in the likeness of sinful flesh, and for sin, condemned sin in the flesh. Let me quote to you a few sentences out of that Christmas sermon, for it was the centre and keystone of the year's teaching, even as the doctrine of which it treated, the Incarnation of our Lord, is the centre and keystone of the system of Christian doctrines. After striving to shew how He was sent in the likeness of sinful flesh, viz. in perfect manhood, and for sin, viz. to take away our sins, I went on to say, "Now this taking away our sins He accomplished by two great things which He did: by his life, and by his death. The Apostle Paul puts this very plainly and clearly before us: 'If,' he says, 'when we were enemies, we were reconciled to God by the Death of His Son, much more being reconciled we shall be saved through His Life.' The whole process of this wonderful matter—how His Death reconciled us, how His Life saves us, will come before us, please God, hereafter." And then soon after I said, "The Son of God has become Man: our nature is united to the Godhead. A new and righteous seed is implanted in it: a second and perfect Head is granted. The first Adam was tried and fell: but this new Adam shall be tried and shall gloriously conquer. The first Adam, being created liable to Death, lost by sin the means of escaping death, and bound it as a lasting curse on himself and his posterity: the second Adam, also born liable to death, was pleased to become obedient unto death for our sakes; thus condemning sin, the cause of death, in our flesh. The first Adam brought the penalty of his sin on us, the Head on the members: the second Adam suffered the penalty of our sin for us, the Head for the members." Now you see where we at present stand. The Son of God was, like the first Adam in his innocence, born liable to death. Death was in fact more a certainty for Him than it was at first for Adam. Adam was of the earth, earthy: and even without sin, he must eventually have been subject to decay and dissolution, if he did not first take of the tree of life and thus live for ever. This liability became by his sin a definite sentence of death on him and his race: and thus the second Adam, who was the Lord from heaven, took on him a nature which, however personally pure as dwelt in by Him, was yet under, not the possibility or the probability of decay, but this definite sentence of death owing to sin. So that, although the death of the Son of God was a voluntary self-sacrifice, even at the last moment, yet it was not, so to speak, an act outside of his human nature, brought in upon it, but an act belonging to it and involved in his taking it upon him, unless, which He could have done at any time if He had pleased, He had exerted his divine Power and saved himself from it.

Now then our question returns upon us,—WHY then did Christ suffer? And this you will see resolves itself, as concerned with the matter of fact of His sufferings revealed in Scripture, into *two* questions: why did He die *at all?* and, why did He die *as He did?*

Now for the sake of reverence, and that we may keep ourselves, in every man's mind, in our proper position, let me say that we do not for a moment ask either of these questions, as if we could ever answer them by any unaided speculations of our own. It is impossible that we can understand even the simplest truth of redemption, except by the light which God's record of redemption sheds. It is in that light, it is as Christian believers, that we ask these questions. Holy Scripture has been pleased to assert, or to imply, sufficient answers to both of these. What Scripture asserts, it is the preacher's duty to enforce: what Scripture implies, it is his privilege to unfold. And all we have to say in replying to these questions will fall under one or other of these descriptions: will be an attempt either to enforce what Scripture has asserted, or to unfold what it has implied.

Why then did Christ DIE? And we may boldly answer, with certain warrant of Scripture, that if He had not died, we could not have been saved. I have dwelt often, I dwelt in the next sermon of this course to that on Christmas day, on the vast share in our redemption which is due to our Blessed Lord's life of holy and spotless obedience. And I then insisted on this point; that that obedience went even beyond all absolute law and covenant binding the blessed Mediator as obedient to the law for man : it went to a further point, to which the Lord was not, even when under the law, bound by a law ; to which He was constrained by nothing but transcendent Love. That Love had indeed bound Him of his own will in the bonds of an everlasting Covenant to do this thing, because this thing was necessary in order that we, the race whom He undertook to save, should be redeemed.

And now look on the matter itself. The Son of God takes on him human nature : takes it entire : in St. Augustine's words, once before quoted during these sermons, takes it "from the very highest boundary of the rational soul down to the very lowest boundary of the animal body." And our whole manhood is summed up in Him. He who does not apprehend this, has yet to learn the very first principles of Christian doctrine. The Lord Christ, in His work of Redemption, carries all men in Himself: *is* all men, for the purposes of that work.

Now then contemplate Him thus standing in the human nature, and intending to redeem the human nature. See Him brought face to face with Death. Which of two things shall He do? He bears about

Him this human nature, which is doomed to death for sin. That He has not personally sinned, and could not sin, makes absolutely no difference to the matter: physical death is not the consequence of each man's sins, it is the consequence of Adam's sin, whereby the stock of the whole race passed under it. Christ then bears this death-sentenced nature. But being the eternal Son of God, the everlasting and immortal, shall He, as beyond doubt He has power, cast this sentence from him, —stand with his disciples, say, on Mount Olivet at any time during His ministry, and ascend to heaven in their sight, and thus glorify the body of humiliation which He had taken on him?

With all reverence, because treading in the sure path of inspired teaching, we answer, that this might not be, according to any right view of the consistency of God's dealings with themselves. And we surely are bound to require that consistency most of all, when the highest and most exemplary of those dealings is before us. And even if this had been possible,—the likeness of sinful flesh would thus have been made partaker of the throne of the Father. Flesh and blood would have inherited the kingdom of God. There would have been in it this manifest violation of divine justice: that the taint of the race, of which the sentence of death was the token and retribution, would have remained unaccounted for, untaken away. In fact we are dealing with a supposition in itself inconceivable: so much so, that, on the other side, among Christians, the ascension of the Lord into heaven is ever regarded as the crowning and decisive proof that the sin of the world is taken away, and that all manhood, which He bears upon Him, stands accepted and clear before the Father.

Let us then ask again, why does the Son of God die? The answer is very simple;—as a SACRIFICE FOR THE SIN OF THE WORLD. It was the ultimate and perfecting act of His obedience, to carry down into death that death-sentenced nature which He had taken into the Godhead: to subject His divine Person to the dark and to us utterly mysterious contact with the actuality of death, and to *put by* His almighty power of casting off from himself the sentence of death which He bore about him. That this was so, was the testimony of his Forerunner, when he said, " Behold the Lamb of God, that taketh away the sin of the world :" is His own testimony in many places, and especially when He says that He came to give his life a ransom for many: is the testimony of his holy Apostles, Paul, Peter, and John, frequently and solemnly in their writings: is the belief of his holy catholic Church, in an unbroken line from the earliest primitive times even to the present: and I may add, is the foundation and source of spiritual life, and hope of salvation, to a multitude whom no man can number, of Christian believers in all nations of the world.

This is why Christ died: that He might in his own body, as the second Head and including representative of mankind, pay the penalty of death, which rested on that manhood which was summed up in Him.

Now without waiting to meet the objection which this offence of the Death of Christ is sure to raise in the minds of worldly and of disputatious men, let me say one word before I pass on to our other enquiry. The GODHEAD of our blessed Lord is an element absolutely necessary to the belief of even the least portion of the benefits and effects of His death. If a man do not firmly and clearly hold that, he has not a notion of what is meant by the doctrine of Christ's Atonement for sin. His entire oneness with the Father lies at the very root of all. We are apt far too much to take a divided and separated view of the great covenant work of our Redemption, and especially of this part of it. You must regard the Father and the Son as One in it, or you cannot see it in its justice, holiness, and love. No doubt there is solemn and necessary truth in the words which express the Father as exacting, the Son as paying; the Father as requiring, the Son as rendering satisfaction: but we must never forget, in using them, that there is not for a moment to be imagined want of union, or diversity of purpose, or any thing but the most entire and holy accord in the great work of redeeming mankind. Scripture is in many places very explicit on this point; and no words can more strikingly illustrate this combination of the two truths, than those wonderful ones of our Lord Himself: "Therefore doth my Father love me, because I lay down my life that I may take it again. No one taketh it from me, but I lay it down of myself. I have power to lay it down, and I have power to take it again. This commandment have I received of my Father." We see in these words the purely voluntary act in the blessed Redeemer set forth to us as the object of holy love on the part of the Father: and at the same time, that which is so purely voluntary in Him is placed before us as a commandment and appointment of the Father, received and consented in by Him.

I proceed to our second enquiry. Granted, that it was necessary for Christ to submit to death in order to the taking away of the sin of the world, why did He die AS HE DID? For it would appear perhaps at first sight that, death being the penalty of the sin of that nature which the Lord took upon him, the mere fact of death might have sufficed: and then the mind would go on perhaps to suggest that as the divine Person who was to make this satisfaction by death was transcendently great and glorious, it might have been well that circumstances of shame and publicity had been spared, nay even that the avenues to death by weakness and pain should not have been trodden in this case, but a painless and honoured decease have been secured; seeing that, as I said, the act itself seems to be all that was required.

I am reluctant, when on such a subject, to put before you any hypothesis of human imagination; but I do it, that the great truth of the matter may be brought more plainly and clearly into view. First then, I say in answer, that we have no right to speak thus, because we cannot tell how much of deep humiliation and desertion and anguish was absolutely necessary, in the covenant which infinite wisdom arranged, to make that Death the full and sufficient sacrifice, oblation, and satisfaction, for the sins of the whole world. It is not for us to say that, even for this main purpose of the Lord's death, any one pang was borne in vain,

WHY CHRIST SUFFERED. 175

any one insult or mockery endured, any one circumstance of shame undergone. The analogy of the Redeemer's whole life on earth leads us to the humble inference, that nothing less than such an amount of self-denial, and endurance of pain, and contradiction of sinners, was enough for the accomplishment of His mighty purpose, even in its hidden and unfathomable recesses, where it flowed forth from unity with the Father's will.

But if we look at this same matter from another and a human point of view, even to *us* there may be made plain a full and sufficient reason why these sufferings should have been undertaken. Our Blessed Lord Himself sums it up for us in a few simple words: "I, if I be lifted up, will draw all men unto me." And the beloved disciple adds: "This he said, signifying what death he should die." Not only was the Lord's death to make satisfaction for the sins of the world, but it was also to draw all men unto him. It was not enough for His great work that the penalty of sin should be paid, but it was its object to provide that strong constraining love, which might melt the hard heart of the careless sons of men, and attract them to Himself as their Saviour and their Consoler. He came, that he might fathom the very depths of human sorrow: that there might be no dejection in which He might not be seen as the companion and sympathizer;—no pain of which it might be felt that he never knew it, no shame that should ever shrink from pouring out all its penitent tears before Him, who had been signally put to shame. We want such a Saviour: such an one, who is also a Consoler in all human trouble. For this our life is full of trouble, full of pain, dejection, anxiety, bereavement;—and such times are our times of good,—our softening times, when we think seriously, and look for one to save and bless us. But if the Saviour set forth to us were a stranger to our sufferings,—if He who is Head of our humanity in heaven had led a life which had nothing in common with the suffering, the stricken, the guilty, the shamed,—how should they fly to Him in their anguish? So then the way which the Lord took to draw all men unto Him was this. He was born of humble birth,—in a condition of manual toil: he had not where to lay his head;—he was despised and rejected of men,—a man of sorrows, and acquainted with grief: he underwent contradiction, insult, persecution, and finally a shameful and agonizing and accursed death. So that all through the depths of human misery and ignominy, His footsteps are to be seen: out of every one of them may the sufferer reflect, "The Lord has gone even hence up into glory:" and there is no chamber of anguish so dark, but the blessed light of His presence and His triumph is there. Surely then, my brethren, even if not in what was before said, we have a sufficient reply to the question, "Why did our Blessed Lord suffer and die as He did?" We know not that every pang of His suffering was not necessary in His work *for* man: and we do know that every one was necessary for his work *on* man: to bring in that constraining love which should draw all men to Him, and make them live to Him who thus sacrificed Himself for them.

Now look at the effects of this life of suffering—of this death of shame. Has it not, ever since it happened, been drawing men to Him? Have not untold thousands lived in His love, and died for His love? Has not nation after nation and creed after creed been drawn within the irresistible impulse of this constraining love,—so that it has proved more powerful than the persuasions of human wisdom, more attractive than the charms of worldly power and pleasure, yea a mightier coercion than the chains of bondage and the terrors of the oppressors of the earth?

How this constraining works in men, and what it effects within them, will come before us, if God will, at other times in our course: let us now conclude with applying to ourselves that of which we have spoken to-day. These stupendous sufferings of the Son of God were undertaken to put away sin; the sin of the world; the sin of each man: and they were undertaken that each man may be mightily constrained, by the power of the divine Love shewn in them, to take up the freedom thus purchased for him; to see himself complete in Christ His satisfaction before God; to live as Christ's freeman, prevailing over and conquering sin, and daily renewed with God. Is this, my brethren, our state and mind? Are we gaining continually fresh victories over sin, the world, and the devil? Are we subduing our tempers, restraining our tongues, living in brotherly peace and love and forgiveness, following Christ and His blessed example? O let me impress on you the danger of being but half-Christians. Listen to Christ's message to the Church of Laodicea—"I know thy works that thou art neither cold nor hot: I would thou wert cold or hot: so then because thou art lukewarm and neither cold nor hot, I will spue thee out of my mouth." To hear of the sufferings of Christ, and hear of them unmoved: to know why they were undertaken, and then in our own persons to hold them of no account: to profess ourselves members of Christ, and to be mere dead members, exercising no life: branches of the true vine, and to be clad merely with the leaves and tendrils of a fair profession, but to bear no fruit:—there is nothing against which our Lord more frequently lifts up His voice than this hypocrisy: there is nothing which He will so sorely and so signally punish wherever it be found, at the great day of His appearing.

Doctrines are of no use, except as leading to practice: sermons on doctrine are of no avail, unless they clear, and quicken, and bring into new vigour and energy, the Christian lives of those that hear them. And it is the sole purpose with which I have undertaken this course of doctrinal sermons—with which I have deserted for this year the more attractive paths of unwritten exhortation, and bound you down to a regular statement of the things believed among us,—that we may be better grounded, more assured, more thoroughly convinced, not for speculation, but for hope sure and stedfast: not for disputation, but for faith working by love: not for condemnation of others, but for that all-enduring and all-believing charity of which you have heard that it is the greatest of Christian graces, being the very essence of GOD Himself.

SERMON XIV.

(PREACHED ON THE FIRST SUNDAY IN LENT, MARCH 9, 1862.)

OUR LORD'S TEMPTATION.

HEB. iv. 15.

" He was in all points tempted like as we are, yet without sin."

IN considering those Christian doctrines which group around the person and work of our blessed Lord, His Temptation, brought before us at this season, and by the Gospel this day, is far too important a matter to be passed over, though we have spoken on it to you from this place before. I shall deal with it however to-day not minutely and in detail, but on general grounds and with immediate reference to the subject of our present course.

HE WAS TEMPTED. Here is our fact: and in this fact is much matter for our consideration.

I will first then speak of our Lord's temptation as a portion of His great mediatorial work in redeeming us. That work, as you know, was carried on and brought to perfection by two things: by His unsinning Life of righteousness, in which He wrought for us perfect obedience to God's laws, and by His atoning Death, in which He paid the penalty of the sin of the world. Now our Lord, in his spotless childhood and youth and early manhood,—all passed at Nazareth in humble daily duties,—had already accomplished a vast amount of this perfect obedience. It now remained for Him to come forward publicly, and present himself to men as the Saviour: healing and teaching in the power of the Holy Spirit, which was given to Him without measure. And for this his public ministry, He has been especially inaugurated and set apart at His baptism by John his forerunner: at which time also the Almighty Father by a voice from heaven gave His solemn testimony to Him;—"This is my beloved Son, in whom I am well pleased." Now then begins the open and decisive work of the Son of God as the second Adam, as the champion of our human nature, as One who was to make us more than conquerors through His conflict, and His victory over our Foe. His power has been hitherto hidden in obscurity: it is now to be put forth. And where and how shall its first conquests be achieved? Here is our Head, our Champion, our Substitute,—bearing the nature of man upon the Person and nature of God. He stands forth for the ends of the earth to look to Him and to be saved. Even so stood the first man in Paradise, and was tried, and fell, entailing, as we have seen, death and misery upon us his progeny. And the second Adam is to reverse this: to bring in life, to bring in righteousness; to overcome, where the other was defeated; to stand gloriously, where the other shamefully fell.

So that the Temptation, consisting as it did of a conflict with the personal malignant power of evil, bringing in as it did a decisive victory over him, proving as it did that the Foe had nothing in our Lord, no power to touch or to allure Him, was the very first and most obvious work to be undertaken in the great public process of our redemption. Henceforward, in our Lord's earthly course, it is not of temptation that we hear any longer. The evil one is vanquished; falls as lightning from heaven. The power of darkness indeed returns for a while in Gethsemane, and on the Cross: but not the hour of evil suggestion from without, only of the weakness of the flesh, unequal to the willingness of the Spirit. This Temptation with its decisive victory was indeed Paradise Regained: not regained *for us*, without much more that our blessed Redeemer did and suffered, but regained in the completeness of the evidence thus furnished absolutely and once for all, that our Lord was not to be solicited, not to be tempted, by the approaches of sin. And so the Temptation bears its part in the actual work of Redemption done for us by Christ.

But now look at it in another light. If it was necessary that this Temptation should be undergone, and that the Son of God should overcome the evil one, it was equally necessary that the details and manner of the Temptation should be set before us as we have them in the holy Gospels. And that for two reasons. First, that we may be possessed of the absolute certainty of the humble and self-denying character of our blessed Lord. Nothing gives certainty, like detail. We may have even overwhelming reasons to believe that He was free from unlawful appetite, from presumption, from ambition: but when we see that He actually was tried with each of these, and did in his own Person repel them, we feel, with infinitely more reality and vividness than we otherwise could have done, that He is the humble self-sacrificing Redeemer, who came not to seek his own, but to seek and to save that which was lost. And this detail was necessary secondly, that we might have His temptation before us as our model and pattern, how we are to resist the temptations which beset us. We want to be shewn the best way to meet and to overcome the allurements enticing to sin. He was tempted like as we are. As He resisted and overcame, so must we: by the same means, and in the same spirit. As our Captain fought, even so must we his soldiers fight; with the sword of the Spirit, the word of God. Where He planted his feet so firmly, there alone likewise is our safe standing-ground in the combat with our spiritual foe; even on the footing of our humble obedience and bounden duty. The same holy wisdom which He shewed must also be ours, not shrinking from the use of God's word because the enemy misapplied it, but rather persisting in its truth against the untruth which it was made to tell. And thus also we needed to know of Christ's temptation, that it might be our example and model.

But now a question comes before us, all-important as regards our Lord's sacred Person, and his entire freedom from sin. It may be said, Is not all temptation, was not His temptation, a solicitation to sin? How then could it have any reality for Him, who knew no sin? "Every man," says St. James, "is tempted, when he is drawn aside by his own lust and enticed." How then was this with our Lord? Because if there was in Him, though ever so slight or faint, any desire tending towards sin, then we have not the pure and spotless Redeemer whom we need; then He could not be one with the holy and sin-hating Father; then, in a word, our Redemption could not have been accomplished by Him.

Now do not put by this question as an unprofitable one; for it is not. It is for us to study the acts and sayings and Person of our blessed Lord, wherever they are revealed to us—for in the knowledge of Christ stands our eternal life, and it is in that knowledge that we are to grow and make progress. How then was temptation possible for our Lord? How did it get its reality? How is our text true, that He was in all points tempted like as we are, sin only being excepted?

Now in answer to this I say, Let us observe carefully the manner in which, and the channels through which, the Lord was tempted. If you look at the two scenes of temptation, that in Paradise and that in the wilderness, you will see that there is one remarkable circumstance common to them both; viz., that in both cases the temptation came from *without, not from within*. Our first parents were created good: in them were no present sinful tendencies. Therefore when the enemy would tempt them to sin, he outwardly approached them under the guise of the subtlest beast of the field, and he put into their minds thoughts which were not there before: or rather, to speak quite accurately, he did this to Eve, and she, when she had fallen, did the same to her husband. The first approach of and the partial attraction to evil to a sinless being cannot be from within, but must be from without. It is another and a widely differing consideration when the evil does not partially attract, but, as in the case of the fall of a sinless spirit, absolutely possesses the whole being. We are not now speaking of that, but of temptation happening to man, compounded of body and spirit. And even so was it with our Saviour. The tempter *came to* Him; held converse with Him. It was necessary that this should be so: other conflict with evil could he have none. It was a like temptation to our temptations, with the sole exception of sin, which in our case gives the Tempter a handle within us to lay hold of, whereas in our Lord the enemy had and could have nothing. And hence you may see the excessive folly of those who would view this whole narrative of the Temptation as merely a figurative account of something which passed within the mind of our Lord, but is ascribed to another person coming and speaking to Him. Why, if a single thought of all these that were suggested ever originated in the mind of our Lord Himself, he was not the Son of God, he was not the Saviour of men.

So much for the *manner* of His temptation, as contributing to the answer to the question, How was it possible for Him to be tempted? And now let us go to the channels through which the temptation acted on Him. It may be said, Suppose the Tempter *did* come to Him and try Him by these suggestions: what were they to His perfectly sinless soul? Would not they glance as idle darts from the surface of a polished shield? How could they ever become to Him matter of conflict or of victory, seeing that He had nothing in common with them? Now here let us give some careful thought to what are the channels of temptation in our own case. Our temptations attack us through some lawful, some appointed desire or tendency of the body or mind. That desire or tendency in itself is not sin: but the temptation is to use it in some unlawful way, and thus to commit sin. "The woman saw that the tree was good for food, and that it was pleasant to the eyes, and to be desired to make one wise." The faculty to discern what is good for food, the desire to take that in which the eyes delighted, the desire to know and be made wise—these were not in themselves sinful: they were implanted by the Creator in that nature which was as yet perfectly good: but the exercising these tendencies and desires in a matter respecting which there was a direct prohibition from God,—this it was which was sinful: this it was which was the letting in of temptation and the giving the Tempter the victory. Now look at the case of our Lord. He had fasted forty days and forty nights, and was worn out with hunger and weakness. In this feeling there was no sin. When the angels came and ministered to Him, we may presume that that appetite of hunger was yielded to, and satisfied. But the Tempter's suggestion was to satisfy it by departing from his path of humble obedience: by exerting supernatural power out of the course of the will of His heavenly Father. Well then, trust in God being now asserted by our Lord to be his chosen path,—

through even this does the Tempter again assail him. He places Him on the high roof of the temple, and bids him cast himself down, trusting to God's preserving hand. Thus would trust be turned to presumption. This having also failed, he next attacks Him through the blessed desire of his soul for the advancement of His kingdom of Redemption on earth. He suggests to Him that for the accomplishment of this, the purpose and yearning of his heart, there is a short way, better than the long and painful one which He was about to tread;—that of falling down and worshipping him. Thus we have, in each case, lawful and laudable desires and feelings made the channel of temptation to our Lord.

And now let us bestow some more thought on the way in which He met the suggestions of unlawful use of lawful means, thus made to Him from without. And observe that He, in his conflict with the Tempter, was not, like us, liable to be led astray by his fallacies, or confounded by his subtlety. There was no more danger of this when the most powerful of evil spirits was set against him, than there was when his adversaries were the Jewish Scribes and Pharisees, of whom we read that no man was able to resist the power and wisdom with which He spake. But of this irresistible power and wisdom he makes no use here. If He had done so, His victory might have been more notable and complete; but it would not have been, as it now is, the most precious of lessons for us. It was not his purpose to confound and wither the Adversary by the mighty exercise of his divine power and infinite wisdom: this, though angels might have admired, men could not have imitated:—but it was His purpose to combat and to conquer as Man, and *for* man, with weapons accessible to the meanest of His disciples, from a standing-point common to Himself and the lowest of us. He answered and said, "It is written." Here spoke humble obedience: the submission of himself to His Father's written word: the waiving and putting aside of all thoughts and all reasons of His own, and sheltering himself under the expressed will of His heavenly Father. And notice that He does this not in general only, as man, but in particular, as under that special form of God's will which was revealed to the children of Abraham, from whom He was sprung according to the flesh. All His citations of Holy Scripture are from one book: and that one contains the summary of the law given on Mount Sinai. He answers the Tempter, not as God manifest in the flesh: not as possessed of any wisdom or power beyond the common: not even as when He spoke with the doctors at twelve years of age, and all were astonished at his understanding and his answers: but as the ordinary Jewish man might do who knew and applied the law under which he was born. And with these three texts, thus plain in their meaning, thus ordinarily and simply applied, He puts to flight all the arts and devices of the Evil One, and breaks his power for ever.

O what a precious lesson is this for us, my brethren: —for us who are daily tempted with common temptations, and not seldom tried with greater ones, more than our own strength can bear! Are we not often disposed, in the prospect of such trials, to say within ourselves, Now must I put forth all my strength: now is the time to shew my powers of reasoning, my firm determination to stand fast in the faith: to recollect all I have read and been taught, and to meet the Tempter with it, that my victory may be complete? Ah, my brethren, and how do we deceive ourselves if we think so! The subtle spirit who tempts us is infinitely superior to us in all these arts which we think to bring against him: his fallacies will confound our best reasoning, his allurements will shake our firmest determination, his wiles will elude our utmost vigilance. There is one way, and but one way, in which the meanest, youngest, least skilled of Christ's servants is superior to his fallacies, his allurements, his wiles, be they never so subtle, never so attractive, never so deeply laid, and that one way is, the simple path of humble unreasoning obedience. "I cannot do as thou wouldest have me, for I am God's servant, a member of Christ. His vows are upon me,—His cross is on my brow; How can I do this wickedness?" And the shape which this answer will take in those who know and study their Bibles (and woe, woe to those of *us* who know and study them *not*) will commonly and most safely be some saying of our divine Master, pointedly and practically applied to the sin to which we are tempted. For *us*, these are found in rich abundance, and are so plain that none can miss them. Are we tempted to high thoughts of ourselves? It is written, "Blessed are the poor in spirit." To hard thoughts of others? It is written, "Judge not, that ye be not judged." To a vindictive unforgiving spirit? It is written, "If ye forgive not, neither will my Father forgive you." To distrust of God? It is written, "How much more shall He care for you, O ye of little faith?" And so we might go on through the whole circle of human temptations and divine commands and assurances, shewing how rich is God's armoury for the tempted Christian, and how entirely every weapon in it is within the reach of all, even the least learned, and least able, and least experienced, amongst us.

But we have one more view of our Lord's Temptation to deal with, and that of no small importance and interest. His Temptation was *His training*, that He might better be able to help us when we are tempted. What saith the Scripture? "In that He himself hath suffered being tempted, He is able to succour them that are tempted." This is a wonderful part of our subject. God knows all things. Most true; and therefore He knows all suffering and all pain and all shame, what they are, and how heavy is their burden. But there is one *kind* of knowledge which God as such does not possess: and it is that kind of knowledge which we call personal experience, of these infirmities of men. God is not any one of us. He has not, except by the incarnation of His blessed Son, personally known human sorrow and suffering. And every one of us is surrounded by, and grows and lives in, a continually increasing mass of personal experiences of which another man knows nothing as we do. About these, which are our own facts, our intensest and most living realities, the great solid rocks so to speak which underlie our lives, twine the very fibres of all the roots of our interests, our affections, our longings, our sympathies. Speak to a man of things he never witnessed, places he never saw, feelings he never underwent, and you shall have a listener more or less attentive according as you do or do not approach the inner circle of his own experiences; but take your place within that circle, speak of what he has known and felt, run your words along the channels where tears have gushed before, and the listener will at once be changed: it will be as if light were kindled, and a day-spring had quickened: your words no longer fall on the outer ear: they enter within: they are heard in the inner chamber of his heart: they take him and lead him after them: you have gained the man, and you do with him almost what you will.

And it was this marvellous power of personal sympathy, which God out of manhood had not, which the Son of God by entering manhood and suffering in manhood and dying in manhood, and being tempted in manhood, gained, and possesses everlastingly. Are you tempted, my poor brother or sister, tempted beyond your power, tempted as that it seems you must fall? Does it appear to you as if Scripture had for you lost its power, as if the Church had ceased to strengthen you, as if you were cut adrift on the boiling ocean of human passions without anchor or compass, and must founder in the storm? O what a comfort, if you could find some wise and kind and true counsellor, who had gone through it all before, who would receive you in secret, and minister to you hidden strength; who you are sure would never reproach you, never expose you, never put you off to a further day; whose will to help you you could not for a moment doubt, and whose power to help you was infinite and inexhaustible! Well, blessed be God, such an one there is provided for us—for every one of us: even Jesus the Son of God, who is passed into the heavens. "For," it continues, "we have not an High Priest which cannot be touched with a feeling of our infirmities: but was in all points tempted like as we are, yet without sin." He is ever present: ever dwelling in the hearts of those that believe on Him: ever to be found in His ordinances and means of grace: ever to be found in His holy Gospels, where His acts and words are recorded for us: nay more—He is ever with us when we think Him far away. When we forget Him, He does not forget us. He bears every sorrow of every member of His Body evermore in His heart, and succours us in our temptations without our seeing Him.

Such then, my brethren, are some of the doctrines and of the practical lessons which seem to belong to this subject,—the Temptation of our Blessed Lord. You will observe that as last Sunday, in dealing with His atoning sufferings and death, I had reason to press His eternal Godhead as that which formed the key to the whole doctrine of His satisfaction for sin, so to-day we have been much and indeed principally concerned with the truth of His manhood in its sinless obedience. But as it was impossible then in the midst of His sufferings to forget that He was One with the Eternal

Father, if we would see the truth and significance of them: so let it be impossible to forget it now also, though His humanity has been more than ever before us. "If thou be the Son of God," was evermore the Tempter's challenge to Him: and He proved himself to be the Son of God, not indeed by complying with, but by refusing compliance with, that which was demanded of Him. His victory over temptation as man shews him to be the holy and divine Son of the Father. We must evermore join together in our thoughts, as the Gospel narrative ever joins together, His human example, His human suffering, His human sympathy, with His divine power to save: He is our God, as well as our brother: one with the Father in glory, as He is one with us in sympathy.

May you and I, my brethren, ever find Him near to help us when we are tempted, to hold us up when we are sinking: may He be our trust in life, our stay in death, our portion in everlasting glory!

SERMON XV.

(PREACHED ON THE FIFTH SUNDAY IN LENT, APRIL 6, 1862.)

THE HIGH PRIESTHOOD OF CHRIST.

HEB. ix. 11.
"Christ being come an High Priest of good things to come."

THE High Priesthood of our blessed Lord and Saviour is a matter full of important consequences to us relating to his sacred Person and his work in our Redemption. And that High Priesthood is specially brought before us in the Epistle this day, when we stand as it were on the very threshold of the celebration of His sufferings and His death. I therefore propose to devote this sermon to the consideration of the High Priesthood of Christ.

Of course the term is one derived from the Jewish ceremonial worship: and it is to the books in which that worship is ordained, that we must look for its explanation. Turning then to them, I find the first ordinances respecting the High Priest's office in Exod. xxviii. There Moses is ordered to take to him Aaron his brother, and with many prescribed ceremonies and adornments to consecrate him as priest; i. e. as afterwards abundantly appears, as *chief,* or *high* priest. We need not follow these prescribed ceremonies, further than to cull out from among them the general character of each portion of them, as applying to the office of our blessed Lord. The first part of the chapter is occupied with the description of the holy garments which he was to wear, as it is said, for glory and beauty: and in the twenty-first chapter of Leviticus we learn respecting the priests themselves, that they were to be without blemish or deformity. And this is a point to be noted in entering on the consideration of Christ's High Priesthood, which was represented by these. As they were to be without blemish or deformity, as they were to be clothed in holy garments for glory and beauty, as they were not to defile themselves with any uncleanness, so was He, as the very first condition of this His office, holy, harmless, undefiled, and separate from sinners. They, these priests of Israel, were like their brethren in outward form, but, unlike them, were not to be made unclean by things which rendered others unclean. And even so it was with Christ: He took on Him the likeness of sinful flesh, but, as we saw before in this course, He did not become sinful: He partook of the infirmities of our nature to the full, but He did not partake of its pollution: He stands before God pure and accepted, clad in the white and holy robes of His own perfect and unsinning righteousness, having upon Him all glory, and being for beauty the chief among ten thousand, and altogether lovely. But, when the High

Priest is thus constituted and thus apparelled, what is the first matter of which we read, belonging to His special duty and office? Precious stones are to be taken, two sets: upon both the sets are to be graven the names of the tribes of the children of Israel: once, on two onyx stones, which are to be worn on the shoulders of the High Priest: the other time, on twelve separate stones, whose names are specially detailed;— and this last tablet is to be worn on his heart. "Aaron shall bear the names of the children of Israel in the breastplate of judgment upon his heart, when he goeth in unto the holy place, for a memorial before the Lord continually." We have here a double feature of the office. The High Priest is judge; the High Priest is intercessor. He judges between man and man: He presents the people of the Lord, thus ordered by him, as a memorial before God in his ministrations. And this too belongs to the reality of the High Priesthood of Christ. All judgment is committed to Him: the Father judgeth no man, but hath entrusted all judgment unto the Son. And thus judging, thus ordering His Church, He bears His people written on His heart; they are precious to Him as the apple of His eye: they are graven on the palms of His hands: He can never forget them, for He represents them, and He loves them as Himself, and He bears them on Himself as a memorial before God continually. Think thus of your High Priest, all ye that believe in and obey your Saviour. He bears your judgment upon him; He will right you, and will order all for your good and your blessing; and He has your names, even the least of them, even those whom men forget and make no account of, borne among the precious ornaments of His glorious vesture in heaven: He wears your memorial before God: your wants are known, your tears are offered, your prayers are presented, even before the inner throne amidst the light inaccessible, by Him who abideth for ever your glorious High Priest and Judge.

The next point which requires our notice is important, as introducing a whole class of duties which mainly constituted the High Priest's office. "Thou shalt make a plate of pure gold, and grave upon it, like to the engravings of a signet, Holiness to the Lord. ... And it shall be upon Aaron's forehead, that Aaron may bear the iniquity of the holy things which the children of Israel shall hallow in all their holy gifts: and it shall be always upon his forehead, that they may be accepted before the Lord." Here we have the High Priest in a new character: that of one bearing the iniquity of others, who are made acceptable to God by that his bearing of their iniquity. The plate of pure gold,—the "Holiness to the Lord" inscribed on it,—must of course be taken as indicating, in connexion with his bearing their iniquity, the acceptance before God, as holy, of the people of the Lord whom he represents.

It will be enough at this part of our sermon to say, that our blessed Redeemer here also fulfils the reality of which these High Priests were the shadow. Not only does he carry his people engraven on his heart before God, but He presents them to God as Holiness to Him, by virtue of his having Himself borne their iniquities. Take the Apostle's testimony to this in Eph. v. 25: "Christ loved the church, and gave himself for it, that he might sanctify and cleanse it with the washing of water by the word, that he might present it to himself a glorious church, not having spot or wrinkle or any such thing: but that it should be holy and without blemish."

Then come, in the book of Exodus, the rites and ceremonies of the consecration, or setting apart of the priests to minister before God. Concerning these, one remark before all is suggested to us by the writer of this Epistle to the Hebrews:—viz., that no man took the office unto himself, but only those who were selected and consecrated by God, as was Aaron. And even so, he tells us, Christ did not take this High Priesthood to himself, but He that said to Him, "Thou art my Son, this day have I begotten thee,"—and, "Thou art a priest for ever after the order of Melchisedek:" even the Father, of whom He said that He had sanctified (or consecrated) Him and sent Him into the world. Of those ceremonies themselves, the ANOINTING deserves our special attention. The very name of the Lord by which we call Him, Messiah or Christ, signifies the ANOINTED.

But we now come to that which was by far the larger portion of the duty of the priests of old, and of which we shall have much to say as concerning our great High Priest Himself. "Every high priest," says our Epistle, "is ordained to offer gifts and sacrifices." This was the priest's especial office; to minister for the people in the things concerning God, and to offer sacrifices for sin. And this it is concerning which the directions in the Levitical books are the most careful and precise. Let me enumerate briefly a few of these ministrations. First of all, day by day, every morning and evening, the high priest was to offer incense upon the altar of incense. (Exod. xxx. 1 ff.) Then we have, through the early chapters of the Book of Leviticus, directions concerning the various offerings which were to be made for different sins, and on different occasions; and all these were to be brought to the sanctuary by the person concerned, and there offered up by Aaron and his sons the priests. The ordinary manner of these offerings may be thus described. The person concerned brought the animal which was ordered in the law, and put it into the hands of the ministering priest, who killed it, and sprinkled of the blood of the sin-offering on the altar, pouring out the remainder at its foot. Or, if it were a burnt-offering, the priest simply took it and burnt it on the altar. The result, as it affected the person bringing the offering, was always the same, and may be stated once for all in the words used of one such occasion (Lev. iii. 13): "And the priest shall make an atonement for him as touching his sin that he hath sinned, and it shall be forgiven him." Moreover, what the priest did for others in this matter, that he did also for himself. He offered for his own sins, when he went in to appear before the Lord, as well as for the sins of the people. (Levit. ix. 7 ff.) And so it was ordained for all sin, and all uncleanness, and every occasion when any of the people drew near to God for any purpose of devotion:—the offering was brought to the priest, and the priest offered it to God, and thus atonement was made for sin. And the ordinary rule of the law was, that which is stated in this Epistle:—that without shedding of blood by the priest for the people, there was no remission of sin for any one.

There was however one especial day in the year, the ordinances of which are above all instructive to us, and are especially alluded to more than once by the writer of this Epistle to the Hebrews. Once a year, on the tenth day of the seventh month, the High Priest was to make a general atonement for the sins of the whole people. The day was kept as a very solemn one. They were to afflict their souls, and to do no work at all on that day. It is on that day especially, that the *High* Priest's office and work appear pre-eminent: for its principal solemnities were performed by him *alone*.

To set them clearly before you, I must remind you of the divinely prescribed construction of the tabernacle, in which these ministrations were performed. This very matter is laid down by the writer of the Epistle in the verses preceding my text.

After the outer portions or courts were passed, in which the people prayed, and waited while their sacrifices were offered,—there were two chambers or divisions; which remained also the same in the temple, which succeeded the tabernacle as its more permanent form. First, there was the holy place, where the priests always entered day by day about their ministrations. In that place was the table of shewbread, and the golden candlesticks, and the altar of incense: it was there that Zacharias the father of John the Baptist was sacrificing, when the angel appeared to him announcing to him the future birth of a son. At the end of that chamber hung a thick and costly veil, screening off a second smaller chamber, called the most holy place, or the holy of holies: the holiest of all, as it is named in the passage of the Epistle to the Hebrews. In this were the especial symbols of God's immediate presence: there was the ark of the mercy seat, with the figures of the cherubim above it, on which and between which figures the peculiar place of God's dwelling was ever said to be. "Thou that dwellest between the cherubim," is a well-known appellation of the God of Israel. There, on the mercy seat, God was pleased to appear on those occasions when He made his glory manifest to His servants.

Now bearing all this in mind, let us further reflect, that this inner and holiest chamber was never entered by any of the ordinary priests, but by the High Priest alone: nor might the High Priest himself enter it, except once a year only, viz. on this great day of atonement of which we are speaking. And I must request your attention for a moment, seeing it is very important for our great subject, to the directions for his thus entering the holiest place once a year. He was first to offer sin-offerings for himself and for the people of Israel. Notice the character of the latter of these. Two goats were to be taken. One was to be slain, and his blood sprinkled over the vessels of the tabernacle, and to be carried into the holy of holies, and sprinkled on the mercy seat itself, making, as the expression is, an atonement for the holy place itself. Over the head of the other goat Aaron was to lay both his hands, and to confess his sins, and the sins of the children of Israel, and then he was to be taken and let go in the wilderness, "bearing upon him (so it is written) all their iniquities into a land not inhabited."

Now almost every particular here is explained by the inspired Writer of this Epistle to have immediate reference to our blessed Lord: and of those not so mentioned several are so obvious as to be unmistakeable by any intelligent Christian.

First of all, why all these ordinances of sacrifice at all? Why all this taking away of animal life, and this sprinkling of blood, ceremonies of a kind painful and revolting now to our minds and habits? Could it be,—can we for a moment conceive, that the sin of the soul of man could be removed by the shedding of the blood of an animal? No such thing can be imagined; and the writer of this Epistle appeals to this as a matter too plain to need proving: "the blood of bulls and of goats," he says, "can never take away sin." All these sacrifices, thus divinely appointed, thus introduced by the words, "The Lord spake unto Moses, saying," were ordained to signify greater and spiritual truths: "the Holy Ghost this signifying," as we have it written here: God having a matter to make known in His good time, which should be no type nor shadow, but His own very truth: and that matter being, the death and satisfaction of our blessed Lord, His Eternal Son.

But let us follow this out, considering Him as our

High Priest. "If he be a priest," says the writer of our Epistle, "he must of necessity have something to offer." We saw that it is of the very essence of a priest, that he offer gifts and sacrifices. And here we have God's High Priest, whom He hath consecrated and sent into the world—who has all judgment committed to him, who bears in his heart the names and wants of his people. By what offering shall He propitiate God towards those His people? For they are guilty, sinful, rebellious: they have done, and they do, the things they ought not to have done, and they have not done, and do not, the things they ought to have done. How shall He render them accepted before God? The blood of thousands of rams will not suffice: the pouring out of ten thousand rivers of oil will not accomplish it: burnt-offerings and offerings for sin God will not have, nor does He take any pleasure in them: what, my brethren, has our great High Priest to offer, which may render us acceptable to God? On whom shall our iniquities meet and be laid? Who shall shed the blood that may sprinkle our holy things and make them pure? Who shall go far, far away, bearing upon his head the iniquities of us all? Hear his answer—"Lo *I* come, to do thy will, O God." The High Priest, standing perfect in our humanity, can offer no other;—He shall offer Himself:—the Priest and Victim shall be the same:—the blood of sprinkling shall be none other than His own. He is spotless, He is perfectly holy: He unites in Himself our whole nature: strike Him, and we are stricken: let His sacrifice be accepted, and we are cleared from guilt: let that Blood of His be carried into the Holy place of God's presence in Heaven, and an atonement is made for us.

And thus, even thus, did our blessed Redeemer. He shed His own most precious Blood: He went, through the veil of His flesh, up before God, into God's presence, bearing with Him the all-sufficient virtue of that atoning sacrifice. And there is He now, our accepted ransom, our merciful Intercessor, our righteous Judge: "Holiness to the Lord" is written on Him, and through Him is written on his accepted people, who are holy in Him.

There are several other, apparently minor, but really not less interesting points of comparison, between the High Priests of old and our blessed High Priest and Redeemer. Their sacrifices were imperfect, and of no intrinsic value or avail. They therefore needed renewing continually, day by day. But His is perfect and all-sufficing. "By one offering He hath perfected for ever them that are sanctified." By His one oblation of Himself once offered, He made a sufficient sacrifice, oblation and satisfaction, for the sins of the whole world. Therefore His sacrifice needs no renewing. It needs only to be believed in, and applied by the obedience of living faith to the heart. It needs only that a man make real to himself his state as a member of Christ, and live in the power of it, and he is accepted of God,—holy, as Christ is holy;—taught by the same Spirit which dwelt so richly in Him, and a child of the same Father who testified to Him that He was his beloved Son in whom He was well pleased.

So that now, properly speaking, we have in Christ's

church no such thing as a priest, and no such thing as a sacrifice. We use indeed the words, but their meaning is different. Our word *priest* is only a short way of writing *presbyter* or elder, and has absolutely nothing to do with the office of a sacrificer. Our sacrifice in the Lord's Supper is not,—God forbid the thought, for it is a blasphemy and a denial of Christ,—is not a renewal of Christ's offering of Himself, but it is simply a sacrifice of praise and thanksgiving, a sacrifice of ourselves, bodies, souls and spirits, to the service of our God.

Again: those High Priests, by reason of their being mortal men, were continually renewed from time to time. None of them was permanent: they came as shadows, and so departed: theirs was no abiding priesthood, to which all men might look for atonement and acceptance. But the Son of God abideth for ever: He dieth no more, death hath no more dominion over him: in that He died, He died for sin once: in that He liveth, He liveth unto God. For ever and for ever does the virtue of His blood endure: for ever and for ever does His holy Priesthood avail. There is with Him no wearing out, no forgetting, no failure of earnestness, no vacillating affection, no exhausted pleading. He is for all, He is over all, He is sufficient for all, He cares for all.

So then, once more;—inasmuch as they were human High Priests, they were fellows with their brethren. Was then theirs any advantage over Him? In that land of Judæa, under the shade of those walls of Jerusalem, you might perchance see the High Priest holding conference with the erring or the penitent: might see the venerable man of God, on whose brow was His anointing, with the hand of the young offender laid in his, pleading eye to eye till the tears chased one another down the cheek glowing with shame: and then might trace the Judge of Israel watching, reminding, building up the returning sinner in holiness. Shall we envy them? Were they better off than we? Ah no, my brethren! The sympathizing High Priest on earth, what is he to the sympathizing High Priest in heaven? Few indeed, and interrupted could be such interviews: narrow indeed and partial such sympathies. But our High Priest is not one who lacks leisure or power to receive all who come to him at any time. He is not one who cannot be touched with a feeling of every human infirmity. We saw what knowledge He gained, even over and above His divine omniscience, by the experience of personal suffering: and that knowledge is to Him as all knowledge to every possessor, power also:—in that He hath suffered being tempted, He is able to succour them that are tempted. And though we see Him not,— though He does not take our hand in His, nor look on us with His blessed countenance, yet we have even thereby an especial blessing. Faith triumphs even over the defeat of sense:—for He himself hath said, "Blessed are they that have not seen and yet have believed."

Then, my beloved brethren, what is our conclusion? Have I said all this merely for the sake of explaining the ancient ordinances, and shewing how our blessed Lord fulfilled them? Even if I had, your time would not have been lost, nor your attention bespoken in vain. For it is our wisdom to strive to understand that which has been written for our profit, even where it may not seem immediately to concern us. But this matter is not one of mere understanding; not one at a distance from our hearts and lives; it is one which concerns our very lives themselves, and ought to hold a place in all our hearts. It is for us, for each of us, for the lowliest and the least among us, that the eternal Son of God is thus constituted a High Priest: for our sins, for our wants, for our daily feeling, and obeying, and approaching to God. It is to purge our conscience from dead works to serve the living God, that His holy blood was offered: to make us pure, upright, clear in purpose, and like to our God and Father.

And I would say to each of you, speaking with regard to your inner life and secret springs of action,— Do you know Him thus as your High Priest? Do you find access to God by Him? Are your days spent in the light of His countenance, and under the teaching of His blessed Spirit? Listen to the exhortation of the writer of this Epistle, with which he concludes this portion of his argument. "Having therefore, brethren, boldness to enter into the holiest by the blood of Jesus, by a new and living way, which he hath consecrated for us, through the veil, that is to say, his flesh; and having an High Priest over the house of God; let us draw near with a true heart in full assurance of faith, having our hearts sprinkled from an evil conscience, and our bodies washed with pure water. Let us hold fast the profession of our faith without wavering; (for he is faithful that promised;) and let us consider one another to provoke unto love and to good works: not forsaking the assembling of ourselves together, as the manner of some is: but exhorting one another: and so much the more, as ye see the day approaching." Such will be your attitude, such your resolution, if you are upright and honourable believers in Christ your great High Priest.

Such it will be always, and such in the case of all. But to-day the season, and the circumstances, suggest to us two special applications of what has been spoken. The season—for as I said in the beginning, do we not stand on the very threshold of those holy sufferings by which our great High Priest accomplished his sacrifice of Himself? And ought not our thoughts which at all times should be familiar with these foundations of our inner life, at such a time to be more specially and intentionally directed towards them? would it not be an advantage to each of us, during the coming fortnight, to follow our blessed Lord through that last journey, and through every point of His sufferings day by day, suffering with Him in thought and mind, communing with God through the sacred narrative, and building ourselves up on our most holy faith?

But the circumstances also of our present meeting here to-day admonish me, that there are some among us, to whom every such subject as this speaks with a voice of no ordinary solemnity. I mean of course those who in two days' time will ratify in their own persons the vows undertaken for them in their baptism. There is something peculiarly pointing at you in those words, "Draw near with a true heart in full assurance of faith, having your hearts sprinkled from an evil conscience and your bodies washed in pure water." For this state described in these latter words is and long has been yours. The washing of water by the word;—the accepted state of membership of Christ's Church by Holy Baptism; this has for years been upon you:—and now you are about, by special profession in the face of the Church, and before her chief minister, to adopt the faith and the duties of the state as your own. You are about to seek, I would hope in humility and with prayer, the grace which may follow the laying on of his hands after the example of the holy Apostles. God grant that the following words may be found fulfilled in you,—"that you may hold fast the profession of your faith without wavering,—provoking one another to love and good works,"—and making this your confirmation a new starting-point for Christian energy, in serving Him who shed His Blood for you.

One parting word for us all. Our text speaks of Christ as an High Priest of good things *to come*. True indeed is this in the fullest sense. How little do we know now, of those blessings which He came to bring! How very small a part of that which we do know, ever gets interwoven with our hearts' life or shewn forth in our every-day conduct! But there will be a day when our High Priest, like those High Priests of old, shall again come forth from the holy place to bless us with His glorious presence. Then, and not till then, we shall fully comprehend all that man can know of the glorious High Priesthood of Christ. Then we shall also *be* that which we know, being filled with all the fulness of God in His heavenly kingdom.

Unto which may He vouchsafe to bring us all for Jesus Christ's sake.

SERMON XVI.

(PREACHED ON THE SUNDAY NEXT BEFORE EASTER, APRIL 13, 1862.)

CHRIST CRUCIFIED.

1 Cor. i. 13.

"We preach Christ crucified."

These, my brethren, are very familiar words to you: words very often quoted: very often preached upon. They are sometimes quoted, and sometimes preached upon, as embodying a particular set of views or opinions, to be distinguished from other views and opinions about religion and the church: sometimes also used as if they gave undue prominence to one among all the holy doctrines of the Gospel. Let us try to see what they really do import: and especially at this entrance to Passion week, when the subject to which they refer is so much in all our thoughts.

St. Paul, who wrote them, was employed in preaching, or proclaiming, the glad tidings of salvation to two very different sets of persons. There were the Jews, who had long been in possession of God's laws and ordinances, and who in order to be influenced by what he had to say, required a sign,—i.e. wanted some outward miraculous convincing proof of his assertions, and without it would not receive them. Then there were the Greeks, who had preserved no direct revelations from God, but followed the light, poor as it was, of human reason and acuteness; and they required wisdom:—wanted to be shewn, by argument, and logical subtlety, the force of those things which were announced to them.

Now St. Paul did not comply with either of these demands, but he steered his way between them, with one object ever before his eyes, and one proclamation ever in his mouth: and that was—CHRIST CRUCIFIED. That is, in the simple acceptation of the words, he announced to them the fact that a certain person, whom he affirmed to be the Christ, or Messiah of the Jews, had been nailed to a cross, the common death at that time of notorious evil-doers.

To say no more of this at present, let us note the effect which it had upon both classes of his hearers.

It was to the Jews, an *offence*. They expected their Messiah to be a great and powerful prince, who should revive the Kingdom of David, and set their nation again on high among the peoples of the earth. That he should die the death of a miscreant and a slave, wounded the pride, and offended every expectation and prejudice, of the Jew.

Then as to the other hearer, there was nothing in the proclamation of this fact which could in any way flatter his love of wisdom and acuteness. It was to him *foolishness*; simply ridiculous, for one to go about proclaiming that a man had been crucified;—a thing which he could not conceive to be productive of any consequences at all.

However St. Paul persisted, and gives his plain reasons for doing so. He says that this fact, expressed in the words "Christ crucified," contained something which was both for Jews and Greeks the power of God and the wisdom of God: the most notable sign that could be required by the Jew: deeper far than the profoundest wisdom that the Greek could demand. He persisted: and the consequences were in his time, and have been since, such as to shew that he was abundantly justified in doing so. Multitudes, both of Jews and Greeks, became, by the force of these words, changed men: forsook dumb idols, or dead works, to serve the living God: the body of believers thus got together spread into all nations, and has reformed the manners, the morals, the social life, of half mankind. Thousands of suffering men and women, of poor, of sick, of dying,— labourers in their toil, youth in their temptations, mourners in their desertion, penitents in their shame and sorrow,—men and women of all ages, all stations, all languages,—have been made happy, and comforted, and strengthened, and lifted higher in the scale of being, by hearing and by knowing this thing,— CHRIST CRUCIFIED. The shameful cross on which Christ died, has been taken out of the place of shame, and made the boast and the banner of wise and holy men: there is no memory, there is no symbol, which has ever exercised such a spell and charm over human thoughts and ways. It is stamped on the majestic area of the Christian

Cathedral, and signed on the soft brow of the Christian babe: it gilds the point of the spire which directs our thoughts to heaven, and it marks the hallowed place where we have laid our beloved ones in the earth.

But all this is as nothing—nothing compared with the triumphs of the Cross within man's heart. There it is, that high thoughts have been cast down by it, and the true majesty of meekness implanted: that the selfishness of man has been turned into self-sacrifice: that the wise has become a fool, in order that he may be wise: and the babe has received wisdom which might baffle the sage.

It seems then that this conduct of St. Paul in proclaiming Christ crucified has its justification; it seems then that his assertion about its being the power and the wisdom of God was not without foundation in truth.

But may not we, my brethren, may not you and I, be permitted to enter somewhat into the grounds of this his justification, and to see on what foundation his assertion rests? Let this be our endeavour, in dependence on God's help. Let us try and make plain to you how "Christ crucified," which offended the Jews and seemed foolishness to the Greeks, was, and is yet, the power and the wisdom of God.

Of course the question for us resolves itself into this, —"What did this death of Christ, so inflicted, mean and imply?" Now let us carefully weigh this. Consider it thus. There must have been something very different indeed about this crucifixion, from any other crucifixion, for this to be able to be said of it. A crucifixion may have been an unjust and shameful act, as doubtless thousands of them were; it may have been a cruel act, as certainly all such were: it may have been inflicted on a holy and harmless man, on a helpless and supplicating woman, on an innocent unoffending child: it may have been the end of some pitiable, or some instructive story: nay it may have even made great changes in the world,—have led to empires being crushed, or dynasties being founded: but I cannot see how any event of this kind on earth could ever have become the subject of St. Paul's proclamation, as this did,—could ever have made such changes in men and in nations as this has,—could ever have been proved to be the power of God and the wisdom of God,—unless there was something in it totally different from any thing whatever in the history of mere worldly transactions.

Perhaps you say, it may have been some very noble example;—some death of love for others, some rendering up of self to shame and suffering that others might escape them. Well, but what then? Are there not in history, thank God, plenty of such examples of self-denying love? Have we not read of them from our childhood, have we not seen such among us in our own time? But what effect do these produce? Sometimes a noble effect, no doubt: a nation is stirred to honour such persons, and their names survive as watchwords in the wreck of ages. But that is nothing, when compared to the effect of this of which we speak. What instance of noble self-sacrifice ever wrought in the conscience of a sinner, to turn him from his sins? What bright example of love ever made a proud man humble? What illustrious name of a victim to philanthropy ever cheered a dying soul, and gilded the dark valley with gleams of hope? The matter is altogether different; and again I say, there must be something in this crucifixion of Christ, totally and essentially distinct from all other events of the same kind.

And do not suppose that I am now labouring to establish a small matter; or wasting words to shew what every body is aware of. The greatest difference I know between one man and another among us Christians is that between the man who is aware of this distinction and the man who is not aware of it. Let a man look on the crucifixion of Christ as the most unjust and cruel of all recorded acts of oppression; let him weep ever so much over the undeserved sufferings of its Victim : let him look on it as the most glorious instance on record of self-sacrificing Love, and prefer it to all others in history : with all this he knows not, he cannot know, any thing of the spell which it exercised over these Jews and Greeks;—neither knows such a man, nor can he know, any thing of " Christ crucified, the power of God and the wisdom of God," unless he knows another thing about it, which does not belong to any human event of the kind :—viz. that which St. Paul knew well, and of which he so often writes; that it was *the sacrifice offered for the sin of this whole world.*

This it is—this, in connexion with the consideration of WHO it was that suffered, and WHY He suffered, which makes this fact of Christ crucified to be all it is, and all it ever has been—the conversion of sinners, the stay of the faithful, the comfort of the mourner, the drier up of the penitent's tears, the hope of the dying, the glory and boast of the Church of God. Keep it as a tragic tale, exalt it as you will as a mere example of human love, and it is a weapon with which you may fight against wrath and terror in vain; but give it this its own true character,—let it be the propitiation for the sin of man,—and it becomes God's bow set in the cloud of His wrath, the sure sign of covenant mercy, the unfailing pledge of reconciled love.

Let us then now, my brethren, with the solemn words of this day's services in our minds, draw near to that Cross where Christ is crucified; and try whether we cannot by what we see there justify St. Paul's resolution and substantiate his description. One hangs crucified there; but WHO is he? Is He the noblest, the most innocent, the most self-denying of men? Alas, what were that for our purpose? Our answer is other than this: we look on, and reply, as the Centurion, "Truly, He was the Son of God." He has come down from heaven from the bosom of His Father, from bliss inconceivable and ineffable, because He, because the Father, loved the sons of men with a love surpassing all our powers of thought. He determined from eternity to submit to this death of shame and pain, in order to pay the penalty of the wrong which the sons of men had done, and to ransom them for Himself and for their eternal happiness in Him.

This is the account *for us*. There are other mysteries in that Death, which we may only behold afar off; but this is near to us, to every one of us. In order to this His gracious purpose, He became *man* like ourselves:

not to reign over us, but to die for us : rather, not to reign over us except by dying for us. Now do you not see as we stand beneath that Cross, and look upon what is done there, how it lays hold on our hearts and weaves itself into our lives and our thoughts of ourselves? Unworthy as I am, each one of us may say, less than the least of all God's outward mercies, for me that Holy One was offered up;—for my sins, as much as if my sins were the only sins in the world. But how do I know this? By what means am I to be assured of it? By something in myself? In the first place, and as regards its intrinsic worth,—surely not: because if any feeling of mine is wanting to make Christ's death efficacious for me, then without that feeling it was not efficacious, and thus was incomplete. CHRIST CRUCIFIED, as preached by us, is an outward fact, historical and final, on which our firm belief may lay hold and rest: not an inward feeling, now here, now there, shifting as our moods and frames are changed. When St. Paul came to these Corinthians, when we come to you and proclaim Christ crucified, we proclaim to you that this Lamb of God has been sacrificed for the sins of every one among you. And we call upon you to act upon this truth as the foundation of your lives and hopes.

But there is more than this contained in the proclamation. The fact itself is, it is true, applicable to every man separately, as much, as we just now said, as if there were no other man in the world. It is the very ground which this same Apostle states why he is not ashamed of the Gospel of Christ, " because it is the power of God unto salvation to every one that believeth." But this is not the ordinary method of receiving the tidings and their consequences. Life might be sustained, if a man were alone. But it is not good for man to be alone. We are not solitary creatures in this world; nor has God so framed the proclamation of his salvation, as to cause us to be such in receiving it. He has called out from the world, and constituted by ordinances of His own, a body of men, which we name the Church. He has commanded that such as receive this fact of Christ crucified shall be made members of that body by an ordinance of His own prescribing,—viz., Holy Baptism: that that ordinance shall be to them the token and pledge of their membership, and assurance to them of their part, in Christ crucified. And if you or I, or any baptized member of Christ's Church, is asked the question, "How do you know that that sacrifice on the Cross is the taking away of your sins and the making you acceptable to God?" the answer, if we are faithful and honest men, will be simply this, "Because I have been baptized in the name of the Father, Son, and Holy Ghost, the three Persons in the blessed Trinity covenanted together for my salvation by that sacrifice of the Lamb of God."

But it may be said, how if a man thus received into Christ's Church,—how if one of you, my brethren, men already baptized and called Christians,—be totally insensible to the great fact and its proper influence on his life,—what are we to do then? What are we to proclaim to such an one? Are we to say, "You have yet to be admitted among the Lord's people—go and repent and believe, and come again, and you may some day be fit to receive the benefits of Christ crucified?" No, my brethren, nothing of the kind. We are to go on proclaiming Christ crucified: to tell him not about himself, but about Christ: Christ in His Death, and in His Resurrection, and in His pleading in heaven;—Christ in the ordinances of His Church;—Christ in His word, and on His throne of grace. This will be the way to deal with such a man;—and to tell him, "All this is yours;—Christ is yours in all these ways of imparting Himself:—draw near and partake of Him: take up this your freedom, and cast off the bondage of sin: come with us, and see the salvation of the Lord. If you will not, our course is not altered—on your own head be the blame and the condemnation."

And so we go on proclaiming, not this or that fashion of the day, not this or that religious system, but evermore and to the end this same thing, CHRIST CRUCIFIED: Christ the atonement for every man's sin: Christ put on in Baptism: Christ to be put on in heart and life.

But, as in the Apostle's day, so now, there are two classes of persons, whom this setting forth of Christ and of Him crucified does not please.

First there are those who require a sign: who are not contented with publishing God's good tidings of salvation for all, and as a testimony to all, but require each man to shew something in his own state, and detail something in his own experience, which may, as they think, manifest that he has a part in Christ. To these persons the offence of the Cross is necessarily great: they cannot imagine how a simple receiving of these good tidings of Christ crucified,—a humble unpretending membership of Christ's Church,—should be salvation to a man: but they want him evermore to contribute something of his own, and to stand in his own strength in this matter of his salvation; forgetting that all growth in grace, and good works, and repentance, and knowledge, must be made on the foundation of acceptance in Christ, and not as a preliminary step to it:—that our obligation to renounce sin, and believe, and obey, were undertaken when we became members of Christ,—not in order that we might become such.

Then again, this preaching of Christ crucified is not likely to please those who seek after wisdom: after that which may satisfy their human ways of judging and thinking of things. And thus we have whole classes of worldly men and of intellectual men in our own as well as in other days, finding the preaching of Christ's Cross foolishness to them: something beneath their notice. And when from any cause they are brought to the outward profession of belief in the doctrine, they deal untruly with it, and try to explain it away: and deny its atoning power, and apply to it the maxims and dealings of human wisdom, and despise those who simply receive and believe it as it is.

Yet, my brethren, for all that both these say or do, CHRIST CRUCIFIED is still the power of God, and the wisdom of God. The effects of the doctrine of the Cross have not ceased, nor have its wonders been exhausted. For all that they can say or do, we, the ministers of Christ, will not cease to proclaim Christ crucified, as our fathers did of old. Let every one of us, in his heart and mind, be determined on this point. We of God's Church are to be in the world witnesses of the death of Christ. Not only in the ordinance which He specially appointed for this very purpose,—to shew forth His death till He come ; but in our whole lives, and words, and thoughts of ourselves, this foundation fact is to underlie all, "CHRIST CRUCIFIED."

I say, let us *determine* that this shall be so,—because it requires determination and firmness in this our time. On one side we have those who want of us more than Christ crucified in religion,—and would rob us of our acceptance before God by the Cross, unless we can shew them a sign,—human feeling,—past experience,— the day and manner of our conversion,—or the like :— and on the other side we have those who would reason us out of our simple faith in the all-sufficient atonement for sin, and try to persuade us that we have no sin at all, or that Christ's death was not a sacrifice for its remission.

May we by God's grace stand firm against both: ministers determined to proclaim,—people resolved to hold fast,—both fixed in purpose to become witnesses to,—Christ crucified. And thus will the mighty Power of the Cross be made known in our hearts and lives— thus will self be thrown down, and Christ and His Love set up as our central motive :—thus will the taint of our old nature be purged away by the virtue of that blood which cleanseth from all sin : and thus too will God's wisdom in this His appointed salvation become gradually and surely revealed to us :—not by signs and tokens which may be watched and recorded,—but by the ripening growth in a life of grace, and the increasing knowledge of our Master and Saviour Jesus Christ.

Especially at this time would I recommend to you these thoughts and this determination. Each day this week we shall be following the sacred narrative in its record of that Holy Death of our Lord of which we have been speaking. Now therefore, if ever, is an opportunity given us of strengthening this foundation of our Christian life, and renewing our vows as soldiers of the Cross.

May this week, with its sacred commemorations and solemn readings of Scripture, and daily liftings up of the Cross in our sight, root and ground us in the Apostle's determination, to know nothing, for this world or the next, as the centre of our motives, and the source of our hopes, save JESUS CHRIST AND HIM CRUCIFIED.

SERMON XVII.

(PREACHED ON GOOD FRIDAY, APRIL 18, 1862: ALSO AT ST. MARY'S, OXFORD, ON FRIDAY EVENING, APRIL 11, 1862.)

OUR LORD IN DEATH.

JOHN x. 17, 18.

"Therefore doth my Father love me, because I lay down my life, that I might take it again. No man taketh it from me, but I lay it down of myself. I have power to lay it down, and I have power to take it again. This commandment have I received of my Father."

I NEED hardly remind you, that there are many and various aspects of this great day's great subject. What that Death of the Lord was as effecting our Redemption;—what it was as our great example of love;— these are the most commonly treated, and perhaps for us the most important. But there is one, which is brought before us by the solemn words which I have just read:—viz. what it was to HIMSELF. Let us then speak to-day of OUR LORD IN DEATH.

But how many different lines of thought open before us as we begin to ponder on these words! First of all, what do we know of any man in death? Who has ever gone down that solitary passage, and passed beyond the thick curtain which hangs before that mysterious chamber that divides time from eternity, and then come back to tell us? What mere stander-by knows aught of that receding personality of which we discern so little even in ordinary intercourse, when it is full in our sight? And those that are dearest and closest knit in life, what have they to look on at the bedside, what have they to think on in the dreary years of separation, but a precious fragment or two of blessed thought and feeling, cast up to the surface in that hour of the last surging tempest? What are these, but perhaps the least part of that which is at that moment being transacted? Amidst the sharp inroads of victorious pain in the sack of the fortress of life, amidst the tearing up of the roots of that life's attachments, amidst the self-accusings of the parting soul looking back from the frontier of the kingdom of grace;—when the faces of the surrounding beloved ones are thickening over with the mists of evening, and morning is dawning on the innumerable company of angels, when all strength and all weakness are met, all hopes and all fears summed up in a point, when mercy must be brighter than mercy, if it would shine through the gathering gloom, and terror must be darker than terror, if it would shade the blessed sunrise of God's salvation,—O who shall tell what any man is in death?

And if this be so,—if we all die alone, and if, as we believe and know, our blessed Lord was very man, man in life and man in death, then for Him too was there, if His death was a real human death, this secret conflict, this unknown last passage—this track in His path where no human eye may penetrate. And seeing that the mightier spirit is ever the lonelier :—seeing that the deaths of the first and noblest of the sons of men are, even in the fragments which they disclose, ever the most obscure and the least satisfactory,—how shall we presume to judge of Him in death, who bore upon the divine person of the Son of God our perfect humanity— in whom such strange conditions met; for in Him was no sin, which is the sting of death—on Him was no compulsion, but every step down the dark valley was a separate voluntary act?

And may we not go on further to ask, Does such enquiry become us? Is the Lord in death a proper subject for us to meditate on, before whose dying pangs the Sun hid his face, that nature and that man might not witness them?

But, my brethren, as these questions are ready to present themselves when we begin to ponder on the words with which I began, so are the answers to them not far off, nor inadequate. And first, though we know but little of any man in death, that little may be most important—may be inexpressibly consoling; may be a potent spell to restrain or to excite to action. The character of the moment imparts solemnity and power to men's dying words, and the same character of the moment gives them an intense burning reality, that pierces through all outward shells and shews, down to the very central reality of things. Courses of conduct have been adopted or abandoned, well-springs of life-long love or of bitterest hate have first gushed up, nay, empires

Q

have been guided for ages, and the destinies of the great human family moulded, by the sayings and acts of dying men. And as they are potent in working without, so are they also in revealing that which is within. He must be lost indeed who can play the hypocrite when dying. Such men doubtless have been: but we do not take the possibility into account, and we ought not: what a dying man says, it is well for us to believe comes from his heart of hearts, is a drop straight from the fountain of his inner being: and not seldom such a word lights up a life which was dark to us before, and gives us a master-key to a character whose intricacies had long continued to baffle our penetration.

Now if such things be true of dying men in general, were they otherwise with Him when He died? Though in Him was no guile, yet doubtless there was an outer, and an inner, and yet still an inner circle of thought and of self-impartment to those with whom He communicated. He spoke not to the Jews as He spoke to the family at Bethany; nor to them as to the Twelve. Was there aught in His death, which came forth from the deepest and holiest centre of His blessed soul? Was there act or word of concentrated power, greater than those of which we spoke but now, as He is greater than we are? Of such things we can judge: in this particular, such as others were in death, such also was He. He suffered, He acted, He spake: the sacred record tells us what, and in what manner. And the same consideration is an answer to our other question as to the lawfulness of such enquiries. Nay, in His case it is more than an ordinary answer: it is even a compelling motive. The deaths of other men happen not by chance; in every one of them our Heavenly Father has His aim and purpose, for those who see it and hear of it, for the bereaved, and for the dwellers round. But this death of His was not only no accident, but it was the one great event in the history of this our world: it was the final satisfaction of divine justice, and the crowning triumph of divine love: it was that by which, according to his own words, all men were to be drawn to Him: that whereon all penitent sinners in all ages were to trust for acceptance with God, and on which as its brightest example all human self-sacrifice was to be based. No wonder then that the sacred narrative should linger lovingly round the precincts of that Cross of shame: no wonder that each of the four holy Evangelists should gather up the details of those hours of the Saviour's Death, and tell them as he saw and heard them, or as they were told to him by those who did. And thus we believe ourselves fully justified in considering our present subject: nay, if it did not enter into such a course as this on the doctrines which gather round the Person of our Blessed Lord, the course would be defective in one of its most important elements.

Let us then draw near with reverence, as humble disciples and accepted members of Him concerning whom we speak, and let us contemplate our Lord in Death. Let us do this, even though it may be with us to-day as it ever seems to be when treating on the very greatest themes; that our thoughts flow freely, and want not fitting expression in words, as long as we dwell merely on the approaches and preliminaries to our subject, but as soon as we have arrived at it, and stand in its presence, our own thoughts fail us, and our own words refuse to come; its commonest detail transcends our capacities; its simplest utterance is a depth before which our speculation is baffled. This must not discourage us, for it is the very condition of our meditations on such matters as these. Over our paths of human feeling and sympathy they cast a light by which we can think and speak; but their own glory is too bright for us to gaze upon, and our powers quail and are prostrated before it.

And in thus approaching our subject, there is one prefatory portion of it which on all accounts must be first treated: I mean, our Lord's *anticipations* of His Death. And here a few words must be said on the meaning of such an expression, as applied to Him. It is the most difficult of all things, in meditating on our blessed Lord's life, to attain the medium, in our thoughts of Him, between perfect omniscience, which would destroy the reality of his manhood, and a condition of limited knowledge like our own, which would be incompatible with the attributes of His Godhead. I know that the definite apportionment of these seemingly incompatible conditions is a matter lying beyond our reach: but at the same time it is one on which, if we would read our Lord's life intelligently at all, we cannot avoid coming to some conclusion or other. Did He always, in his humiliation, know all things? or was His knowledge in kind such as ours is, with all allowance for the vast difference between the manhood in Him perfect and pure, in us maimed and unclean? In answer I would say, not presuming to lay down a rule for the opinion of others, but merely stating my own, that neither of these seems to have been the case. Had He been, in his humanity, absolutely omniscient from the first, it could never have been written of Him that He increased in wisdom as in stature. And we know enough of the history of ancient heresy, to shrink from the idea that omniscience could at any particular moment have descended on his hitherto non-omniscient humanity. Nay, His own most solemn words may here assure us. "Of that day and hour (viz. of His second appearing) knoweth no one, no not the angels in heaven, nor the Son, but the Father only:" words which cannot, I submit, be explained away by saying that He knew it not "for us," but must enunciate a solemn and mysterious truth of His mediatorial exinanition.

But on the other hand we are withheld from imagining that His knowledge was but as ours, even with the largest possible allowance for the difference between Him and us. He knew the thoughts of men's hearts, He saw through the wiles of His enemies at once; He went forth, knowing all things that should come upon Him. Now it is most true that we cannot understand a state so apparently self-contradictory: but carefully guarding and guiding ourselves by what is written, we can say this, that our Lord appears ever to have had superhuman knowledge within His grasp, and on certain occasions, when it pleased Him, when He saw it to be necessary for his blessed work on earth, He made use of it: yet that on ordinary occasions and in the common progress and course of things, He was pleased to withhold from Himself that knowledge which He might have grasped if He would, and to be dependent on human means and appliances for its acquisition.

This view is certainly confirmed by expressions in the Gospels. The Evangelists do not scruple to tell us that "Jesus, when he had heard that John was cast into prison, departed into Galilee:" that after John's martyrdom, "when Jesus heard of it, he departed into a desert place alone:" that "when he had heard that Lazarus was sick, he abode still two days where he was:" and in the last case this acting on ordinary intelligence is remarkably coupled with superhuman knowledge of the death of Lazarus, a few verses further on.

Let us then ask, How was this as regarded His death? Are we to suppose that the whole circumstances of it were ever before Him, in His holy childhood, in His retirement at Nazareth during youth and early manhood—all through every hour of His ministry and conflict with the Jews? And here I believe our answer must be of that mixed kind which we have just given to the general question. In this, as in other things, the Lord in His humanity seems to have grown and ripened into the apprehension of that knowledge which in His Godhead He absolutely possessed. We find Him first uttering that saying about being employed in the matters of his Father, when He was now twelve years old:—first uttering it, I say, because we are expressly told that his parents understood not the saying which He spake to them: but His mother kept it in her heart. And I believe those have been right, who have seen in that act and saying of His, the first stirring consciousness, issuing in action, of the great mission on which He had come into this world of ours. And so I would believe it to have been with that which was the end and crown of His mission—His death itself. It may have come before him in occasional anticipation even in early childhood. It was at least a beautiful and not unfitting thought of a Christian painter, to represent Him in the workshop at Nazareth gazing thoughtfully on some splinters of wood which had fallen in the form of the predestined and accepted Cross. It may have been with Him in an eminent degree as it sometimes is seen to be with us His brethren : the great purpose of life is as it were held over us in youth by heavenly hands, and before it fills our horizon entirely, is made visible to us in partial glimpses, as we require, and as we attain, strength and encouragement in reaching its accomplishment. But concerning all this we are left in uncertainty : some day we may be found worthy to hear of it all : but it was not necessary for us at present to know.

We advance to a period when we are treading on safer ground. Even in the earlier portions of the ministry, we cannot fail to discover traces that the Lord's death was ever present to Him. What can be plainer than that "lifting up as Moses lifted up the serpent in the wilderness?" How otherwise can we interpret such expressions as "taking up the Cross and following Him," than by believing that the street of sorrows with its fatal burden was before His eyes when others saw it not?

But as we pass on, even such plain indications as

these are replaced by others of yet surer and larger import. At a definite period of our Lord's ministry, the sacred narrative seems to enter the first circle of the ever-deepening shadow of His approaching death. And that period may be said to begin with the martyrdom of the great Forerunner. It appears as if our Blessed Lord received those tidings not otherwise than we hear of the striking down of a friend, or companion, or of one whose course is in any way bound on to our own:—as a solemn presage and note of preparation for His own final conflict. "When Jesus heard of it, he departed into a desert place alone." Can any doubt for what purpose? Can we be wrong in attributing to Him the yearning of our own nature at such a time for solitude and for communion with God? As we pass onwards, if I am not mistaken, we may presume to trace the current of thought in the holy soul of the Redeemer setting henceforth very decidedly in this direction. What is the feeding of the five thousand?—what is the great sacramental discourse delivered after it in the synagogue at Capernaum, but a new and public, though as yet mysterious announcement of that death, in which He would give His Flesh for the life of the world? What the repetition of the same act in the feeding afterwards of the four thousand, but a touching and earnest reassurance, to His own soul and to us, of the same great truth? From this point the announcements become clearer and more frequent: the shadows gather apace. It is almost needless to lengthen any more this portion of our sermon. "From that time forth began Jesus to shew to his disciples how that He must go unto Jerusalem and suffer many things of the elders and chief priests and scribes, and be killed, and rise again the third day." From that time forth His words were full of the anticipation. His face was set toward Jerusalem. His very manner and gait made the disciples wonder and fear. One great and glorious event must not be forgotten as specially marking the entrance to this period. I mean, the Transfiguration. We are told by St. Luke that when Moses and Elias appeared in glory and communed with Jesus, they spake of His decease which He should accomplish at Jerusalem. O wonderful theme of discourse with Him whose face did shine as the sun, and whose raiment was white as the snow, so as no fuller on earth can white them! O strange and marvellous theme for those bright ones in glory! for one of them had never seen death; and the other had not died as do the rest of us. Was it that He to whom angels ministered was pleased, in this matter of His deepest concern, to take counsel and comfort rather of the glorified sons of men, than even of the holy angels themselves?

And then at the end of this heavenly scene, Jesus is again left alone, in the power of the Father's voice, which had also accompanied Him as He went up from His baptism, to go on and to suffer.

Thus may be said to open the final portion of His ministry and His life on earth. Before this, intimations of His death were rare: now they are scattered thick, and ever increase in careful specification. Nor can there be a doubt that during this period, our Lord's holy spirit was ever dwelling on the conflict to come:

gathering up its determination to drink every drop of the appointed cup of suffering: full of zeal to accomplish the baptism of blood wherewith he was straitened till He was baptized.

O, my brethren, what a sight it is, even for us who can see so little of it, this solitary spirit of Christ thus passing under the deepening shadow of His sufferings! What can we discern of that which weighed on Him,— we who live on hope, and know nothing beyond the moment, of Him before whom was every detail of all that should come upon him. Every scoff and taunt of His enemies, every keen pang of physical suffering, every one of the great waterfloods of anguish which swept afterwards over His soul,—He saw them all, He felt them all long days before: and if He knew of the joy before Him, He knew too of the Cross, He knew of the shame. O think you not that days of bitter anticipation, nights of conflict in prayer, had left their marks on His outward frame, long ere the ruthless tracks of the buffeting and the scourge were ploughed upon it? How must His visage even then have been marred more than any man! How wasted those cheeks on which the traitor's kiss was to be pressed! How pale those lips, which were ere long to speak the agonized words in Gethsemane and on the Cross! How bowed, as if with premature age, that sacred Head, which was soon to be anointed for burial! Let us suffer with Him; let us enter under the cloud with Him; let us chasten our thoughts and hold our very breath in reverence: let us take our shoes from off our feet, as we presume to draw near to that holy ground where He is brought out to die. And when we stand there, and listen to the words which fall from Him, let us not forget what was said in the beginning: how very little we can discern of what is passing in that holiest place of His inner spirit. May He himself, by His own presence here, and His guiding, lead us by the hand, and grant us rightly to speak of as much as we are permitted to know.

It will be best perhaps to trace through that final scene the action of those great leading motives and affections which we know to have been active in our blessed Redeemer.

And first of all these, beyond a doubt, must be placed OBEDIENCE. "He became obedient even as far as unto Death." His Death is the crowning act of holy subjection to His heavenly Father's will. "The cup which my Father hath given me, shall I not drink it?" "Thinkest thou not that I could presently pray to my Father, and He should send me, twelve legions of angels? But how then should the Scriptures be fulfilled that thus it must be?" "Not my will, but thine be done." In order to arrive at any estimate of the greatness of this obedience, weigh well the freedom of choice, as implied in these words. Power to cast off the humiliation—power to divest himself of the suffering, was not at any moment wanting to Him. "No man taketh my life from me: I have power to lay it down, and I have power to take it again. This commandment have I received of my Father." The holy command is ever before Him, and His own human will is, after the conflict with the weakness of the flesh, absolutely in subjection to it. He permits himself to be apprehended, to be buffeted, to be scourged, to be led out to be crucified, to be nailed to the tree, to linger in the unknown pangs of that most cruel death—all in the ever-renewed self-devotion of unflinching obedience.

And let the opening words of our text never be forgotten in connexion with this thought. "Therefore doth my Father love me, because I lay down my life that I may take it again." We must not for a moment imagine estrangement,—we must not imagine diversity of purpose,—between the Father and the Son in the act of the Lord's death. Nay, it is the especial reason, it is the sweetest and the innermost fountain, of that blessed love of the Father for the Son which is the earnest of our acceptance with God: "THEREFORE doth my Father love me." And all through the final scene, behold this holy accord, behold this self-devoting obedience. Not a restless word, not an impatient gesture, escapes the Lamb of God in His suffering. When they stretch His limbs on the Cross, when they pierce his hands and feet with the nails, when they lift him with rude shock on high, amidst the taunts of His triumphant enemies, amidst the desertion of His followers and friends,—in the burning fever of the death-thirst and the horror of great darkness which fell around Him, there was ever but one frame, one attitude of His holy soul; subjection without murmur, obedience without limit:—"Lo, I come to do thy will, O God." And when now all was accomplished, when He knew that the moment was come that He should depart out of this world unto the Father, then, still free of purpose, and still in the voluntary submission of obedience, by no compulsion, constrained by no physical necessity, dying not because vital power had forsaken him, but because His Father's commandment constrained Him, He bowed His head, and gave forth the breath of life,—" Father, into thy hands I deliver up my spirit." He became obedient, even as far as unto death.

But let us not be thought to deprive this obedience of its merit and value, by seeming to forget the Redeemer's awful SUFFERING at that hour. If it was an example of surpassing obedience, so was it of keenest anguish. And this must be measured, not by any mere deductions of ours respecting that most agonizing of deaths, still less by any speculation on that which His spirit endured when bowed under the weight of the sin of the world and suffering its penalty; but by His own utterances. Was it to record any common degree of physical suffering, that one of the solemn sayings of the Cross is an expression of the agony of the exhausted frame? And do we not all feel that those mysterious words, "My God, my God, why hast thou forsaken me?" impenetrable as their depths are by us, bespeak a degree of spiritual suffering and desertion, exhausting and surpassing all that we can imagine? How He could have been forsaken by God in the act of doing that for which above all other things the Father loves Him,—how the crowning act of holy obedience would bring Him at the same time under the hiding of the Father's face,—if it passes our power to comprehend this, we must set it down to the very horror and strangeness of that which He was then going through : the Lord of Life grappling with and submitting to be overcome by Death : the pure and spotless One crushed under the world's sin ; the Blessing and the Blessed hanging on an accursed tree, and Himself made a curse.

But from that suffering, whose expressions were so few, let us come to that Love, which in His death-scene was so abundantly manifested. The first word from the Cross,—hardly from the Cross, but when His murderers are beginning their work, is a saying of love : " Father, forgive them : for they know not what they do." And it is of a kind deeply instructive and consoling to us, as in many ways, so in this, that it is not merely the love of a human forgiving spirit : it is the love of a divine Intercessor : it is the pleading of the Priest, as He offers the atoning sacrifice. And it testifies too to the blessed accord between the Father and the Son, of which we just now spoke. "Father, forgive them." Beneath these words lie those, "I know that thou always hearest me :" and those, "I and my Father are one." There is no bar between the suffering One and the Almighty Father; no exclusion of Him who was made a curse for others from being at the same moment the source of blessing Himself.

Next among the words of love from the Cross comes the promise to the repentant malefactor. And here we have the power of Love already waxed onwards : the grant of forgiveness and of bliss absolutely made by the suffering Lamb of God. The Son of man hath still, as ever, authority upon earth to forgive sins: He openeth, and none can shut. "Verily I say unto thee, This day shalt thou be with me in Paradise."

Nor shall the Love of intercession alone, nor the love of divine condescension alone, be here manifested. Is the Son of God perfect man, and shall there be in His death no expression of those human affections which speak so earnestly from the dying beds of His brethren? It was fitting, that she who was nearest to the Lord in the flesh, should be last before His sight, and last on His lips as their accents were about to be quenched in death. It was fitting that that loving care of His, which had warned them who came to take Him to spare his disciples, should find one object more even nearer than them, when its exercise became more rare and more wonderful.

Obedience, Suffering, Love: but is there not something of TRIUMPH also in those dying hours of the Lord? Strange indeed it would have been, if there were not, when the last enemy was now vanquished; when the Son of man was now so lifted up that He should draw all men unto him; when the handwriting of ordinances which was against us was now nailed to His cross, and the stain of the world's sin was purged away. And even thus it dawns upon us as we read, that this obedience of His is a glorious victory: that this suffering is no catastrophe of failure, but is the very aim and end of all He did and said: that this Love is no mere human farewell, no sad recollection of the past, no anticipation of distant hopes, but the voice of one to whom is given all power in heaven and in earth. The Cross is no longer a tree of shame, but that in which He spoiled principalities and powers, and made a shew of them openly, triumphing over them while on it. Of all these last words, hardly one is a sad one :—almost all are penetrated with the same spirit of victory and of power. " With me in Paradise :"—then already the joy that was set before Him has risen far above his dark horizon of anguish and suffering. And what triumph bursts from his lips in that cry, " It is finished :" gathering up the humiliation now past : looking on the glory now become present. It was thus that He delivered up His spirit; with yet another cry, the purport of which we are not told, but of which we read "when the centurion which stood over against him saw that he so cried out, and gave up the ghost, he said, Truly this was the Son of God."

Thus was testimony borne to Him, and thus did He bear witness to Himself, in his last and agonizing hour. Further, we may not penetrate. His words are ours, and on them we may ponder ; His outward aspect and gestures belonged for a time to those who looked on, but even from them they were withdrawn by the darkness of nature herself: but His own most sacred inner thoughts none might witness :—that heart knew its own bitterness,—and the stranger did not intermeddle with its joy.

Yet here is abundance revealed for us : both for our thought and for our life.

For such a death it is, my brethren, to which we are to be made conformable ; of which our lives are ever to bear about the remembrance: of which we are to keep up the solemn memorial till He come: of which our deaths, if we be His, will be the faint and imperfect resemblance. In an age of coldness and unbelief, when the atoning virtue of this holy Death is questioned in a world which stands by its efficacy, and in the face of Scriptures which give us these its undeniable testimonies, be we ever more and more in meditation on it, and on that which has come to us by it. Let us not fear to stand by, and dwell in heart and mind on its tokens and details. These are days when the outward facts of the Redeemer's history, when the spoken words of the Redeemer's lips, need to be more in men's view than they are. Of all objects of our contemplation, He himself is our first and best. Of all confirmations of our faith, the record of His sufferings and triumph is the most decisive and the most eloquent. He who has most studied this Death, will be best prepared to meet his own: he who has stood longest by the Redeemer's Cross, will be least dismayed in the hour when his own comes to be laid upon him.

May we so live with Him, that we may die like Him: may we ever, in life and in death, so die with Him, that we may live with Him for ever.

SERMON XVIII.

(PREACHED ON EASTER DAY, APRIL 20, 1862.)

IN CHRIST ALL MADE ALIVE.

1 COR. xv. 12.

"Now if Christ be preached that He rose from the dead, how say some among you that there is no resurrection of the dead?"

REMARKABLE as is the Apostle's argument in several places in this chapter, it is no where more so than in this former part, where he links so closely together the resurrection of our Lord and the doctrine of the general resurrection of all men. He puts it in this way: If Christ rose, then all men must rise: if all men are not to rise, then Christ never rose.

I say this way of arguing appears at first sight strange. A man might feel disposed to answer, "Yes, but Christ was the eternal Son of God, the Lord of life, over whom Death could have no power, and therefore He rose again: but we are vile worms of this earth, born in sin and guilty of sin, and therefore Death has power over us, and we shall not rise again." How are we to answer this, my brethren? This is the point to which I wish to direct your attention this morning. God enlighten us and bless us while we endeavour to make it clear!

Our first consideration must be, WHO THIS IS, of whom this is spoken,—that if He rose from the dead, then all men must rise. It seems a strange necessity, that what happened to one person should therefore be the lot of all: but so it seems to be here laid down. If this be so, there must, you see, be some very close link indeed which binds that Person to all of us. Let us try to explain this by a few examples in history, as given us in Holy Scripture. And on searching for these the very first which occurs is exactly to the point. "In Adam all die." There was something in Adam's position and character, which made that which happened to him of necessity happen to all mankind. Let us go on further. Enoch never died. "He was not: for God took him." But we do not read that because Enoch never died, all we are not to die. Several persons in the sacred record were raised from the dead: but we do not hear of any of them that his resurrection involved us in it in any way. It was just simply an event of his own life, and had no consequences except in any impression it might have made on those who saw or heard of it at the time. Of two persons only do we read that they involved all mankind in themselves and in what happened to them. And those two are, Adam and Christ.

Now I hope I am carrying your minds with me, when I go on to say that, in order for this to be so, there must have been something very different in the position of these two persons from that of any other persons. And if we ask what this was, and begin with the first of them, Adam, we have no difficulty in seeing at once what it was in his case. Adam was the FIRST MAN. There was a time when Adam was the only representative of all mankind. And even when this was not so, he was the father and source of every one that was to be born after. So that when Adam by his disobedience brought in death into his own nature as a certainty and necessity, that death came upon all men, because all were included in him, and derive their being by a regular succession from him. The taint in the source is transmitted to every drop which comes from that source. We have no difficulty in comprehending this: it is to us very plain that it could hardly have been otherwise. And this I think is plain to us also: that in order for an universal effect like this to be again produced on all our race, there must be some fresh relation like this of Adam: some general connexion with us all, or it could not take place.

But now let us come to the other Person, of whom this is said, that because He rose from the dead, all shall rise from the dead; and that if all are not to rise from the dead, then neither did He rise. Who is this, so closely connected with the whole race of mankind? Is it a man like ourselves? Clearly not, by what has already been said. Is it the Son of God, one over whom Death could have no power, become one of ourselves, and having died and risen again? Let us see whether this description will answer our purpose.

I think not. "Become one of ourselves." Not sinful, not unclean, for this the Son of God could not be: but become a man as you or I, in all things like us, sin only excepted. Let us follow such a person through Death and through Resurrection. A glorious fact it would be in the history of our race, that a man like ourselves had been dwelt in by the Son of God, had been brought up out of the grave by divine Power, and was sitting at God's right hand in glory: a thing to be more proud of than the most illustrious events which have ever happened to us. Still, I miss entirely in such a triumph one thing. Where is the link to connect such a divine Person with you and me? How have we any more portion in Him, than in Enoch or in Elijah? If you answer, that we are to believe in Him and pray to Him and try to live like Him, I reply, that I cannot get any real benefit by believing, unless I have something to believe in, which touches my own hopes and fears and state and wants: and I do not see how the triumph of one among all mankind, even though that one were the Son of God, can affect me.

Look at this closer. My body is weak, sinful, decaying. I cannot despise my body. I cannot be healed unless it is healed. I cannot be happy, if my faith is to have no effect on this weak, decaying body. But according to this view of Christ, you give me no hope in my body. Nothing has been done for it. For his own body, according to this view, He did much: even so was there much done by God for Enoch's body, for that of Elijah: but how did this salvation of the body go any further? I must have something plainer than this to trust to. I see how Adam's sin has made my body what it is. This is, alas, plain enough every day that I live. I want some blessed fact about Christ, which shall make it at least as plain to my faith that He has done something, which has been to me, and in my body, the saving from the consequences of Adam's sin.

And then as to my soul: the saving of my soul. I am aware that though Scripture does sometimes sum up the end of our faith inclusively in this term [1], using it in its wider sense, yet it is hardly an adequate, or a Christian way of speaking, to make all consist, in the narrower sense, in the saving of a man's soul: the whole man, body, soul, and spirit, is the subject of God's salvation, not a part of him only. But using the words, as commonly used, to signify the rescuing from eternal punishment of the spiritual part of man,—as to the saving of my soul, can I be satisfied with a Christ who was thus bound up in His own individual being? Where are the merits of His Death? How do I know they are mine? How come they to pass on to me? Because I read, "Every man shall bear his own burden:" and "No man may deliver his brother, or make agreement unto God for him." If I say, I hope those merits are mine, that hope may be a delusion: if I am bolder, and say I feel they are mine, that feeling may be mere fancy. I want a fact to rest upon: something more certain than my hopes, more constant than my feelings:

[1] See 1 Pet. i. 9.

some sure foundation for a faith, on which I can feed and live, with which I can cheerfully sicken and die, and boldly pass into the world of spirits as a redeemed and triumphant soul. And this I shall never get, as long as I believe in a Christ who is merely a divine man, merely one man dwelt in by the Son of God.

In short we come to our old question. How are we to find in Christ something which connects Him with our whole race, as closely and as entirely as Adam is connected with it? Because without this, I do not see how Christ's death could atone for my sins, nor how Christ's Resurrection could necessarily involve mine. How am I to find this?

I answer, simply by receiving the testimony of Holy Scripture concerning Christ: simply by accepting the truth as it is set before us in this chapter. And that truth is this: that the eternal Son of God took on Him, not the person of an individual man, but manhood entire and complete: our nature in its entireness and completeness. He became its Head, as much as Adam was ever its Head. And just as we can look back in history and see a moment when all mankind was summed up in Adam, and when Adam stood in Paradise bearing on him and representing us all, so ought our faith to see all mankind summed up in Christ, and Christ born, obeying, suffering, dying, rising again, standing at God's right hand in glory, bearing on Him, and representing us all. Only when Christ is thus received and thus believed on, can we be sure of our foundation; can we get solid comfort, and strength not our own, and triumph over Death and sin by Him.

When I know this, and when I enter into it by living faith, I know that my guilt is done away in Christ; not because I hope it, not because I feel it, but because I rest on the fact that on Him all our iniquities were laid: that He, by the satisfaction of His meritorious death, standing in the root of our nature as Adam did, suffered,—exhausted, once for all,—the punishment of the world's sin. And when I look on the body, over which decay and death for the present seem to triumph, I know that it shall rise again, glorious and free from sin and pain and decay, not because it is my opinion, not because I can see through the difficulties of it (which I cannot), but because my Redeemer's body rose again, and in that body of His I have a part: I am His flesh and His bones, because He included every man in Himself; and what He is, that I shall be also. And therefore I can see the body decaying without dismay, because it has a glorious future in Him; and therefore, not knowing nor anxiously caring how it may be when the enemy comes hand to hand with the weakened and weary flesh, I can in prospect defy death, and look across the black rift of the grave to the blessedness beyond it, where He is who is my Head, and the Head of us all. Because He rose again, I shall rise. If I am not to rise, He never rose—the Gospel is a fable—salvation is a dream.

But HE IS RISEN. If there is one fact in the world, it is this. And on this fact, and not on mere hopes, or mere feelings, or mere opinions, does our faith rest.

Shall I stop here? Shall I leave it to yourselves to work out the rest in your own minds—to supply, as any one with common sense can supply, the course of a man's spiritual life based and grounded on this fact of universal redemption by Christ? Better perhaps not to trust altogether to this being done. Better to repeat to you from last Sunday's sermon, how our great Head and Lord has not left this, man's universal part in Him, to float about in our minds a vague and ill-assorted thing, but has sealed it to us by a blessed ordinance of His own appointing, in which we were especially made members of Him: how we are by that outwardly and visibly tied on to this work wrought by Christ, and look back on that as the token that it is ours. Better also to remind you that in this salvation the whole man partakes: that unless he believes it, unless he lives on it and by it, unless he is made holy and just and virtuous and upright by it, unless in a word he is led by the Spirit of Christ, he is none of His. Christ did not come to save us as a jewel is brought up by the diver, unconscious and unaltered: He did not come to cleanse us as a building is cleansed by them that sweep it, and leave us empty and dreary: He came to save us, He came to cleanse us, according to the conditions of our being, and of our rank in the scale of His creatures: as thinking and feeling—as repenting and forsaking sin, as energizing and working for good, as renewed and built up on our most holy faith, as renouncing self, the world, and the devil;—serving Him, fighting for Him against evil, ever more and more unto our lives' end. Without this, though of necessity we shall rise with Him, we shall not be saved by Him: without being Christian men and women on earth, we can never follow Christ into the everlasting light of His home in God's heaven. For it will not be our home: we shall not know its language, nor relish its pursuits, nor love its inhabitants. O remember, all ye who hear me, that there is a resurrection of damnation: that this necessity of rising again with Christ may be to some among you a curse, instead of a blessing.

And if I dismiss you with a hope of better things, with a hope that of those now assembled on this our chief Christian festival not one may be wanting when the Resurrection morning breaks, remember that no wish, no prayer of mine will bring this about. It rests with yourselves, whether you will employ the grace offered you: whether you will be faithful soldiers of Him whom you are bound to serve; persuaded of what He has done for you, and devoting your lives and powers to Him.

SERMON XIX.

(PREACHED ON THE FIRST SUNDAY AFTER EASTER, APRIL 27, 1862.)

THE RESURRECTION OF THE BODY.

1 COR. xv. 20.

"Now is Christ risen from the dead, and become the first-fruits of them that slept."

LAST Sunday morning I spoke to you on the intimate connexion between Christ's resurrection and ours; taking up the Apostle's argument in this chapter, and grounding what was said on the fact that Christ is not one from among ourselves, nor merely a man taken into the Godhead, but is the Son of God become the very root and second Head of our whole nature, as entirely and as literally as Adam was its first root and head. I mention this, not that we may go over the same ground again, but that we may bear this in mind to-day, and go on to say more about the doctrine of the resurrection of the dead. I say, may bear this in mind: for without doing so, we can understand nothing about the doctrine itself. And the reason why so very little is believed, and so very little understood, about the resurrection of the dead, is just this, that people know and care so little about this position of our blessed Lord as the second and glorious Head of our nature. Keep this fact in view, and all is clear about the resurrection of the dead: forget this, as I am afraid most people do, and I really do not see how a man can say with any intelligent meaning, "I believe in the resurrection of the body." This will, I hope, become plainer to us as we go on.

First, let us take care that we know what it is that we are about to speak of. What is THE RESURRECTION OF THE DEAD? What does the word itself mean? Re-surrection is simply a Latin word made English, and it is formed from the verb *re-surgo*, to rise again. To rise *again*, notice. We are familiar in our own English with this meaning of the syllable *re*, prefixed to a word. We say to *re*-appear, to *re*-fit, to *re*-build, and the like. And this is an important matter here. So also is the other part of the word, to *rise*. It is in allusion to the Jewish and Christian practice of burial in a lying position, or of burial under the ground, or more probably to both of these combined. So that, as far as regards the word itself, when we say "resurrection," we mean the rising up again, into an erect position, and above ground, of that which we have buried, lying as in slumber, under the ground. The term "resurrection" has nothing to do with the spiritual part of man. To talk of the *resurrection of the soul* would be absurd. The soul has never been laid down, and can never be raised up again. We have reason to believe, and we do believe, that the souls of men will never be extinguished out of being, but will continue to live on for ever in union with their risen bodies: but that has nothing to do with the resurrection itself. That doctrine regards simply and only the body: that which lies down in death. Of that only can it be said that it shall be *raised again.*

So that by the very meaning of words, when we speak of the resurrection of the dead, we do not speak of what is called the doctrine of a future state. The Apostle treats, throughout this chapter, of the resurrection of the dead, and you observe he speaks all through of men's bodies;—of what is sown in corruption;—of there being different kinds of flesh, and so forth: he no where for a moment speaks of the souls of men.

Now it is wonderful that we should have to guard this matter so much from mistake. But it is necessary to do so. For numbers of Christians in our days, when they hear of, and when they profess belief in, the resurrection of the dead, look on the term as only a sort of expression for the immortality of the soul, and lose all recollection of the fact that it concerns the body. I may remind you, in passing, that the Apostles' Creed has taken care to express this very unmistakeably for us: I BELIEVE IN THE RESURRECTION OF THE BODY.

And it is this which is the distinguishing doctrine of the Christian religion. There hardly ever has been a civilized nation, which has not believed in a future state, and in some kind of a final judgment. But until Christ rose, it was never known,—never believed in definitely as an article of faith, that the *bodies* of men would rise again. It is true that the Old Testament prophecies concerning Christ had put the idea into the minds of the Jews, and the greater part of them professed to receive it as a doctrine, as St. Paul said before Felix,—but others did not: and even when our Lord announced his own Resurrection to his disciples, they questioned among themselves what the rising from the dead should mean. Those very Athenians again, who when they heard of the resurrection of the dead, mocked, had long been taught that the soul was immortal, and that all were to be judged according to their works.

And now with this caution against mistaking that of which we are speaking, let us come to the matter itself. Christ is risen from the dead. There is our central fact. He, in whom was summed up all humanity, every man, woman and child born into this world from the creation to the end, is come up out of death: and we saw last Sunday that therefore all mankind will also come up out of death. This necessity may be regarded as proved and done with.

But there is much more to be looked at here than the mere bare fact of a resurrection of all men. Much light is let in upon the subject,—upon the nature and manner of this general resurrection, by looking at the nature and manner of that resurrection of Christ. Why so? Just because He is as we are: not one separate from us, but one including us in Himself. Let me make this clear by the comparison again of Adam. What was true in Adam, must be true in us his offspring, in the main, and in all matters regarding our common nature. We can take upon ourselves to say how Adam died, by knowing how we his posterity die. The breath forsook his body, the countenance became pallid, and after a time decay set in, and flesh and bones crumbled to dust. He, as gathered into death, might be called, not indeed in point of fact as to time of death, but as the first doomed, the one on whom the approaches of death first took effect,—the firstfruits of the sad harvest of that reaper of our race. Well then—as Adam 'for death, so Christ for life. Christ is become the first-fruits of the dead. Of the same kind and race as the human dead, He rose, in His own order, i. e. first, and they will come after Him, not in a different manner, but in the same manner. His sacred Body, when it came up out of death, was what it was, and seemed what it seemed, not by some strange irregular stroke of creative power, making it afresh, and calling up its resurrection state out of nothing, but by the regular agency on Him, in his own place and order, of that quickening Spirit which also shall act on our dead bodies, in their place and order of time, and bring them up into life also. It is true, that our blessed Lord after His Resurrection, did wonderful things, as He also did before His death,—which belonged specially to His exalted Office and Person, and which do not pertain to all our race: but never let this blot out the truth from our considerations, that as the Lord's Body was after His resurrection, so will our bodies be after their resurrection. And how was that? What do we know about His resurrection body, which we may safely expect in our own case also? One thing, for certain. It was the same Body, that was nailed on the Cross, and laid in the tomb. I need not prove this to you. "He shewed them His hands and His side." "Behold my hands and my feet, that it is I myself." He offered to the doubting Thomas even the material proofs which he had desired. And it was the same not in appearance only but in solid substance, capable of being felt and handled. The women whom He met as they came from the sepulchre, held Him by the feet and worshipped Him. He himself challenged His disciples to this proof of His identity: "Handle me and see that it is I myself: for a spirit hath not flesh and bones as ye see me have." And when they still doubted, He demanded food, and did eat before them. And St. Peter in the Acts (x. 41) asserts of himself and the other witnesses of His Resurrection, that they did eat and drink with Him after God raised him from the dead.

But some one may say, "May not these things also, the being the same Body, the being distinguishable by the marks which it bore before Death, the being able to be handled, the having power to take and assimilate food,—may not all these have been peculiar to our Lord Himself alone, necessary for his identification by those who were to testify to His Resurrection, but not necessarily belonging to all our race, as attributes of their bodies after the resurrection?" To this question I fearlessly answer, No: I cannot conceive this: and for two reasons. First, it would very much deprive our Lord's Resurrection of its matter-of-fact reality, if things so entirely belonging to the character and capacities of the body were merely put on for a special effect, and did not really pertain to it:—and secondly, if it were so, the whole teaching of Scripture about Christ being as we are, and our Resurrection being like His, would tend only to mislead us, and not to guide us. We must carefully distinguish, as I did just now, between the things which belonged to His work and His peculiar aim on earth during these forty days, and that which was of the nature of His risen Body: but we cannot consent to cut down and get rid of all its attributes which we believe to be common to Him and us his brethren. Take an example. We find Him rendering himself sometimes visible, sometimes invisible, to His disciples. We find the same power exercised by Him during His ministry, before His death. We may fairly then set this down among those instances of superhuman power which were reserved to Him as the Son of God, and not as belonging to any capacity of the resurrection body. But on the other hand, when He commands them to handle him, and eats before them, to prove to them that it was He himself, surely it would deprive these proofs of all their force, if we are to assume that He made his body solid and tangible, and took food into it, by some divine power separate from its own actually existing nature. It was that nature of which He would persuade them, not of His almighty power: and of that nature He does persuade them, by shewing out before them its phænomena as they were found and already existed in it.

So then I believe it is shewn us by this Resurrection

s

of Him who is the first-fruits of the dead, that we shall rise again with these same bodies, bearing upon them those outward differences from one another by which we were known on earth, having real substance capable of being perceived and recognized by each other. Of course I do not forget, that there are many difficulties in the way of understanding thoroughly how this can be, and many difficult questions arising as we approach the consideration of it: as for instance, whether the body will present the aspect which it had at the end of life,—in old age, or in sickness, or at the point of death,—or some former appearance, more comely and in its prime. But this is partly answered by the nature of the case; for surely we cannot conceive of that state where all will be joy and immortality, that the saints should appear otherwise than glorious and joyous: and partly also by the example of our risen Lord Himself. Mary Magdalene thought him to be the gardener, an ordinary man about his daily work: the disciples were glad, when they saw the Lord: we may safely conclude then, that He did not appear as in the last moments of pallor and exhaustion on the Cross, but though with the same body, in a form more like that which He wore in the ordinary life of former years.

I know that there may be other details of objection made. It may be said, for instance, in the case of our Lord's Body there was no difficulty about its identity. It had lain but three days in the grave, and it saw not corruption. Here it was, entire: of the same material as in the moment of death. But how will this be with bodies which have mouldered into dust for ages upon ages;

whose material particles have passed into other bodies perhaps again and again, or have been taken up into the solid substance of the earth? I answer, that I am quite willing to leave such considerations in His hands who made the body; in His care, who so wonderfully preserves its identity here on earth, that the aged man carries the features and the scars of his youth, though not a particle of matter in his body is the same, but all has been changed many times over.

But there is yet another point in our Lord's resurrection state, which will be in ours also. His Body underwent a change, in passing through death. From being a body of humiliation, it had become a body of glory. "Christ being raised from the dead, dieth no more: death hath no more dominion over him." Even so shall we all be changed, so as to be like the body of His glory. "Flesh and blood," St. Paul teaches us, "cannot inherit the kingdom of God;" the natural body will in the act of the resurrection become a spiritual body, no longer liable to decay, or sickness, or death. And the same change will pass upon those who shall be alive on earth at the time of the appearing of the Lord, and of the rising again from the dead.

If we further enquire into the process and manner of the resurrection, Holy Scripture teaches us thus much;—that all men shall not rise together at the same time, but the dead in Christ, the saints of the Lord, shall rise first, and shall be with Him in glory for a considerable period of time before the rest of the dead are summoned into life, to be judged according to their works. "Blessed and holy," says the beloved

Apostle, "is he that hath part in the first Resurrection." On this portion of our subject I addressed you when speaking of the prophecies in the Revelation of St. John in the Advent of the year before last, and endeavoured to rescue these words just quoted from being explained away by the foolish fiction of a spiritual resurrection being meant by them.

And now, my brethren, does Holy Scripture give us any information as to the condition of those who are thus raised again with glorified bodies, and known to each other, and for ever in bliss? Here and there a few hints are furnished us, on which our hopes may dwell, and our chastened imagination may expatiate. We shall be like the Lord Himself. Thus much have we heard in our Lesson this evening service,—"We know not yet what we shall be; but when He (or better, when *it*) shall be manifested, we shall be like Him; for we shall see Him as He is." The very sight, face to face, of Him, our glorious Head, all pure, all perfect, all lovely, will transform us into His likeness: not destroying our individual identity, but rendering us all, according to the measure of each, as He is. How that is, we can here only imagine by negatives. All that is unholy, unlovely, unquiet, will have passed away: there will be no evil tempers ruffling the serenity of the countenance, no evil words passing from those tongues devoted to praise: no envy, no misinterpretation, no coldness, no contempt. What a change it must be, for pride to have disappeared. What a change, for each to have fallen into his own place, and no longer to be busy with the acts and characters of others. How different men must have become, when there will be no longer any distinction of stations, yet all will be orderly and contented; when all will have enough, without the necessity of labour, and without the danger of idleness: when all will be bound together in holy love, and yet earth's dearest relations exist as such no more.

For we are further told by our Lord Himself, that they who are counted worthy to obtain that first blessed resurrection from among the dead neither marry nor are given in marriage, but are as the angels of God in heaven. Not that we can for a moment believe, that the blessed union of kindred hearts on earth will there be severed, nor that they who have during life been united in the Lord, will be disunited when present with the Lord: nay, God forbid, for this is the very golden thread of hope that runs through the saddened and tangled woof of this life's affections,—and without it they would be imperfect and unblest. But what is meant is doubtless this, that no such relation there being required, its purpose and all that belonged to it having in that state passed away, it will no longer hold that first and exclusive position there which it does here, but will take its blessed place according to the degree of love and union of souls which may have subsisted in it, and not according to any right and privilege of its own: the little stream, with its flowery banks and its mirrored pools, will be lost in the broad bright ocean of universal love.

If it be asked, what is the further employment of those who are thus raised in the body, and thus live for ever with each other and the Lord, our reply must be, that this matter has not been specially revealed to us, doubtless because we cannot now comprehend its actual details. The state itself is one out of our limits and comprehension; how much more its surrounding circumstances and interests. Yet if we think a moment, we can hardly be entirely at a loss for some answer to the question, however scanty and insufficient. "They shall be," said our blessed Lord, "like the angels of God in heaven." And that must mean, they shall be the servants and messengers of God's holy will; adopted into His heavenly household, to do His behests. Then again, can we suppose that He who has given us minds to search His wondrous works, and has yet limited us, in this present state, to so imperfect a comprehension of them, intends to confine us to this—the yearning after knowledge which we cannot obtain? Will there not in that resurrection state be an ever-advancing search into the wonders of His handy-work? What is all that starry universe which night unveils to us? What is all the wonderful mystery of the union of life and matter? What the still more wonderful mystery of the laws of thought, and association, and sympathy? Why are these just shewn to us here in mere tantalizing glimpses? Is this all that infinite goodness has provided for us of the highest of all enjoyments? Are we to spend a blissful eternity in only knowing that we cannot know? Are we to stand for ever outside the door of the temple of truth, and thus to be supremely contented and happy? If so, then I say that the kingdom of heaven will be not an exaltation, but a degradation of our being. God forbid. In that resurrection state will be the perfection of man : and it cannot be wrong to believe of it all that is highest and noblest in the employments of our nature. To do God's bidding in blessed works of which we now know nothing,—to be ministers of His will in the use of faculties which we now do not possess ; in worlds whose existence we now only guess at ;—to witness and to observe His manifold loving-kindness in schemes of Love ever unfolding brighter and brighter as they are nearer and nearer to Himself :—here surely is employment active enough for an angel's strength, high enough for a seraph's intelligence.

And who can tell what there may be belonging to this portion of our employ there, of mutual help, and the offices of pure affection to one another ? Here on earth the spirit high in knowledge dwells apart, and will not, or as often cannot, share that knowledge with others: infirmity rests on both : he too proud to teach, they too proud to learn :—but there he that is greatest will be the minister of all, the glorified Lord Himself ministering most of all to all. And when we remember what a mixed multitude that will be ;—how varied in knowledge, in experience, in power, what an infinite employ does such a thought open to us. There will be a blessed company, from every age in the world's lifetime, of dear children, who have passed away into the Lord's mercy before knowledge dawned on them : shall we tell them of that which they knew not—or will they perhaps not rather teach us? Or likelier still, will not our longer knowledge of earth, and their longer knowledge of heaven, mutually supply and fill up one another?

Then in addition to these active employments, there will be opened there the books of Creation, of Providence, of Redemption; Creation, as He sees it who made it,—ranging from the secrets of the central law which moves firmaments round His throne, to those of the lowest and meanest forms of organized life:— Providence, embracing all the world's history, stretched out as in a map before the renovated memory, with not the meanest incident unrecorded, nor the lightest word forgotten: Redemption, laid out before the view of the redeemed, not as in our inspired books, in the earthen vessels of human languages: but thought to thought, even to the fullest capacity of the glorified Spirit, and with the present Lord Himself for its Expounder: think, I say, of all these, and surely we can be at no loss to conceive how the sons and daughters of the resurrection will find employ even of these kinds for a blessed and undying eternity.

I have said nothing to-day of the individual's share in that state and his spiritual life as there brought to perfection. I purposely reserve this for another time.

Well then, my brethren, what of us in the presence of these truths? What of us who are here, resting for an hour on our journey to the grave, that we may think of these things, and better believe them? Should not this thought be uppermost in our minds after this our meditation—What manner of persons ought we to be, in all purity, and uprightness, and constant preparation for our summons into this blessed final state?

What have we heard to-day? "Every man that hath this hope in Him," this hope founded on, brought in by, resting upon the Lord Christ his Saviour, "purifieth himself, even as He is pure."

If this body of ours, this battle-field of God's army and the devil's army,—may be the happy scene of so many triumphs, and at last become the region of God's everlasting peace, O how manfully ought we to fight this battle—how earnestly to strive against all that is impure and unholy in it—how humbly and constantly to follow the signals and commands of God's holy Spirit, that dwelleth in us and teacheth us!

SERMON XX.

(PREACHED ON THE SECOND SUNDAY AFTER EASTER, MAY 4, 1862.)

THE HOPE OF THE RESURRECTION.

TITUS ii. 13.
" Looking for that blessed hope."

WE have been speaking, for two Sundays during this Easter season, of the doctrine of the Resurrection of the dead. We have seen how it has become a necessity that all men should be brought up out of their graves with their bodies, seeing that Christ is risen, who includes in Himself all of us as our righteous Head,—the second and glorious Adam.

We have seen too, something of what our Resurrection will be, by thinking what His was. Our bodies will be the same, able to be touched and recognized by others, but changed from humility to glory, from decay to incorruption. Our employ will be that of the holy angels, to do God's will: to advance, in all likelihood, ever more and more in knowledge of Him, and His works, and His ways, in Creation, in Providence, and in Redemption.

But there is one part of our subject left: the application of this blessed doctrine to our individual hopes and prospects. And of that I wish to treat to-day, by God's help.

Of this kind then will be the Resurrection: this its glory, this, in the main, its employ. And now, what should you and I think of ourselves as connected with it? You will observe it is an article of our faith: "I believe in the Resurrection of the body." And what does this imply? Does it merely mean, that we assent to there being such a thing, as a bare truth in the abstract? Does it mean, "I believe that men's bodies shall rise?" And when we continue, "And in the Life Everlasting," do we merely intend by this, "I believe that some shall live for ever?" O surely not: we cannot have such a cold unworthy idea of the articles of the Christian faith as this. They are assuredly confessed with the mouth, not as cold bare facts, but as living realities; not as objects of thought, but as objects of reliance and hope. And when the Christian child, or the Christian man, professes his belief in them, it is as being his own in Christ, as real in his own case, and not only in that of other men.

When I utter these words in church, when I profess them as my belief, I must surely mean that I regard them as facts in my own life and course. I take the words as they stand in the Nicene Creed, where the very same expression is used as in our text: "I look for the Resurrection of the dead, and the life of the world to come." That is, I expect in my own case,

I look forward to witnessing, and sharing in, the things thus spoken of.

If you ask me, what reason have I in my own case to look for such blessed participation in the resurrection to life eternal, my answer is plain and decisive. I look for it, because of God's covenant with me as a member of Christ, sealed to me in my Baptism. Christ's work in our flesh, as we saw a few Sundays since, has given all men an equal right in Him, and in all that He came to do and to bring in. But He has commanded that men shall enter into this their right in Him, by a certain ordinance which He appointed: that they shall be made His disciples by being baptized in the name of the Father, and of the Son, and of the Holy Ghost. When you and I were children, we were thus made His disciples; we were baptized in this form, and in this thrice Holy Name. And that fact,—God's covenant with us thus sealed to us, is our title to the blessed hope of resurrection unto life. This fact, I say, and not any thing that has passed in ourselves:— let that come in in its own place:—but this hope of our salvation is not in any way of ourselves, but entirely of God: His doing, not ours.

Now let me be understood aright. Do not suppose me to say for a moment, that every baptized person is to be saved. You know well that I could not say that; that no man in his senses could say any such thing. Any baptized person may—and thousands of baptized persons do—forget, neglect, despise, forfeit in all its substance and reality, their membership of Christ. There are many branches in Christ, as He himself has told us expressly, which do not bring forth fruit, and which the heavenly Husbandman taketh away. But whenever such unworthy members are by God's grace led to repentance, and to turn back to Him whom they have forsaken, it is not their conversion back to God which is their evidence of acceptance and the cause of their reliance; it is not any thing in themselves at all; it is, even if repentance and conversion have to be repeated again and again and again, simply and only this first and plain fact—God's original covenant with them, in his Son Jesus Christ, which was sealed to them in Baptism. "I was then made a member of Christ, the child of God, and an inheritor of the kingdom of heaven." Note especially these last words. We have every reason to be thankful to God that the venerable reformers, the compilers of our Catechism, had the boldness to speak thus manfully and scripturally on this truth, which lies at the very foundation of our individual spiritual life: that it is God's covenant with us, not any thing which has passed since, on which our hopes of eternal life are founded. For it is even thus that St. Paul speaks in his great argument in the Epistle to the Romans. All his powerful persuasions to holiness of life are grounded on this, that our covenant state with God is one of death to sin, and life to Him:—that we are (I am quoting St. Paul's own words) "buried with Christ by baptism into death: that like as Christ was raised up from the dead by the glory of the Father, even so we also should walk in newness of life."

And now let us look back, my brethren, and see how far we have advanced. "I look for the resurrection of the Body, and the life everlasting," because God has assured these blessings to me in my covenant relation with Him in Christ as a member of Christ's body. Now many of you are aware, that in saying this, I am touching on a question much debated among religious writers of a certain stamp: I mean the question as to what is called *personal assurance :* the question as to whether it is, or is not, an essential portion of the Christian's faith to be assured of his own part in Christ, and his own ultimate share in Christ's salvation. Now this is a question, which no Christian churchman can be at any loss how to answer. He will answer it as we have done above; and tell the enquirer that his own personal part in God's covenant and God's promises is not a matter which can be left to uncertain and easily mistaken feelings and experiences of his own, but is, as we said before, at the foundation of his whole spiritual life, which is built up upon it, as it is built on the fact of God's mercies to him in Christ. And here again I must say, Do not mistake me. Do not suppose me to say that any man can be, or ever ought to be, certain of his own ultimate salvation. No man who lives by faith in Christ ever will be; for he will see more and more of his own utter unworthiness, and even to the last moment of a long and useful life, will humble himself in the dust before the Searcher of hearts, and trust implicitly in His infinite mercy in Christ. But then he *will trust:* and ever, all through life, he will in faith look upon himself as a member of Christ, and as one of God's chosen ones, according to that command of St. Jude: "But ye, beloved, building yourselves up on your most holy faith, praying in the Holy Ghost, keep yourselves in the love of God, looking for the mercy of our Lord Jesus Christ unto eternal life."

So then I dwell no longer on this point, which it was necessary to put clearly before you, and to free from objections, before going on. We are ready now to say,—This blessed Resurrection,—this life eternal in the glorified body,—is the covenanted inheritance and is the glorious hope of the faithful members of God's Church. I say of the *faithful* members: because a man may not live in sin, and hope for it: a man may not live in neglect of God, and hope for it: but every man, who knows and puts in practice his state of a member of Christ's Body, is bound to hope for it, must hope for it, in order to live as a member of that Body at all. And thus you and I, though we can never say that our own unworthiness may not after all shut us out, though we carry out this our safety with fear and trembling, yet must, and do in the main take for granted, and look for, this resurrection, and this life eternal.

And this being so, important effects are produced, or ought to be produced, on our views of several things, either present, or in prospect.

The first of which I shall speak, is our view of DEATH. If a blessed resurrection in an incorruptible body is to be ours, any one can easily see that the act and state of death, so terrible where this hope is not, at once loses its formidable character, and shrinks up into utter insignificance. It is very striking to compare heathen authors with the sacred writers, even of the Old Testament, when this hope was but dimly seen,— and to notice, while those who knew not God are full of descriptions of the terrors of death, how few such there are even in the earlier portion of our Bibles. And still more remarkable it is to notice, how entirely absent from the whole of the New Testament is almost any mention of death at all. Our Lord absolutely makes nothing of it. "He that believeth in Me shall never die;" as if bodily death was not worth taking into account at all. Truly is it written that He "hath abolished death" for us. And not one Apostle ever speaks about death, ever preaches on it, ever exhorts concerning it. It is evermore the *coming of the Lord* for which we are to watch, and for which we are to wait. Death is gone; put an end to; only alluded to in speaking of those most glorious things which follow it. It forms no part of our message to the world to tell men of it, or strictly speaking to prepare men for it; but to tell them of Christ, and of His salvation, by which it has become to them as it were nothing. Even the name was unheard in the earliest and freshest ages of the Church. *Sleep* in Christ was always used instead; a term full of comfort and hope,—leading on the thought to the day of glorious awakening. And such will be the change produced in the view regarding Death, of every one who looks for the resurrection of the body, and the life everlasting. There will be no more gloomy and morbid dwelling on the act and accessories of dying: the light of the coming morning fills that dread chamber, and it is no longer dark to the faithful Christian. Doubtless it will and must be a conflict when it comes, that solemn moment of parting from the body: but what is a conflict, where victory is assured to us? What soldier ever dwells long and gloomily on the fearful incidents of battle, by way of bracing his courage to meet it? Is it not ever the rule, and should it not ever be our rule, to dwell on the triumph beyond, and so to forget the struggle by which it is to be reached?

One thing then we shall do, if we are faithful members of Christ's church, and do indeed expect the resurrection to life eternal: we shall look on that inevitable day which must come, without morbid anticipation or cowardly fear, leaving the manner and time of it to Him who doeth all things well for us, and reckoning its conflict as not worthy to be compared with the glory which is to be revealed beyond it.

And as this confidence of hope will alter our view of death, so will it also of LIFE. What is life, my brethren, to the man of this world — to the poor creature who does not know whether it is not to be cut short for ever at the day of death? Life, to him, is simply a snatching-time: to get as much as he can out of it, to eat, and drink, and amass gain, and earn repute, and win importance, and fill as large a space as he can with what credit he may: and there is an end of it. Thousands on thousands are leading just this life and nothing more: often varnished over with pure and bright colours,—decent charities, expected attendance on religion, and the like: but none can deny that, judging by the practice of most men, such is the general view of life; that as to eternity, and so on, it is an uncertainty after all, and it is better to take the present good in hand, not to lay up for such an uncertainty.

Now then, does a man, in his heart, in his deepest thoughts and views of the future, look for the resurrection of the body and the life everlasting? And can he any longer think thus of life? Why, to the other man, this life is *all*: he knows of nothing beyond it; but to this man, what is beyond it is almost all, and this life is as compared to it almost as nothing. But how? Even as the seed-time, which though in a certain field it may be but one morning in a year, yet on that one morning depends all the use and produce of that field for that year,—so is it with the Christian believer's estimate of this life. It is, as compared with that beyond the grave, but as a moment,—but as a point hardly to be appreciated: yet in the use of this moment, in the complexion of this little point, is involved the whole character and degree of blessedness of that immeasurable eternity. O what does time become to one who views life thus? What does duty become? What does mere present advantage become? What becomes of the opinion of the world about him, in matters which have any reference to that other and final state? Life is now not a snatching-time, but a laying-up time: a time of treasuring up things which may be of account there.

And coming closer to the Christian's faith and

obedience,—looking at Him who is the Christian's Example as He is his Lord,—what did HE think of life? "I must work the work of Him that sent me while it is day: the night cometh, when no man can work." Thus will the Christian live: sinking himself in God's work, that He may be able, when he stands, as the Redeemer stood, at the threshold of life, to look back and say, "Father, I have glorified thee on earth: I have finished the work which Thou gavest me to do." What holy zeal, what caution, what self-denial, what fruits of charity and mercy, will such a view of life produce! What a turning of the clay of this earth into heaven's gold, and blessing the relations of our frail homes with an everlasting blessing.

There is another thing concerning which, if we look in our own persons for the resurrection of the dead and the life everlasting, our views will necessarily undergo a change; and that is, the BODY.

It may not be very easy to say, what the mere worldly man thinks of the body in which he finds himself dwelling. But I am afraid we should not be far wrong in believing, that the very last thing which he expects is, that it will rise from the grave, and be his dwelling for ever. This doctrine, at which the wise Athenians scoffed, is still despised by those who think themselves wise after this world's measure. They have some vague notion of a probability of the immortality of the soul, and a future judgment, without ever reflecting that we shall be judged in the body for the deeds done in the body. And the consequence is that in their view the man is not one, but two persons, soul and body: the soul is meant to be saved by religion, but the body has little or nothing to do with religion. And so their religion is all what they call *spiritual;* i. e. it has nothing to do with common life, its temptations, its duties, its tempers, its toil, and its repose,— but is confined to Sundays, and to one book only, and one kind of work, and one kind of talking:—and the body, with all its interests, and all its manifold ways of glorifying God, is put out of sight, and neglected, and supposed to have no concern with religion at all.

And then those who are not only worldly, but irreligious, go further than this; and pretend to tell us, from the speculations of misused science, that the life which is so mysteriously placed in the body is necessarily and inseparably united to it, and therefore perishes when the body decays. Now I need not tell you that he who believes in the resurrection of the dead, is of course directly opposed to such a view of the body: but I mention the speculations of these last, just to remark how, in as far as they are grounded on real research, they give strong confirmation to that Christian doctrine. If it be true that our personal life is so intimately bound up with certain organic arrangements in the body, then at least we see still stronger reason why those organic arrangements should be preserved in that final state which is to be the perfection of our personal being. The righteous souls, during the time of their severance from the body, are in the hand of God: and there we are contented to leave them, satisfied that He can keep them in being and in bliss till the day of reunion; but it is something for modern science to have taught us, that the revelation made to us by Him who hath brought immortality to light is a truth to which physical research also seems to lead us.

But to return. How different an aspect do the things of the body present to him who regards it as his companion through a blessed eternity — to him who reads and feels what the Apostle tells us, that Christ is the Saviour of the body;—that we are now waiting for the adoption, that is, the redemption of the body. How careful will he be to train this his future servant for its blessed ministrations there;—to put it entirely under the power of God's purifying Spirit of grace:—to subdue in it all impure and unholy desires, all inordinate indulgences of lawful appetite, and render it an habitation if it may be worthy of Him whose temple it ought to be.

Yet another change will be wrought by looking for the resurrection of the body, and the life everlasting: and that will be, in our views of, and affections towards, OTHERS AROUND US. And here again perhaps we are apt to be at the same time too vague and general, and too earthly and carnal, in our ordinary expressions and anticipations. The hope of reunion to those who have gone before us in Christ, the hope that our present ties of blood and affection may subsist beyond the grave, these are common enough, but either are merely a fancy that this world's situations may be renewed there, or, if searched into as to their ground, seem to give way under us altogether. I am persuaded that neither of these need be the case, if we apprehend rightly the glorious doctrine of the Resurrection. That this world's relations cannot be renewed there as such, a moment's thought may convince us. They are dependent on this world's necessities and circumstances, and, as we saw last Sunday, when those are passed away, these, as such, will have passed away likewise. But the holy love, and intercourse of word and thought which was the real charm and hallower of all these relations, that will subsist, and in an undisturbed and pure form utterly unknown here. And this being so, will not he who looks for this, walk with those whom he loves on earth differently from him who regards it not? If the painter who painted for posterity needed more care in every touch than the other, who painted merely for the day, will not he who loves for eternity love more wisely, more tenderly, more cautiously and self-denyingly, than he who merely gratifies a present predilection? A fellow-member of the Body of Christ, —one with whom I hope to hold converse which shall never know parting nor end in the presence of Him who is Love,—if I remember this, and act on this, can I wantonly wound the feelings of such an one? Can I hinder such an one in the path to glory? Can I to such an one act a part, and put on guile, to serve any worldly purpose? "They take the sun out of heaven, who take away friendship out of life:" thus wrote the heathen philosopher: but we may say a worthier thing,—they take away the sun out of heaven, who take the hope of the Resurrection out of friendship.

Once more: he who looks for the Resurrection of the

dead and the life everlasting, will, in proportion as this blessed hope is present to him, find his thoughts of CHRIST evermore changed, and exalted, and made more precious to him. From a distant historical character, to a present Saviour,—this is the first great change in a man's thoughts of Christ. From a present Saviour, to be the desire of his soul,—One whose likeness, and nothing else, will satisfy him; this is the next change; and it is no less an one than the former :— it is, after all, that which constrains a man, that which leads him on, that which will transform him into Christ's image from glory to glory. And I see not how this latter change can take place, without a man's looking for this blessed hope of the Resurrection. Even the old Psalmist, gazing on through the coming centuries, before life and immortality were brought to light, could say, "When I awake up I shall be satisfied with thy likeness:" and the beloved Apostle has told us, "We shall be like Him, when we shall see Him as He is."

And when a man thus hopes, how sweet and consoling does such a character of Christ become to him as that which is set before us in our services to-day— Christ the GOOD SHEPHERD of his people! He sees not only the scattered flock led through the wilderness on earth, but the many folds united in one flock in the blessed pastures above: the shadowed valley lies between, but there is the rod and the staff supporting him through it: there is his own unworthiness when he was as a sheep going astray: but he is returned unto the Shepherd and Bishop of his soul. And there he will abide: his treasure, his heart, his home, where Christ is :—looking for the Resurrection of the dead, and the life of the world to come :—looking for that blessed hope, and the glorious appearing of the great God and our Saviour Jesus Christ: who will change the body of our humiliation, that it may be fashioned like unto the body of His glory, according to the mighty working whereby He is able to subdue even all things unto Himself.

SERMON XXI.

(PREACHED ON THE THIRD SUNDAY AFTER EASTER, MAY 11, 1862.)

JUSTIFICATION BY FAITH.

Rom. i. 17. Heb. x. 38.
"The just shall live by faith."

THESE, my brethren, are very memorable words. They are quoted from the prophet Habakkuk both by St. Paul and by the writer of the Epistle to the Hebrews. By the latter they are made the introduction to his illustrious catalogue of the triumph of faith, and by the Apostle they are placed as an authority for that great doctrine which he is about to lay down and to prove in his Epistle to the Romans. They express very shortly that which our eleventh Article asserts more at length,—the doctrine of Justification by Faith: "We are accounted righteous before God," says our Article, "only for the merit of our Lord and Saviour Jesus Christ by faith, and not for our own works or deservings. Wherefore, that we are justified by faith only is a most wholesome doctrine, and very full of comfort." It is on that doctrine that I wish to speak to you to-day: and if God enable me, to make plain what it means, and how we are to take it as affecting our daily Christian life.

Now this is the more necessary, as we seem at first sight to find, in the writings of the Apostles, something very like conflicting statements on this subject. For example, St. Paul, in Rom. iii. 28, says, "We conclude that a man is justified by faith without the deeds of the law." But St. James, in his Epistle (ii. 24), says, "Ye see then how that by works a man is justified, and not by faith only." This certainly is startling, until we come to examine what it is of which each Apostle is speaking. When we do, all the difficulty vanishes. Let us see, how this is.

First, what do we mean by the word "justify?" Our Article, which I just now quoted, will supply us with an explanation. To justify, in the Scripture sense, is to "account righteous." When we say that some men are justified before God, we mean, that whereas they are by birth and practice sinners, some reason has been found, for which God regards them as being righteous. And if we ask, what thing can have produced so great a change, we surely, at this period of our course of sermons this year, can have no difficulty in answering the question. There can be but one reason why God reckons a sinful man righteous;— and that must be on account of the righteousness of the One Man, the Second and righteous Head of our human nature, Jesus Christ, the Son of God incarnate in our flesh. That righteousness of His, perfect, all-sufficing, was wrought out, as we have abundantly seen, in the very root of our nature, and extends over it all, He having once for all put away sin by the sacrifice of Himself. But, as we have also abundantly seen, it is not enough for a man's personal salvation that Christ thus wrought out perfect righteousness for all mankind: nor is it enough that he should have been brought by a holy ordinance into personal covenant with Christ, and made a member of Him. Both of these are unspeakably important, as we have also seen: but both, if there be no more, fall short of the great effect which Christ's righteousness was intended to produce on every man, which is, to change us into the holy image of that pure and righteous Saviour, whose name was called Jesus, because He shall save His people, not in their sins, but from their sins: bring them out from the practice, the guilt, the consequences of sin. Now remember what has been said about sin in our former sermons: and then ask yourselves, How can a man ever be saved from his sins, from his love and practice of what is evil, except by something which enters into his very inmost heart, takes possession of his thoughts, wishes, desires, turns round the current of his tendencies at their fountain? Nothing short of this will ever change a man to be another character from what he formerly was. So that in order for any man to become personally, and in his own real life, a partaker in the righteousness which the Son of God has wrought out for our whole race, he must receive that righteousness into his innermost heart, that it may take possession of his thoughts and desires, and gradually change him to a new and a better man. How does he do this? What do we call the doing it? He does it by receiving as a living fact, real to him day by day, that which the Son of God has done in our nature; by receiving it as *his own* living fact, true in his own soul, true in his own body, true as to his own past, true as to his own future, working on him and constraining him in his own present being, because Christ hath wrought it, and because he is a member of Christ. This is how he does it. And the act of doing it we call *believing:* and the state of one so doing, we call FAITH.

Now I want it to be evident to you all, that nothing less than this, and nothing but this, is required for a man to be accounted righteous before God as a member of Christ. Nothing less than this. For suppose a man, for instance, to stop short of it, by receiving the facts of Redemption merely as things which have happened, without any idea of his own personal share in them, without any application of them to his own case, —looking on Christ as the Saviour of the world, but not as his Saviour: regarding Him vaguely as the Lord of all, but not peculiarly as his own Lord and Master: what good can such a belief do him? Can it work any change on him? Did a man ever become strong like Samson, by crediting the history of Samson? No more can a man become righteous before God, by merely an historical belief in the acts and sufferings of Jesus Christ. So that faith of this kind, although it is a necessary step to the higher kind, is perfectly worthless of itself towards the object of which we are speaking: it can never justify a man before God.

Again, let us make another supposition, to shew that nothing short of the transforming faith of which we spoke ever can do this. Let us suppose that a man does much more in appearance than the last mentioned: that he holds and maintains a far higher standard of belief than the other: professing that he receives, and thinking that he receives, the work and merits of Christ in all their heart-constraining, life-renewing power. But unfortunately there is in his case that slip so often found between profession and practice: his tongue speaks great things, but there is no evidence of their power in his life: he requires much from others, but he brings forth no fruit himself: zeal, love, obedience, self-denial, heavenly-mindedness, these are ever on his lips, but his character belies them all: no doctrine is high enough for his profession, no selfishness and worldliness too low for his daily practice. Now think you that such a faith can justify a man before God? Can such an one make his own the righteousness of the Saviour of men? How will such a faith ever constrain him;—ever change him into Christ's image? With such a faith, a man may be in Christ, but Christ is not in him: he may be a branch in the vine, full of leaves, and making shew of great usefulness, but inasmuch as there is no fruit, the great Husbandman will take away all such branches, and they will be cast out. No man can on these terms be accounted righteous before God.

And here seems to be the best place, before trying

to shew you that nothing but true faith is required for that purpose, to recur again to the two Apostles, who seemed to say two things so opposite to one another. For we shall thus be also gaining a step at this point in our own course. When St. Paul speaks of faith, he leaves no doubt what he means by the word. At the very opening of his Epistle to the Romans, he describes the Gospel as being preached among all nations for *the obedience of faith:* and he uses the same words again at the end. And his argument in the course of the Epistle is directed to shew that faith does not encourage sin—does not make void God's law—requires and ensures the becoming dead to sin, and living unto God. Let any one, with the average exercise of common sense, read the Epistle, and there can be no doubt about this: that St. Paul does mean by faith, that living inward reception of Christ's work, and subjection to Christ's Spirit, which furnishes constraining motives to a man to yield himself up to God: —to make his members instruments of righteousness, and have wrought in him that righteousness, into which by that living faith he enters. According to his own words elsewhere,—in Christ Jesus no mere ordinance, no outward performance is any thing, but Faith which worketh by Love.

Now let us come to St. James. St. Paul and St. James were building up the same church of God at different points. And at these different points there were different enemies to be resisted.

Where St. Paul, the Apostle of the Gentiles, was building, there were rebellious Jews, clamouring that there was no leaving out the law of Moses and its works; —insisting that the Apostle must work the materials of the old temple into his foundation, or there would be no salvation. Against them it was his glorious work to lift up the standard on which was written, "No foundation but Christ:" and to assure those living stones whom he built on that foundation, that union with it by faith was all that they needed. And with all the energy of his fervid character, he threw himself into this work.

On the other hand, where St. James, the holy Jewish Christian, the Apostle of the Mother Church of Jerusalem, was building, there were licentious Gentiles and renegade Jews, proclaiming that the faith of mere assent was all;—that if a man say he have faith, and have no works, it will save him. And it was his equally glorious work to protest against this monstrous perversion of the great truth which his brother Apostle was upholding: and thus,—whether with knowledge or without knowledge of what St. Paul wrote, matters but little,—he gives forth that faith, such a faith as this which enters not into the heart and leaves no fruit in the life, cannot save a man; that we are justified by works, by faith in its fruits, and not by faith only —faith of such a sort that it is dead, being alone. And so both holy Apostles were at one:—St. Paul defending faith from the imputation of needing the works of the law for its help or its foundation;—St. James, defending faith from the attempt to rob it of its essential character of working by love and holiness. Both have recourse to the same illustrious example, that of Abraham, who believed God, and it was counted to him for righteousness: this belief being manifested by implicit obedience to God's command, when the shews of things were against it.

So that there is no real opposition between these two sayings of Holy Writ; and the lessons to be learned from their occurrence in the same infallible word of God are,—first, that God has chosen thus to leave them on record for us, to teach us that right doctrine on this momentous subject is inestimably important, seeing it is fenced by these strong sayings on both sides; and secondly, that it is ever dangerous to take out sayings of Holy Scripture from their context,—and essential to their right understanding to enquire what is really meant, in the place where they occur, with reference to the writer who uses them, and to those for whom they were written.

And now, returning to the main line of our argument, I do not think we shall find the last few minutes wasted. We have tried to shew that nothing *short of* this living faith will serve the purpose of justification before God: let us now try to shew, that nothing *but* this is required.

He that is joined to the Lord is one Spirit, says St. Paul; adapting his words from those used by the great Creator respecting the closest of human relations. The man and the wife are one: dealt with as one, enriched, impoverished, in prosperity or in adversity, together. And even so it is with Christ and the believing man. A partaker of Christ in his nature, a member of Christ in his church, a lover and obeyer of Christ in his life: receiving Him in his heart, following Him in his conduct, praying to Him, and living on Him, and becoming like Him,—approaching the Father through the Son of His Love, taught by the Comforter, who proceedeth from the blessed union of Father and Son, guided by God's counsel and prepared for God's glory, what more can he want as the means of entering into the state of righteousness before God than this oneness with the righteous Head, in whom all the members are righteous also?

And surely it must be plain to you, that such a state of a man's acceptance with God does not and cannot in the least degree depend for its acceptability on works of his own wrought previously to its beginning in order to bring it in. For how can it be so? There is but one righteous work in the world; the obedience of the one man Jesus Christ. There is but one way in the world of doing things acceptable to God; the being united to that obedience. No work done by any who is not united to that obedience by living faith is or can be acceptable to God. Here again we have very certain and very safe teaching in the thirteenth Article of the Church: "Works done before the grace of Christ and the inspiration of His Spirit, are not pleasant to God, forasmuch as they spring not of faith in Jesus Christ." So that it is impossible that our acceptance with God can rest on such works.

If it be here asked, Where then do our good works come in? Again, though this question has been in the main answered already, when we shewed that the only real faith is that which worketh by love, we may most

U

satisfactorily reply in the words of another article (the twelfth), "Albeit that good works, which are the fruits of faith, and follow after justification, cannot put away our sins, and endure the severity of God's judgment: yet are they pleasing and acceptable to God in Christ, and do spring necessarily out of a true and lively faith: insomuch that by them a lively faith may be as evidently known, as a tree discerned by the fruit."

So you see nothing can be plainer than the teaching of the Church on this matter. We cannot deserve the favour of God, we cannot earn our own salvation: in and of ourselves we have only sin and guilt, and are rebellious against God. But this deserving God's favour, this earning salvation by merit, has been done for our whole race by its One righteous Head Jesus Christ. And only those are in God's favour, only those inherit salvation, who make that merit of His their own by a belief in Him which unites their lives to His, and makes them like Him. And if they have this, then in power and capacity for progress, as regards God and themselves, they have all; not all *yet*,— for there is much to be done, and much to be suffered, before faith and patience have had their perfect work; but all that is needed to set them free for God's service, and enable them to glorify Him in the work which He has for them to do.

Let me make just three remarks before I dismiss you. First, as to our subject to-day. Do not, I entreat you, put these words from you as profitless. Go not home, saying, "He preached us a sermon all about justification by faith, and as I do not pretend to understand such doctrines, I brought away nothing." There is a sort of fashion of thus speaking about sermons in our day. Men fancy they must all be about familiar household things, or they are not profitable. And so preachers have followed the popular clamour, and far too much left out Christian doctrine from their sermons.

But after all, what is Christian doctrine? What is the doctrine of justification by faith? Just one of the very foundations of all Christian practice: what a man must know, if he would serve God at all in his capacity as a member of Christ. These people seem to forget, that preaching must be teaching; that we are bound to declare to you the whole counsel of God, not merely to exhort you about the duties of common life. It is these doctrines which furnish the motives for those duties. We want, as much as these men can do, to steer the vessel into a right course: but we prefer to do it by turning the helm, not by losing labour in applying our force to each portion of the ship in turn.

Secondly, you may in these days hear this particular doctrine of justification by faith made the subject of the unbeliever's cavil. To such cavils I trust we have our answer ready. "It is the clear revelation of the Bible: it is the indisputable teaching of the Church. Till you can disprove the one, and set aside the other, it shall be my belief." It has nothing unreasonable in it: men are led by faith to do and suffer some of the most remarkable things in their earthly lives: why should not the same power in a higher degree belong to it in our spiritual lives, which must of necessity be so much more closely dependent on it, because we cannot in them walk by sight, but must be guided by what we believe?

Then, thirdly, take care that you rightly understand what has been said to-day about faith, and put that Christian grace in its right office and position. Faith is not righteousness. Faith is not meritorious. Faith is not an object to strive after for itself. It is simply a means to an end. It is merely the attitude of mind in which we must put ourselves, in order to receive Christ's salvation. It is primarily Christ, and not our faith, that saves us. It is only as leading us to Him that our faith can be said to do so. It is our membership of Christ's Church, not our own belief in it, which originally gives us a part in Christ. That belief is our entering into, our making real, a state which exists whether we believe it or not; is a making it to be a blessing to us, not a condemnation. In one word, Christ is the Bread of Life:—faith is the hand put forth to reach it. We must not over-estimate Faith; it is only the road, not the end of the journey: along it we must ever be passing, forgetting the former stages in our anxiety to reach those which are yet to come. It is not the fruit, but it is only the necessary condition for bringing forth fruit. We are created anew in Christ Jesus unto good works, *not unto faith*. Keep these things in their right places, and all will be well.

Finally, if by this true and living faith we are to stand approved before God, by entering into Christ's finished work, let each one of us ask himself, How is this with me? Am I standing in this faith? And on this point there need be no doubt. Weak, irresolute, unworthy, short-coming—this all must be: and the degree of our faith and the achievements of our faith may be matters of shame to us, which we hardly dare pronounce upon: but the existence or non-existence of faith at all,—this can surely be no matter of doubt.

May God grant that all of us may so perfectly believe in his Son Jesus Christ, that our faith in His sight may never be reproved.

SERMON XXII.

(PREACHED ON THE SUNDAY AFTER ASCENSION DAY, JUNE 1, 1862.)

THE DOCTRINE OF THE LORD'S SUPPER.

JOHN vi. 53.
"Except ye eat the flesh of the Son of man, and drink his blood, ye have no life in you."

THERE is one great doctrine which is in direct connexion with a right apprehension of the fact of our Lord's Ascension: I mean, the doctrine of the Holy Communion. Of that doctrine, and in that connexion, I mean, by God's help, to treat to-day.

Let me first recall to your minds what was said in these sermons about the Resurrection of Christ. He came up out of the grave with the same Body which He had before He died. He himself plainly shewed this, by appealing to certain tokens in his risen body to prove his identity with his former self. In that risen body He wrought miracles, as He had done in the Body which He had before death. Those miracles proved his Almighty power, but they did not take away the nature of his risen body. That body was glorified, but it had not ceased to be a body. And no further change passed upon it after that time. As it was after his Resurrection, so He took it up into heaven. While He was blessing his disciples, He slowly rose in their sight, and His form was lost in the clouds of heaven, and they saw Him no more. The Body in which He appeared to Mary Magdalen in the garden, —the Body in which He was made manifest to the disciples at Emmaus, the Body in which He stood when He challenged the eleven to prove his identity, and in which He ate and drank with them then, and at the sea of Galilee,—that same Body He has taken up into heaven, and in that Body He at this moment is sitting at the right hand of God.

Now let us contemplate that glorified Body of His. What is it? What do we know of it? Of its absolute and transcendent majesty and blessedness, little or nothing. But some things about it we do know; and those are of immense importance to us to-day. And one of these is, that it is, and must be, essentially what other bodies are. It must possess the qualities which are necessary to all bodies, or it is not a body at all. Now one of the very first of these qualities is that which has been affirmed for us by the Church in the important doctrinal declaration at the end of the Communion Service in the Prayer Book: where we read, "It is against the truth of Christ's natural Body, to be at one time in more places than one." Christ is in heaven. Whatever is meant by heaven, we are certain that some blessed place there is, which answers to that mysterious name: some place, which is above all others favoured in being the very centre and special abode of God's majesty and power. And there, wherever it be, is our glorified Redeemer in His human Body: and in His human Body, no where else. As the angels said of the tomb, "He is not here, but risen," on the morning of the Resurrection: so we must say of this earth, "He is not here, He is ascended," from the day of the Ascension. The same universal Presence indeed of the Lord Jesus, which fills heaven and earth, was yet in that sepulchre when the sons of light pronounced him absent from it: and that Presence still continues to fill all things, though in his Human body He is not here. To assert that His Body was risen, and yet in the tomb, would manifestly have been to deny its reality as a body at all: to assert that He is ascended, and yet hold his Body to be present on earth, is just as much to deny the reality of His glorified humanity now. We shall all see that Body of His one day: but in order for that, it will *come* on the clouds of heaven, and He, clothed in it, will make his approach to this earth, as one of the sons of men approaches to and arrives at a place: it will be no unreality, no multiplied vision, but that very Body of the Lord Himself which we shall see; the Body which was born of the Virgin, the Body which was nailed to the Cross, the Body which arose from the tomb, the Body which ascended into heaven. And till then no man will see Him: none at least in the ordinary methods of sight, or common means of grace. Holy visions of Him may have been vouchsafed to some, and may yet be; but He himself is withdrawn from us.

Now I hinted just now, and you know well, that there is a Presence of the Lord Jesus, which is never withdrawn from us. Of that I treat not at this moment, but of His bodily Presence; of that concerning which He said, "I leave the world, and go to the Father."

Let us then come at once to the subject of our text. The Lord Jesus had miraculously fed five thousand men by the shores of the lake of Tiberias. Having seen this miracle, the multitudes followed him about, and were disposed to take him by force, and make Him a king. Under these circumstances, He addressed the congregation in the synagogue at Capernaum. He explained to them the true meaning of the miracle which he had wrought. As He had in a wonderful manner given food for the supply of that multitude's natural necessities, so He was about to give Himself, the true bread of life, for the supply of the necessities of the whole world. And that which He would give was His Flesh, bestowed for the life of the world. Then again, as Bread taken into the body is necessary for the sustenance of the body: so that Flesh of His must be partaken, in order for any man to live by His gift of Himself for the life of the world. The act of partaking of ordinary Bread, we call *eating* that Bread: the act of partaking of that Flesh of His, He calls eating that Flesh. But it must be manifest from the first, except to the grossest incapacity, that He does not use that word in the ordinary material sense: if for no other reason, for this, that the life which His gift of Himself is to confer on the world is not the lower animal life of the body, but the higher and nobler life of the spirit, ennobling and giving life to the whole man. And when some of the Jews hearing his discourse said among themselves, "How can this man give us his flesh to eat?" our Lord further and more strongly laid forth to them the same truth, that it was absolutely necessary for that eternal life which He would give at the Resurrection at the last day, that a man should thus not only eat His flesh, but, which would convey a sound abhorrent from their Jewish ideas, drink His blood also: nay, that these two were so absolutely necessary, that except a man did them both, he could have no life in him. Now what was the consequence of our Lord's saying these words? We read that from that time many of his disciples went back, and walked no more with him. They imputed to Him madness, or enthusiasm, and believed His words to be no longer those of truth and soberness. Others again, we are told, said, "This is an hard saying—who can hear it?"

Now note our Lord's answer to them. "Doth this offend you?" He asked: "What if ye shall see the Son of man ascend up where he was before? It is the Spirit that quickeneth: the flesh profiteth nothing: the words that I speak unto you, they are spirit and they are life." That is, if we rightly understand it,— "If you are offended by this mention of eating my flesh and drinking my blood now, when you see me before you present in the body, what will you say, if that body should be withdrawn from you into heaven, and yet the same thing shall remain true, that it is necessary to eat my flesh and drink my blood, in order for a man to have eternal life? What an offence, what an impossibility will such a thing appear then! And yet it will be as true then as now." Well, then, our Lord's next words enter into the reason of their error, and give us the explanation of his hard saying: "You cannot understand me," he says, "because you are taking my words in a gross lower material sense: you forget that it can only be through man's nobler part, his spirit, that true life can be conferred upon him, and through communion with, and partaking of, my Spirit in himself, not through any grosser and material conversion of flesh into the substance of his body: this will profit him nothing. The words that I speak to you are not carnal and material in their meaning, but are themselves, if rightly taken and apprehended, spirit and life."

And now comes the time to ask, Does our Lord mean by this last saying, that these His solemn words may be explained away, spiritualized, as it is called, and understood only to allude to some inward partaking in a man's thoughts of the benefits of His Body and His Blood?

This question will be best answered by passing on to another, and that a very solemn period in his earthly life, even the same night that He was betrayed. Observe what He then did, bearing in mind at the same time what He had said in the synagogue at Capernaum. And in doing so, reflect also, that we have handed down to us but a very small portion of what our Lord from time to time said to his disciples; and that beyond doubt so solemn a subject as this must again and again have formed the subject of his discourses to them. The Holy Evangelists give us only a few principal specimens of what He taught them: and they themselves must have been far more familiar with such sayings from his lips than we who read the Gospels can be. So that the Twelve, who were sitting round our Lord on that eventful evening, were, we have every reason to believe, quite prepared for what He then did, not only by that discourse, but by sayings on the same matter, perhaps plainer and closer, uttered up to that very time. And what did He then? He took some of the bread which lay before them at that paschal supper: He brake it into pieces, and divided it among them, saying, "Take, eat: this is my Body which is given for you." Now, as on that other occasion, His true human Body was there before them; looking on them, breaking, giving to them. It could not be *that* body, which he asserted the bread to be. It would be against the truth of that natural body, to be in more than one place at one time. Nor was it any other body of His, for He had no other: but it was that one which He bore about him: that one which was conceived by the Holy Ghost in the womb of the Virgin Mary. And He also added a remarkable command, pointing on to the future, when that body of His, which they saw before them, would be removed from them into heaven. "This do," said He, "in remembrance of me." How then are we to understand His words, "This is my Body," in connexion with His former discourse, and with this His command? Can there be any question, my brethren, on this matter? "The words that I speak unto you, they are spirit, and they are life." Is not this the key to His meaning in that other solemn saying also? But does not this very saying most plainly shew that of which we are in search,—viz. that our Lord is speaking not merely of a *thought*, to be entered into in a man's spirit, whereby His flesh and blood may be spiritually partaken, but of an outward act also, by which this spiritual truth may be assured and made real to us? What this outward act is, as prescribed by Himself at that solemn evening, we have already seen: and, both by His own words, "Do this in remembrance of me," and by those of his Apostle St. Paul, "Ye do shew forth the Lord's death till He come," it is evident that this prescription of His points on to a lasting and regular ordinance, to be binding on the Church to the end of time.

Let us now regard the form and manner of that ordinance. It consists of two parts;—the eating of bread—the drinking of wine. Of the bread, the Lord said, "This is my Body:" of the wine, "This is my Blood of the New Testament." He chose these material elements of bread and wine, to set forth or represent, to His disciples and to us, His sacred Body and Blood. Their fitness for this high purpose must be obvious to all. BREAD is that whereby the life of man is sustained. It is the commonest food: and is in all languages used to express food in general. "Give us this day our daily bread," is the petition for sustenance which we are taught to put up to our Father in heaven. What then more fit to represent that Bread of Life, which was given for the sustenance of the world,—

without which man's spirit, soul, and body, must dwindle and die,—but sustained by which he will live in life eternal? Again WINE, which maketh glad the heart of man,—whose exhilarating properties are not, as the shallow and ignorant of our days would represent them, evil and noxious elements in nature, but the good gifts of our beneficent Father,—this creature of God is chosen by our Lord to set forth His atoning Blood, by which, applied to man's spirit in a living faith, the guilt of sin is removed, terror and remorse taken away, and the joy of adoption into God's family brought in.

The faithful Christian, in partaking of these elements according to his Lord's command, does take into himself, and feed upon, the Body and Blood of his Lord, as really and actually as his outward body takes into it and feeds upon the material elements which he eats and drinks. There is no unreality, no mere fancy, about the matter. There is a real partaking of Christ, present to him in these symbols of His own ordaining: present to him because and in as far as he is a faithful receiver of them, seeing Christ in them, feeding on Him in them. Listen to the decisive words of the Church, in her twenty-eighth Article: "The Body of Christ is given, taken, and eaten, in the Supper, only after an heavenly and spiritual manner. And the mean, whereby the Body of Christ is received and eaten in the Supper, is Faith."

And now, this being so, there arise two or three matters for our consideration, before we draw to a close.

First, as regards the form and manner of the ordinance itself. To a reader of the sacred word for the first time, it might seem as if our Lord had intended this remembrance of Him to accompany every meal: to be resumed as often as bread is ordinarily eaten, or wine ordinarily partaken. And it would seem from the early part of the Acts of the Apostles, and from 1 Cor. xi., that this idea was at first acted on in the infant church.

But we are not readers of Scripture for the first time; nor is the first apparent meaning of such a command always that which it ought to have for us. We may see even in Holy Scripture itself, and by the following history, that Christ's Church was very soon led, from various considerations, to make the Sacrament of the Lord's Supper a regular and formal ordinance, recurring at stated times, and administered with special solemnity. To her regularly ordained ministers she has ever entrusted the office of setting apart, or consecrating, the elements of Bread and Wine in its administration. This has probably been the case from the very first. The Apostle Paul speaks of the breaking of the Bread and the blessing of the Cup as a ministerial act. In the course of the miracle which gave rise to the discourse of which we have been speaking, our Lord gave the bread to the disciples, and the disciples to the multitude.

Secondly, this holy Sacrament of Christ's Body and Blood is not to be regarded as something superadded to the ordinary means of grace, which a man may or may not receive, as he pleases: but must be looked on as essential to a man's salvation. In this respect, it occupies a similar place to the other sacramental ordinance,—Baptism. Some of you will remember what was said in the early part of this course of sermons on that sacrament. We saw, that Christ is the new and righteous Head of all mankind: that every man has an equal right in Him by virtue of His perfect humanity. But we also saw, that He himself has appointed a special way of entering into and taking up this right and part in Himself: viz. the sacrament of holy Baptism. Even so it is here. Every man may feed on Christ by faith, under varying circumstances, and at varying times. But He himself has appointed a special way of feeding on Him, viz. this holy Sacrament of the Lord's Supper. We cannot and may not refuse, or set aside, either the one or the other. Both of them are generally necessary to salvation: necessary, that is, where they may be had: necessary to all, wherever, as in this Christian land, they are offered to and pressed upon all. He who refuses Baptism, he who turns his back on the Lord's table, does so at his peril. The words of our text, "Except ye eat the flesh of the Son of man and drink His blood, ye have no life in you," have been, by our Lord himself, explained and fixed, in the institution of this holy Sacrament. They have been shewn by that institution no longer to bear merely a vague general meaning, but to apply to the meetings of Christians at that table, and to prescribe, as necessary to salvation, participation in that holy Sacrament.

Next to speaking of the form and manner and the necessity of the Sacrament, it will be expedient in conclusion to say something of the mind with which we, as believers in Christ, and as English Churchmen, ought to regard it. And here there occur to us two extremes to be avoided: the first, irreverence: the second, superstition. Of falling into the former of these, there is at present among those who at all obey the call to the Lord's Table, happily but little danger. Some time ago, when communicating was made a test for the holding of various offices in the state, the danger was great, and many fell into it; but now a better spirit prevails among our people: and I am sure that any of us who has long served God in the sacred ministry of His Church will bear witness to the universal prevalence of an earnest and reverential demeanour on the part of our communicants. Still, for reverence to be true, it ought to be intelligent, and a man ought to know why he feels it. So that it may not be amiss to say something on this point. Let us all, my brethren, reflect what it is that we assemble to do in that holy Sacrament. It is nothing less than to receive the Lord Jesus Himself into our hearts, as we do the symbols of His presence into our bodies. How ought we to abase ourselves, how ought we to prepare ourselves, for the reception of such a heavenly guest! How ought we to exclude worldly thoughts and trifles, as indeed at all times from our devotions, so more especially, and with jealousy more than common, from that most sacred time of all, when we sup with the Lord, and He with us!

And observe, he does not treat the Sacrament of the Lord's Supper with due reverence, who does not expect from it all the blessings which it is pledged to give him. It is the first, holiest, most effectual, of all the means of grace. "He that eateth me, even he shall live by me," are our Lord's own words. In no other ordinance is the contact so close between the believing soul and Christ: from no other may we look to reap such choice and precious blessings, as from this. He who does not look for these, dishonours the ordinance. Expect Christ there. Look for strength to go on your way: grace to gain new victories over sin and the flesh. Reach out the hand, not only to grasp the offered bread and cup, but to take out of the Lord's own hand the inward strength and refreshment which He stands waiting to impart to you. Thus reverence the holy ordinance, and it will be life and joy to your souls.

Again, we must, in our thoughts of it, avoid all superstition. Here, there is undoubtedly more danger. The tendency of all revivals of true principles is to carry weak and ill-balanced minds off into extremes. And it has been found so, and will be found so, in every place where that revival has been truly and earnestly going on. There are ever some ready to adopt unusual postures, and methods of receiving, and to make themselves prominent by a display of extraordinary reverence. But this behaviour is on all such occasions both unwise and unchristian. Unwise, because it is true wisdom, in matters not absolutely commanded or requisite, to follow the ordinary usage of those about us, and not to be conspicuous: unchristian, because by such practices the consciences of weaker brethren are offended, and they may be even induced to absent themselves from the Lord's table altogether.

For do not let us conceal from ourselves, my brethren, how great a thing is at stake in this matter. The corrupt church of Rome, from which we have happily been delivered, but which still spreads its snares around us and imperils the souls of our brethren, even to this day worships as an idol the consecrated bread and wine in the Supper of the Lord. This description of their practice is the language of the Church, not mine. In the same precious declaration at the end of the Communion Service in the Prayer Book, she says, "The Sacramental Bread and Wine remain still in their very natural substances, and therefore may not be adored; for that were Idolatry, to be abhorred of all faithful Christians."

Now this adoration constitutes the very essence and soul of divine service among the members of that corrupt church. The priest lifts up the vessel containing the consecrated elements, and the congregation fall down and adore them.

So that in this matter, the very life of our souls is concerned. You yourself perhaps may bow down to the bread held out to you with no such view, but only as a reverent recognition of Christ spiritually offered: but the weak brother or sister by your side may see your action otherwise, and think the deadly sin of idolatry lies at your door, and at the door of those who teach you. You may adopt an unusual form of reception, from simple motives of reverence to Him whose ordinance it is: but the weak brother, *whose feeling, and not your own, you ought to consult*, may see superstition in your act, and depart with his conscience wounded.

Finally, let your course in this, as in all, be, humble obedience, earnest reverence, manly wisdom, quietness, confidence, charity one to another. So God will bless us: so peace and truth will flourish among us: so we shall help to increase the blessed number who, having met in God's appointed ordinance on earth, shall be called to the marriage Supper of the Lamb when the Kingdom of God shall have come.

SERMON XXIII.

(PREACHED ON WHIT-SUNDAY, JUNE 8, 1862.)

THE GIFT OF THE SPIRIT.

Acts ii. 33.

"Being by the right hand of God exalted, and having received of the Father the promise of the Holy Ghost, He hath shed forth this which ye now see and hear."

WE stand, my brethren, close upon the end of our Sermons on Christian doctrines. The sin of our race, the redemption wrought by God in Christ, His Incarnation, His Obedience, His Temptation, His ministry of healing and teaching, His Sufferings, His Resurrection, His Ascension into glory,—these have all been dealt with, and with them some of those subjects of thought and enquiry which seemed to spring up and demand our attention by the way.

But is all done? When our blessed Lord carried up His risen Body into heaven, His work for us was indeed accomplished: for Him, no more combat, no more offering of himself for sin: by that one dread conflict, His victory was won for evermore: by that one offering,

He has perfected for ever them that are sanctified. But is therefore all accomplished? Nay rather, in the deepest and truest sense, is *any thing* accomplished? The way indeed into the holiest is opened: but how are they to be fitted for it that are to pass in? The foundation has been laid; but where are the hewn stones of which the goodly temple is to be built? The corner-stone is in its everlasting position; but who are to be the wise master-builders, to square and to lay the living walls of the habitation of God? These master-builders are appointed;—designated by the Lord Himself: but what are they? Not mighty, not prudent, not learned: but simple fishermen;—men of this world's ideas, more than of the kingdom that is not of this world: men unapt to learn even the simplest truths concerning Christ and His work: men who dreamt of smiting with the sword for their Master's cause: who forsook Him and fled, in the hour of His glorification by suffering: men even now dazzled with the splendour of the Resurrection morning, and confounded by the strangeness of His appearances among them. True, their understandings have been opened, and Holy Scripture is now seen to have evermore testified of Him: true, they have been breathed upon by those sacred lips, and the foretaste of heavenly influence has been vouchsafed: but power is yet wanting to them:—their high office is as yet only in reversion, not in possession. And those living stones for the building, where are they? Scattered up and down in the world, some in the obstinacy of unpersuaded Judaism, some in the darkness of unenlightened heathendom: walking as yet in the formality of legal obedience, or in the pride of the carnal understanding, or in the degradation of sensual indulgence. Who is to touch those hearts, now dead in trespasses and sins? Who is to go forth and work upon all men, and to draw them to Him who was lifted up that all might look upon Him and live? The Righteous Head of Humanity has indeed perfected the Father's work on earth: man indeed henceforth stands accepted in the Father's sight: but WHY was this done? The penalty of sin has been paid by the Lamb of God on the Cross, and that Blood shed, which cleanseth from all sin; but again, WHY? The new creation has been planned, and its central laws have been laid down, and its necessities have been remembered before God, and its capacities implanted:—it shall live before Him, for He is well pleased with that divine Word of His, in whom is its Life: but as yet all is without form and void. What then is wanting? What, but that first great command again uttered, "Let there be light?" What but that Spirit of God moving again over the face of the waters, going forth over the hearts of men, quickening the dead, shining in the darkness, dropping holy persuasion into men's slow and stagnant minds, and aspirations after purity into their selfish and sensual lives, and changing them into the righteousness of their glorified Head, and into the image of the holiness of the everlasting Father? Without this, all is unfinished, nay all would be in vain. It was for this that Redemption itself was wrought, that man might be again restored after the image of Him that made him in righteousness and true holiness: not that sin might be put away, and man remain as he was: not that man's enemy might be defeated by another, and men win no victory for themselves: not that we might believe in Jesus with the understanding, and confess Him with the mouth, and be saved by that belief and that confession only: but that there might be implanted in men, by virtue of the righteous obedience of their glorified Head, the power of like obedience in each man's measure and degree;—that as He is, so we might be in this world: pure, gentle, loving, self-denying; that earth's wilderness might rejoice and blossom as the rose: that man, and nature, and all things below, might be brought from the bondage of corruption into the glorious liberty of the sons of God. And therefore it was, my brethren, that this gift of the Holy Spirit, which was as on this day bestowed, was described by our Lord as THE PROMISE of the Father; the one great promise, including all other promises in itself. All that He did, and all that He suffered, was in order to win this for us. Without it, his Incarnation would fail of bringing its blessedness to us; his Example would be hopelessly out of our reach: his Death would offer in vain its power of clearing from sin: his victory would be no victory for us; we should have no power of becoming like Him; we could not ascend in heart and mind where He is, nor dwell with Him.

Such was the necessity for this day's event—such its place: the very highest and most blessed among all the events of our Redemption.

THE GIFT OF THE SPIRIT. 313

And now, what was its nature? And what are its effects? We have been preparing the way for answering both these questions already. But let us enter into them more in detail, and more as regards the matter of fact, of which we have read in the portion chosen for our Epistle to-day.

The little company of believers at Jerusalem were assembled with one accord in one place on the day of Pentecost. Suddenly, the Holy Spirit came down upon them, with a rushing sound as of a mighty wind, and in visible shape of cloven fiery tongues. Suddenly, they became endowed with miraculous powers, receiving the gift of tongues, and speaking in various languages the wonderful works of God.

And with respect to these signs and effects of the Spirit's descent, we may remark this: first, that the audible and visible tokens appear never to have been renewed after this occasion: secondly, that the miraculous effects seem to have occurred again occasionally during the apostolic age, but after it; disappeared, and are now no longer found: thirdly, that neither the audible and visible signs, nor the miraculous effects, formed any part of the abiding work of the Holy Spirit as promised by our Lord himself to his disciples. He did indeed, as we read at the end of St. Mark's Gospel, announce such miracles as about to follow on faith in Him: and such we learn did follow for a certain time: but it is observable, that when He described the indwelling and permanent work of the Holy Spirit on men, it is not any thing of this kind on which He dwells, but the inward conviction wrought on men's minds respecting their own sinfulness, and His righteousness, and the true judgment to be formed respecting this vain world.

Now putting these facts together, we infer, that the audible and visible tokens shewn on the day of Pentecost, and not renewed, — and the miraculous powers which then, and for some years after accompanied the being filled with the Holy Ghost,—were not any necessary parts of His abiding influence, but only circumstances then seen to be requisite for the work which the Church had to do, and afterwards withdrawn as having become unnecessary.

And now, my brethren, a most important enquiry opens upon us. WHAT WAS the gift of the Spirit, WHAT WAS the work of the Spirit, which that day was begun, and which had not begun before? Because if there be truth in Christ's word, and in what we have been founding on that word, this greatest of all gifts, which He won for us by his Incarnation and obedience and death and glorification, must be a real and genuine bestowal; something which was not before, and began to be as on this day. And it is manifest that this is the view which the holy Evangelist St. John takes of the gift. For when he is relating our Lord's discourse concerning the living water, he says, "This spake He of the Spirit, which they that believe on Him should receive: for the Spirit was not yet,"—i.e. was not among us—had not His existence as the living water, refreshing and comforting,—"because Jesus was not yet glorified."

Well then, again, what was this, which had not

been before, but began as on this day? Clearly, not the supernatural gifts of the Spirit. These had been known long before. In the Old Testament history, the Spirit of God had many times come mightily upon men, and endowed them with superhuman powers. We read this of Samson, we read it of Gideon, we read it of Saul, we read it of Elijah, we read it of the holy prophets.

As clearly, not the mere powers of wisdom and skill, which are also His gifts; for of these we read, that the Spirit of God was, for example, in Joseph for government, and in Bezaleel for the construction of the tabernacle.

Nor again was it His ordinary work in and upon the consciences of all men, teaching them to choose the good and refuse the evil: for of this we believe, that it has been continued through every age of the world and every degree of human degradation:—that it exists even where Christ has never been named:— that it is the blessed salt which alone keeps man's moral nature from utterly corrupting and perishing. It was none of these His works, which was not before, and began when He descended on those hundred and twenty on this day.

But if we have apprehended the matter aright, this it was,—this it is,—this it will continue to be, till the final triumph of life and light over death and darkness. On this day first the blessed Spirit of God took up His ordinary peaceful abode within the hearts of men, even of all those who are knit unto Christ in His Church by true and living faith. Influences of His began within men, and within the church, which were never before exerted: of such a kind, that the least, in this dispensation of the Spirit, is greater than was the greatest before it began. The Old Testament saints, though they had God's Spirit in a degree, and as far as He could be then said to come upon or to be with men, yet had Him not in the same sense of intimate indwelling, and inward testifying, and abundant bringing forth of fruit, in which He now abides with the Church, in virtue of Christ's accomplished work of redemption, and of the glorification of our humanity in Him. The Old Testament life of the saints of God was not like the New Testament life. That fitful and turbulent character, that strange mingling of worldly purposes with spiritual life, which more or less prevails through all Old Testament examples, at once ceases, when we come to the New Testament dispensation of the Spirit. The new birth by the Spirit of Christ is the opening of an entirely fresh, and continuous, and consistent life. From the time of the descent of the Spirit, a new leaven has begun to penetrate mankind. In spite of all adverse influences, in spite of war, and persecution, and the ever-working uncharitableness of the human heart, there has always been a sure and steady progress, from generation to generation, of maxims of gentleness and purity, of practices of love and beneficence, of sound and wholesome knowledge. With whatever sad exceptions in individuals or in nations, the public conscience of mankind has been more awakened, and its sight more clear, and its standard raised higher and higher, as the ages of the

Christian church have passed on. All our best blessings;—the bright examples of purity and charity which, thank God, abound in Christendom;—the repose of our own hearts in humble confidence in One who doeth all things well;—the peace of our homes, and the mingling of our affections;—and, to descend within, the sense of inward strength against the enemies of our peace, and of easier practice of acts of holy obedience to our divine Master;—all these arise from the working of this same blessed Spirit, the Strengthener and the Comforter, the substitute to us for the removed bodily presence of our glorified Lord, the token and earnest of His continued bearing us in mind where He is, and of our advancing preparation for one day seeing Him as He is.

And now, my brethren, let us conclude with a word of warning and exhortation. This blessed Spirit is dwelling in and working upon those who are Christ's. Without His indwelling, without His working, none can belong to the Lord :—none has part or lot in Him. "If any man have not the Spirit of Christ, he is none of His." It is not for us to limit His influence;—not for us to prescribe to Him that He shall act in this way or in that: but it is for us to say, that His indwelling and His work in a man is the one essential for happiness, and for advance in good, and for salvation in Christ at the last. There is among us, there is in Christ's Church, this blessed work going on :— there is this testimony to purity, to gentleness, to peace, to holiness, broadcast over Christ's kingdom, ready to become the precious possession of all who seek for it: for the Lord himself said, "If ye, being evil, know how to give good gifts to your children, how much more shall your heavenly Father give the Holy Spirit to them that ask Him?"

Then the question for every one among us is—"Am I a partaker in this influence?" And it is not a difficult enquiry to answer: not one whose reply need be sought in doubtful experiences, or in fanciful tokens, or in animal dejections and exultations; but one which can only be solved by the testimony of a life advancing in the fruits and graces of the Spirit; in love, in self-denial, in self-command, in gentle words and acts of kindness.

None have the gift of the Spirit, but those who walk in the Spirit: none but those who are being transformed by His influence into the blessed image of Him whose Spirit He is.

SERMON XXIV.

(PREACHED ON TRINITY SUNDAY, JUNE 15, 1862.)

THE HOLY TRINITY.

MATT. xxviii. 19.

"Baptizing them in the name of the Father, and of the Son, and of the Holy Ghost."

IF we reflect by whom these words were spoken, and when, we cannot fail to see that they require more than ordinary consideration. First of all, they form an undoubted part of the sacred text. There are some few verses and expressions which are found in some of our ancient authorities and not in others; but this is not the case in the present instance. The words are found in all, and received by all. They were spoken by our Lord Himself as part of his last command to his disciples before his Ascension: "Go ye and make disciples of all nations, baptizing them in the name of the Father, and of the Son, and of the Holy Ghost." When we consider that our Lord rarely if ever speaks formally of what we now understand by Christian doctrines;—that He for the most part, and with hardly any exception, left these for the future Comforter, the Holy Spirit, to reveal in His due time,—it does appear somewhat surprising to hear from the mouth of our Lord himself so very plain a declaration of the doctrine of the Holy Trinity. For manifestly this, and nothing else, can be the import of the words in our text. The Name, into which the future converts to Christianity were to be baptized,—i. e. into the confession of, and trust in, and obedience to which, they were to be admitted by that ordinance,—could be none other than that of the God whom Christians were to worship. And in consequence, the plain inference from our Lord's words,—followed as they are by the assurance, "And lo I am with you alway, even to the end of the world,"—can be no other than this: that the God whom His followers, even to the end of time, are to confess, worship, and serve, is to be known as THE FATHER, THE SON, AND THE HOLY GHOST.

And this is not all. The position given to this doctrine by these words of our Lord is as remarkable, as the declaration of the doctrine itself. You will observe, that it is not introduced somewhere in the process of a long and difficult discourse, as a deep truth which the mature disciple may some day arrive at,—a thing the confession and comprehension of which may be the object of a Christian's ambition; but it is made a principal portion of the one great simple command, which our Lord gives to those who were to be the Founders and Governors of His Church; thus teaching us that it is primary and indispensable.

And further notice the place which it is to hold in the Christian life of future disciples. It is to come, not far on in their course, not as the result of much teaching, and the use of their reason; but as the very first fundamental fact, on which their baptism, and its covenant state, is to be founded. "Unto what name wast thou baptized?" would naturally be the very first question asked of the Christian convert, or the Christian child. And then, in all cases where our Lord's command has been obeyed, the answer would at once be, "Into the name of the Father and of the Son and of the Holy Ghost."

So that the doctrine of the Holy Trinity is not a thing which may or may not be held, according as a man apprehends it or not; not a thing which may be kept out of sight, or held back in our instruction and preaching, or which may be reserved till understanding shall be mature; but it is the very first thing to be professed and taught. FATHER, SON, AND HOLY SPIRIT, is the name of the God whom Christians worship. This every Christian ought to know; in the grounds and reasons of this his belief every Christian ought to be instructed. First it is our duty to believe it, and then to prove and confirm it: this is ever the order for us. Life is too short, and our nature is too rebellious, for it ever to be prudent, or safe, to keep our belief back till we are persuaded of every thing respecting the objects of it. We believe in Christ. Christ has commanded us to be baptized into the name of God, the Father, Son, and Holy Ghost. This faith therefore we receive: this command we obey.

If the truth thus conveyed to us, that there are three co-equal Persons in the one God whom we confess, be a dark and difficult one for our understandings, it is only one out of a hundred other things which in our present imperfect state we cannot comprehend, but yet are constrained to believe, and should be foolish indeed if we denied.

If on the other hand, things are found in Scripture, or in nature, tending to clear up, and to confirm, this great doctrine, these we thankfully receive, and turn them to their proper account: not resting our faith upon them, but using them to cheer and encourage us in the maintenance of our faith: using them moreover as its outworks and defences, in our struggle for God's truth with those who do not hold it themselves. All the indirect inferences from Scripture, all the distant analogies of nature, would never have revealed to us the doctrine of the Holy Trinity: the plain words of our Lord have revealed it, and then these other things come in aid, shewing that God's word and God's works are full of tokens that it is so.

But now from these considerations about the doctrine, let us come to the doctrine itself. What is it? First, what is it not? It is *not*, that the one God has been pleased to reveal Himself to us in three different attributes, or three different modes of working, whether we take this as applying to successive revelations at different periods of time, or to revelations co-existing at one and the same time. It is not, that God is Power, is Love, is Wisdom: it is not again, that the Old Testament history reveals His Power, the

Life of the Lord His Love, the dispensation of the Spirit in which we live, His wisdom: all this may be very true, and very good for us to think of, and it may be closely connected with, and flow from, the doctrine of the Holy Trinity; but it is not itself that doctrine. These things no special revelation in words would have been needed to teach us: they are but views and distinctions of our own reason, collecting from facts.

Nor again is the doctrine to be thus expressed, in a manner slightly differing from that cited above:—that God, one and the same divine Person, was pleased in old time to be known by men as the great universal Father, then after that as the incarnate Son, then after that again as the indwelling Spirit. For such an idea would not only not be that which our Lord's words in the text express, but it would be wholly inconsistent with it. Our Lord's words set before us Father, Son, and Holy Ghost, as the living and abiding God of His Church to the end of time: co-existing, and to be confessed and believed in together: whereas this idea would represent each one of these as belonging only to one dispensation in time, and then giving place to another.

Nor again have we any right to say, that this revelation of God, as Father, Son, and Holy Ghost, is only *for us*, and has no connexion with the real essential nature of God Himself. Against this idea, the use of the doctrine made in Scripture testifies. If we are to understand Holy Scripture as setting forth to us plain facts in plain words, we surely cannot avoid the conclusion that this distinction into Three Divine Persons

Y 2

is not one regarding us alone, but one subsisting in the eternal and essential nature of God Himself. However little we can ourselves understand of that nature, thus much is certain: that purposes and operations are ascribed to each of these sacred Persons, absolutely requiring that they should be, not merely aspects of the Deity as concerned with mankind, but self-existing,—and, however mysteriously united in the Godhead, capable from eternity of separate and independent action. To show you that this is so, I would direct your attention, by way of one example among many, to the Apostle Paul's Epistle to the Ephesians. That Epistle, so close in its argument, so minutely and skilfully contrived in every point of its arrangement, is throughout constructed, in its larger portions or chapters, in its paragraphs, nay even in its single sentences and phrases, on the basis of this doctrine of the Holy Trinity. And in this its arrangement, we ever find distinct and personal action ascribed to the Father, Son, and Holy Spirit: the Father counselling our Redemption, calling us with His holy calling: the Son, putting in force the Father's will by giving Himself for His Church, and setting us the great Pattern of Love: the Holy Spirit, carrying out in us, and on earth, and through the ages of time, the great purposes of Redemption: giving to man through the Son his access to the Father. It is only in this light, of the separate personal existence and agency of Father, Son, and Holy Ghost, that St. Paul's words and sentences in this wonderful Epistle carry with them any coherent and intelligible meaning.

And now, by discussing and repudiating these several inadequate views of the doctrine, we have very much prepared the way for speaking of it as it really is. It is then, this: we worship one God in three Persons, and three Persons in One God.

First, ONE GOD IN THREE PERSONS. To worship or confess more than one God, would be folly, and would be superstition. It would be *folly*. For the whole testimony of the history of man serves to shew, if that of nature herself did not enough declare to us, that in the recognition of One Supreme Power as Creator and Governor of the world, lies the only secret of a religion which can harmonize and purify and elevate our conflicting passions, our bewildered thoughts, our yearning affections, our jarring responsibilities. And it would be *superstition:* if at least that term means, abject religious devotion to inadequate and unworthy objects. For if we confess gods many and lords many, who and what are they? They must be the creatures of our own reason, or imagination; deified influences, moral or natural: different in different climates, under different circumstances, and in the views of differently constituted men.

To us therefore there is but one God: the Father, the Creator, the Giver of all: *One* in all His operations: consistent with Himself, however it may appear otherwise to us who only see the lower side of His works: infinitely powerful, though His designs appear to us from time to time to be thwarted: infinitely good and loving, though to us evil and sin may seem to prevail: infinitely wise, though foolishness may be laid to His charge by our poor and blind reasonings. This recognition of one God is, we are persuaded, the only safeguard for man: the only light that will guide him through moral darkness, and cheer him amidst the fearful discouragements of this unintelligible world. I said that the history of man shews us this. Where the unity of God has been held fast, there we find more or less the bright track of moral purity, in spite of all adverse influences, running through the ages of a people's history; where this has been lost sight of, there have followed inevitably moral degradation, and neglect of the testimony of conscience. And therefore we are not surprised to find God Himself, in the laws and ordinances laid down for His chosen people, making this, the unity of His Godhead, the one essential point, impressed on them again and again, and most jealously guarded against infraction. For it was their very life. And though we live not among professed idolaters, and are not in danger of worshipping in groves and at idol altars, it is also our life, as it was theirs.

ONE GOD then we worship. Whatever else may be revealed respecting the Deity, we are quite certain that this fundamental truth, God is One, cannot be interfered with by it. Let none of us therefore for a moment think, and let not any adversary of the Faith presume to say, that in our confession of the faith of the Holy Trinity, we are letting go the Unity of God. That any should do this, and believe what they say, is surprising. The assumption of the name Unitarian by those who deny the doctrine of the Trinity has ever struck me as shewing how little is understood by them of the essential conditions of that holy doctrine itself.

But again, as we are firmly founded on the confession of One God, so in that One God we confess and worship THREE PERSONS, Father, Son, and Holy Ghost. We not only address our adoration and our prayers to that One God, understanding, as we do so, that in that one God these Three Persons are united : but we address our adoration and our prayers to each of these Three Persons separately, as for example in the opening of the Litany. God the Father made us, God the Son redeemed us, God the Holy Ghost sanctifieth us. To God the Father we pray, as to our Creator and Upholder, as to Him who ordereth all things after the counsel of His own will, as to Him who ordained from the first the wonderful and gracious process of our Redemption: to God the Son we pray, as to Him whom the Father hath anointed to be a Prince and a Saviour for us: as to Him who can feel for our infirmities, having borne them upon Himself,—who intercedes for us in heaven, and will one day come to be our Judge : to God the Holy Ghost we pray, as to One ever present among us and in us, dwelling in our hearts,—the life-giving Lord of our spirits, the Comforter, who is to lead us into all the truth, to help us, to enlighten us, to make us holy. Through the Holy Spirit we have access by the Son unto the Father.

Let us observe further, that the whole Three Persons of the blessed Godhead are covenanted together in unity for our Redemption. The Son of God, as we saw before in these sermons, laid down His life of himself, and yet according to the commandment of the Father: the Holy Spirit came down upon the Church, proceeding forth from the Father and from the Son, and being the promise of the Father, won for us by the obedience and sufferings of the Son: and those who shall be found worthy in the end to sit down at the marriage supper of the Lamb, are known to our Blessed Lord as "they whom the Father hath given him," of whom He will not lose one. In Christ the whole building of the Church is said to be framed together, growing unto an holy temple in the Lord, builded together for an habitation of God through the Spirit.

And as to our further knowledge of this great truth, the Creed in which we have this morning confessed it embodies shortly and well the things most necessary to be held and remembered. That these Three divine Persons are co-eternal together and co-equal, is most certain from that which is revealed respecting them. However in point of time the revelation of God the Son the Redeemer may have come after that of God the Father the Creator, and the revelation of God the Holy Ghost the Sanctifier may have followed on the promise of the Father fulfilled owing to the finished work of the Son, yet in the existence of the divine Persons there is no such priority, or such existence could not be an essential and eternal truth. Again, however God the Son in His humiliation as man may be inferior to the Father, and however in the amount of mention and prominence in the Gospels and Epistles, God the Holy Spirit may seem to fall beneath the Father and the Son, yet we are sure that in the essence of the divine Persons there is no such inequality, or each could not be fully and personally God, in the unity of an indivisible Godhead.

Such then, my brethren, is the great doctrine, which forms on this day the subject of the humble meditations of the Church. And being such, it closes the great procession of Christian doctrines of which, during this year, we have been treating. For in it we see all completed: the revelation of God to man on earth fully made: His relation to us, and His existence as He is in Himself, disclosed to us as completely as our present imperfect condition admits.

To take a general survey of the steps by which we have arrived at this great final doctrine, will require more time than a few concluding sentences could allow it, and must be reserved for an entire sermon on another occasion.

Meanwhile, let me remind you of the fulness of the grace and blessing thus conferred on us. Thus, in the consideration of the doctrine of the Holy Trinity manifested to us,—

Behold what manner of love the Father hath bestowed on us. By the Son of His Love, He hath adopted us out of our state of sin and ruin to be His children, and hath given to us the promise of a glorious inheritance, even of the possession and enjoyment of Himself in the perfection of our being for ever.

Behold how the Son hath loved us: coming down

from His glory, emptying Himself of His power, becoming one of us, obeying, teaching, healing, suffering, dying, triumphing, in our behalf,—and now pleading for us at the throne of the Majesty on high.

Behold how the Spirit loveth us: taking up His abode in our unworthy and disloyal hearts, striving with His good against our evil,—witnessing amidst all our self-will and disobedience, that we are not forsaken of God,—that we are still His children, still heirs of His heavenly kingdom.

And with what exhortation shall I conclude, better than with that of St. Jude, framed as it is on the very basis of this holy doctrine?

"But ye, beloved, building up yourselves in your most holy faith, praying in the Holy Ghost, keep yourselves in the love of God, looking for the mercy of our Lord Jesus Christ unto eternal life."

SERMON XXV.

(PREACHED ON THE FIRST SUNDAY AFTER TRINITY, JUNE 22, 1862.)

KNOWLEDGE AND PRACTICE.

John xiii. 17.

"If ye know these things, happy are ye if ye do them."

Our Blessed Lord spoke these words to His disciples concerning an act of self-denying love of which He had just set them the example. But they relate not only to that, nor only to similar acts. They apply to every thing in the Christian life: to every good thing which being known ought to be practised: but which, as sad daily experience teaches us, may be known without being practised. They are therefore very fitting words on which to build up a sermon which forms the last in a course on Christian doctrines; and in which I intend to bring shortly to your remembrance the things of which we have been speaking, that your view of them at the end may be coherent and complete. Every one of these doctrines of which I have been treating, has a directly practical tendency, if understood, and taken into the heart. Those which have not that tendency, but rather contribute to foster speculation, I have carefully avoided: not that they are of no importance, but that it was my wish to lay down the foundations of our holy faith, and to dwell on those matters which all could receive, and in which all were interested.

And in doing this, we first treated of man's universal sinfulness, inherited from our general parent. We insisted on the fact, that our very nature bears token of sin being its enemy, not one of its natural conditions; that we have a moral law within us, which will not let us sin; every man's own heart being God's witness against his sin. And then, having set before you the deceitfulness, and the manifold nature, of sin, and insisted on its guilt and punishment, we thus came to God's great remedy which He hath provided for the sin of all mankind,—even the Incarnation of the Son of His Love. We shewed you how the Son of God was made man, placing Himself in the root of our nature, and becoming its second and righteous Head, and in this His manhood working out for us a perfect righteousness, overcoming the Tempter for us, teaching and healing, suffering and dying, paying the penalty of the world's sin in His own person on the Cross, and thus taking it away in the Father's sight. We saw how He conquered death, bringing in, as our second Adam, life and immortality, so that as in Adam all die, so in Christ shall all be made alive. We dwelt much on this great doctrine of the Resurrection of the Body; on its nature; on the portion which individual Christians have in its reality and blessedness. Then we spoke of Justification by Faith in this finished work of Christ; and of the precious gift of the indwelling and sanctifying Spirit, won for us by its completion. Finally, on Sunday last we dwelt on the crowning doctrine of the Holy Trinity, the most complete revelation of God to man, resulting from the whole comprehensive knowledge of the facts of our redemption. These, together with incidental notices of the means and ordinances whereby it has been our Lord's will that His work should be partaken by, and made real to the members of His Church, have been the subjects on which the teaching of this year of the Christian Festivals and Commemorations has been expended.

On such a course of doctrines, the words of my text form the best possible comment. If ye know these things, happy are ye if ye do them: happy, if they so sink into the heart as to form part of the life; happy, if they are believed in with a living conviction, which leads a man to act upon them, and take them for granted day by day.

Now, in saying this, what do I mean? Because these, like all other phrases and sayings regarding religious things, are apt to pass over the ear without rendering up their meaning; apt to be made into mere watchwords of orthodoxy, or into vehicles of criticism and blame upon others, without bearing any reference to the actual state of the man himself who utters them.

Let me then say something in this sermon, which concludes our course, on the practical effect which the belief of these doctrines may be expected to have on him who receives them. I will not take them one by one and enquire separately about each: but I will take them together, and as forming, which they do, one consistent whole: as making up that which in Holy Scripture and among ourselves, is called THE FAITH.

I suppose a man then to receive and believe the following facts: that he is by nature sinful and guilty, but redeemed by the perfect obedience and the atoning death of the Lord Jesus Christ: that he is a member of Christ's church and flock, admitted thereto by his Baptism, and upheld therein by God's continual grace: that the great reason why he was brought into this state was that he may become pure, holy, loving, like his great example the Lord Christ, by the teaching and cleansing of God's indwelling Spirit: that to this end, the means and ordinances of grace, as offered to him in the Church, of which he is a member, are necessary, and constantly to be resorted to. I suppose him further to believe in the certainty of a resurrection after death, and of a glorious reward hereafter, the measure of which will depend on the amount of fruit borne, by God's grace sought and obtained, in the work which God has appointed him, and for God's glory.

Now before pressing the question which I have mentioned, I must remark, that we are accustomed continually to see persons professing to believe all this, and yet not living in any one thing differently from those who make no such profession, or who profess the contrary. Many a man who is living in sin, with heart and life entirely void of any Christian principle, would yet be deeply offended if he were for a moment suspected of unsoundness in any one of these fundamental Christian doctrines. And other cases not so bad as this are far more numerous: cases of men very insufficiently influenced by the doctrines of their faith; influenced by them, it may be, in one or two points, but not in more. As for example, when a man fully receives, and builds his hopes upon, the atoning death of his Saviour as his ground of acceptance with God, but has no notion whatever of the purpose of this acceptance being, his growth in grace and good works under the teaching of God's Holy Spirit. Or again,—when a man looks forward with hope to be saved by Christ in the day of His appearing, but has no desire and takes no pains to be like Christ, or to know more of Christ, in this life present.

Such instances are very common indeed; in this age of endless variety of thought and opinion, nothing more common. Among people professedly religious, we perpetually find one person exalting and idolizing one doctrine of the faith,—another person, another doctrine; while all the rest, equally important and essential, are put by and neglected.

It is hardly needful to tell you, that none of these courses can be taken with safety; none of them is the right way to salvation. The Faith is one and indivisible. The truth of God must be held in all its essential parts: not indeed understood in all, not perhaps studied in all,—but confessed in all, and followed in all.

And now comes back our original question, What is the effect which we may reasonably expect the confession of the Faith as above specified, to produce in a man's heart and life? Mind, I do not wish to exaggerate or overstrain; my wish is to give such an answer to this enquiry, as may come home to every one here present, and lie within the compass of the ordinary abilities and experiences of all ages.

First, then, I reply, that such a belief cannot be in a man to any purpose, without making him earnest and thoughtful respecting his works and ways. If all this is true, then I am a perishing man, with the means of safety within my reach: then those means of safety have been put into my hands, and it depends on myself whether I hold them fast or let them go. Now this is not a situation to be trifled with. On the one side, ruin; on the other side, safety :—ruin, if we go with the stream, and let our own desires and feelings master us: safety, if we seek for grace and strength, and overcome our own evil with God's good offered to us. Who can believe this, and go trifling through life as if none of it were true? The very first effect, therefore, of a true belief in the doctrines of the Faith, will be, EARNESTNESS. Not moroseness, not bitterness, not a clouded and blighted life; but an earnest life: a life worth living, a fight worth waging, a victory worth obtaining, a prize worth grasping. O how very few people do we see in earnest! How many go on toying life away, shutting their eyes to its realities, and interested only about its trifles! For such to be genuine believers in the doctrines of the Faith, is impossible: that belief could not be in them, without producing earnestness somewhere. And mistake me not. I have already guarded against the idea that this earnestness is to be shewn in moroseness or bitterness: let me now guard against another mistake, that it need be shewn by any decided religious line of action taken up, out of and away from a man's ordinary duties of life. This error is very common: so common, that in a large portion of the Christian world, *religious* persons mean those who shut themselves up in monasteries and convents: and in our own country, even among those who would protest most loudly against that acceptation of the term, a serious conviction of the truth of religion is often supposed to involve retirement from society, and taking up some conspicuous line of self-chosen action separate from the duties of life. No doubt, some are called to do this: but it is far oftener a temptation, than a duty. There is something flattering to pride, something gratifying to our love of singularity, something romantic and inviting, in being different from others, in taking a line of our own,—in making out that our sacred duty is just what we choose to think it to be.

But this is not the earnestness of which I speak. Many persons who are thus in earnest are in real fact worse triflers than their neighbours. The earnestness of which I speak is found in the common pursuits, in the daily tasks, in the recreations also, of a man's own life, to which it has pleased God to call him: is found and exemplified in his being more in earnest in his family, in his business, in his relaxation.

Nor is it a showy thing, always making itself conspicuous. On the outside, he differs little from other men : but there is a core in what he says, there is a heart of hearts in what he does, there is a balance, and a firm step, and an upward bent, and a worthy purpose,

z

in his whole walk and conduct. Look at him for a moment, and you may not perceive it: but watch him for any considerable time, and you see not only the man himself, but a work growing up beside him, a light increasing in the path where he walks: "whatever his hand findeth to do, he doeth it with his might."

And this retiring and unostentatious character of that earnestness, which a sound belief in the faith of the Church will bring about in a man, leads us on to the next effect which it will have on him:—viz. to make him *humble*. Speculations on high and mysterious doctrines may make a man proud: and so may, and often does, the questioning and arguing about holy things. But the simple faith which believes that which has been revealed in the Bible, can never make a man proud: it must, if it have any of its proper effect, keep him humble. For he cannot but see by its light his own utter unworthiness, and want of power to save himself: he cannot but see how great a price was paid that he might be received back into God's family. Moreover he cannot but see, how often he provokes God's Holy Spirit to depart from him, and how the blessed inward Witness remains with him notwithstanding. "Be not high-minded, but fear," is the motto ever written up before his eyes: is the lesson ever sounding in his hearing. FEAR,—lest thou shouldest disgrace by thy thought, word or deed, the Thrice Holy Name into which thou wast baptized, and whereby thou art called. FEAR,—lest when judgment begins at the house of God, it choose thee for one of its victims. FEAR, lest when the cry is made "Behold the Bridegroom cometh," thy carelessness, thy neglect to provide oil in thy vessel for thy lamp of grace, should shut thee out at the last from the joy of thy Lord. FEAR, lest the watchful enemies of the faith, lest the weak brother seeking to justify himself by example, should find that in thy life or words, which may add to the one boldness to attack thy Lord, or take away from the other courage to serve Him.

So that such an one will be humble—self-distrustful— not intruding into things which he hath not seen; not certain, where it is a duty to suspend judgment; nor doubtful, where he is bound to believe and be sure.

And being this, he will not be over-ready, in society or in private converse, with the mention of holy things, and the distinguishing terms of the doctrines of his Faith. We might profit in this matter by remembering the world's judgment on similar conduct, which comes under its cognizance. When a person is fond of telling of his intimacy with great and titled people, we rightly infer that his friends of that class are very few, and his acquaintance with them very slight. And I am afraid it is much the same with men who have ever on their lips those sacred truths, whose place, if they are really believed, is in the very depths of the heart. Do you for yourself know God as your reconciled Father in Christ? Do you approach Him as such in secret? Is your chamber morning and evening filled with His awful presence, and do you go forth to life's duties fresh from the fountain of His grace, and lie down to rest safe under the shadow of His wings? O how precious to you will be such a hiding-place—how sweet these your stolen waters of blessed refreshment! It may be that in the hour of close intercourse with those whom you love, it may be that in the confidence of the written correspondence of personal friendship, you may tell of what you have found : there are communications, there are times, which are to our words like a costly setting, warranting the genuineness of the gem within it. But O not to the idle world, not to the casual acquaintance, not when on ordinary topics of talk, will you take and cast forth your holiest things, for the hypocrite to use again in lifeless counterfeit, for the trampler to crush and reproach you with. The holier and truer the doctrines which you really hold, and on which your soul feeds, the greater will be your reverence in their presence; the greater your unwillingness that they should be misunderstood, or should fall powerless, or furnish matter for scorn to those who know not God. Let your light shine—but how? Not by the idle crackling and sparkling of forward religious talk, but by the calm and growing testimony of a holy life, that men may see your good works, and glorify your Father in heaven.

And lastly, if a man do really in heart believe and feel as his own ground these great doctrines of the Faith, there will be this other effect produced upon him : he will be made charitable in his judgment of others.

This may seem a strange thing to say, in the face of the fact that the keenest and bitterest conflicts on record, and the harshest and most unsparing judgments have ever taken place over these very doctrines of which we speak. And such, it is to be feared, will ever be the case. We cannot ensure the Church against the evils of over-zealous partisanship;—we cannot secure even in the best of Christians, that love and large-heartedness, which ought always to accompany the advocacy of God's truth. But we can and we must assert this,—and the Church asserts it, in choosing for this her first Sunday after Trinity, as her Epistle and Gospel, two great lessons of love,—that the more the real power of the doctrines of the Faith is felt within a man, the less will he be disposed to form uncharitable judgments, or to use bitter words, concerning those who differ from him. For, even to say nothing of his obedience to the command of his divine Master, and his following of His example,—the secrets of his own heart, if he be honest in looking on what the Spirit reveals there, will teach him better. What difficulty we have in keeping up within ourselves the confession and the honest approval of these holy doctrines! What distressing doubts often harass us; what treacherous fears make our prospects dim and our steps unsteady, as we walk in the light of these truths! How often has the thought shot across us, Suppose after all it is all untrue—suppose we perish when we die—suppose there is no resurrection—no redemption—no God—no soul! O how difficult it is to chide down, to extinguish, such sinful and perilous suggestions of the Tempter! And who are we then, that we should despise, that we should anathematize, that we should persecute, others who are divided from us by so narrow a line, not indeed of belief, not indeed of life, but of the effects of human infirmity, and the protection of divine grace?

The sum of all is this: holding fast the doctrines of the faith—confessing our own sinfulness to Him who has provided for our pardon and salvation, believing in the atoning death of Christ, and looking for the glorious hope of our triumph with Him, partaking of the means of grace in the worship of Father, Son, and Holy Ghost in the unity of one Godhead, let us be earnest, let us be humble, let us be loving and charitable. Knowing these things, let us slack no effort to do them: let us prove that we hold the Truth not by angry disputation, not by over-zealous forwardness, not by maintaining a standard of duty which we ourselves take no pains to reach: but by obeying and being like Him who is the Truth itself. For to increase in the doing of His will is the only way to grow in the knowledge of His Doctrine.

THE END.

WORKS

BY

THE DEAN OF CANTERBURY.

The GREEK TESTAMENT; with a Critically revised Text; a Digest of Various Readings; Marginal References to Verbal and Idiomatic Usage; Prolegomena; and a copious Critical and Exegetical Commentary in English. For the use of Theological Students and Ministers. In 4 vols. 8vo. Price 5*l*. 2*s*.

The Volumes are sold separately as follows:—

Vol. I.—THE FOUR GOSPELS. *Fourth Edition.* 28*s*.

Vol. II.—ACTS to II. CORINTHIANS. *Fourth Edition.* 24*s*.

Vol. III.—GALATIANS to PHILEMON. *Third Edition.* 18*s*.

Vol. IV.—HEBREWS to REVELATION. *Second Edition.* 32*s*.

The Fourth Volume may still be had in two Parts.

The NEW TESTAMENT for ENGLISH READERS; consisting of an English Version of the Sacred Text, representing as nearly as possible the Greek Text according to the most ancient Critical Authorities; Marginal References to Verbal and Idiomatic Usage; a Notice of the principal Various Readings; and a Popular Commentary. In 2 vols. 8vo. (*Preparing for publication.*)

WORKS BY THE DEAN OF CANTERBURY.

SERMONS preached at QUEBEC CHAPEL, 1854 to 1857. In Seven Volumes, small 8vo. (*Sold separately.*)

> Vols. I. and II. (A Course for the Year.) *Second Edition.* 12s. 6d.
>
> Vol. III. (On Practical Subjects.) 7s. 6d.
>
> Vol. IV. (On Divine Love.) *Second Edition.* 5s.
>
> Vol. V. (On Christian Practice.) *Second Edition.* 5s.
>
> Vol. VI. (On the Person and Office of Christ.) 5s.
>
> Vol. VII. (Concluding Series.) 6s.

HOMILIES on the former part of the ACTS of the APOSTLES. (Chap. I.—X.) 8vo. 8s.

SERMONS. 1850. 8vo. 10s. 6d.

A MEMORIAL of the REV. HENRY ALFORD, A.M., late Rector of Aston Sandford, Bucks. By his ELDEST SON. 8vo. 7s. 6d.

POETICAL WORKS. *Third Edition.* Crown 8vo. 8s. 6d.

REMINISCENCES by a CLERGYMAN'S WIFE. Edited by the DEAN of CANTERBURY. Crown 8vo. 5s.

RIVINGTONS, WATERLOO PLACE.

OCTOBER, 1862.

NEW WORKS AND NEW EDITIONS,

PUBLISHED BY

MESSRS. RIVINGTON,

3, WATERLOO PLACE, PALL MALL, LONDON.

Alford.—Sermons on Christian Doctrine, preached in Canterbury Cathedral, on the Afternoons of the Sundays in the year 1861-62. By Henry Alford, D.D., Dean of Canterbury. In crown 8vo. 7s. 6d. (*Now ready.*)

McCaul.—Testimonies to the Divine Authority and Inspiration of Holy Scripture, as taught by the Church of England: in reply to Mr. Fitzjames Stephen's Argument. By the Rev. A. McCaul, D.D., Prebendary of St. Paul's, Professor of Ecclesiastical History at King's College, and Rector of St. Magnus. Crown 8vo. 4s. 6d. (*Just published.*)

Goulburn.—Sermons preached on Various Occasions during the last Twenty Years. By Edward Meyrick Goulburn, D.D. In Two Vols., small 8vo., uniform with "Thoughts on Personal Religion." (*In October.*)

Clissold.—Lamps of the Temple ; or, Rays of Light in Faith, Hope, and Love, from the Lives and Deaths of some Eminent Christians, in the Church of England, from the beginning of the Nineteenth Century to the Present Time. By the Rev. H. Clissold, M.A., Author of I. "Last Hours of Eminent Christian Men;" II. "Last Hours of Eminent Christian Women." Crown 8vo., *with Portraits on Steel.* (*In November.*)

RIVINGTONS, WATERLOO PLACE, LONDON.

Gurney.—Sermons on the Acts of the Apostles. By John Hampden Gurney, M.A., late Rector of St. Mary's Church, Marylebone. Small 8vo. (*In the press.*)

Lately published by the same Author,

Sermons on Old Testament Histories. *Second Edition.* 6s.
Sermons on Texts from the Epistles and Gospels. *Second Edition.* 6s.
Miscellaneous Sermons. 6s.

Alford.—The New Testament for English Readers: consisting of an English Version of the Sacred Text, representing as nearly as possible the Greek Text according to the most ancient critical Authorities; marginal references to verbal and idiomatic usage; a notice of the principal Various Readings; and a Popular Commentary. By Henry Alford, D.D., Dean of Canterbury. In Two Volumes, 8vo. (*Preparing for publication.*)

Seymour. Mackarness.—Eighteen Years of a Clerical Meeting: being the Minutes of the Alcester Clerical Association, from 1842 to 1860; with a Preface on the Revival of Ruridecanal Chapters. Edited by Richard Seymour, M.A., Rector of Kinwarton and Rural Dean; and John F. Mackarness, M.A., late Vicar of Tardebigge, in the Diocese of Worcester, now Rector of Honiton. Crown 8vo. 6s. 6d.

"If these records have any merit, it is that they contain a history of Clerical opinion during a not uneventful period, and a proof that the internal conflict of theological parties in the Church, often assumed to be more bitter than it really is, may easily be tempered by good sense and practical wisdom into friendly and not unprofitable discussion."—*Extract from Preface.*

Mackenzie.—Ordination Lectures, delivered in Riseholme Palace Chapel, during Ember Weeks. By the Rev. Henry Mackenzie, M.A., one of the Chaplains to the Lord Bishop of Lincoln, &c. &c. Small 8vo. 3s.

CONTENTS:—Pastoral Government—Educational Work — Self-government in the Pastor — Missions and their Reflex Results—Dissent—Public Teaching—Sunday Schools—Doctrinal Controversy—Secular Aids.

RIVINGTONS, WATERLOO PLACE, LONDON.

NEW WORKS AND NEW EDITIONS.

Wordsworth.—Journal of a Tour in Italy; particularly with reference to the Present Condition and Prospects of Religion in that country. By Chr. Wordsworth, D.D., Canon of Westminster. (*In the press.*)

Goulburn.—Thoughts on Personal Religion. By Edward Meyrick Goulburn, D.D., Prebendary of St. Paul's, and one of Her Majesty's Chaplains in Ordinary. *Second Edition*, in One Volume, small 8vo. 6s. 6d. (*Just published.*)

Adams.—A New Edition of The Shadow of the Cross: an Allegory. By the late Rev. W. Adams, M.A. Elegantly printed in crown 8vo., with Illustrations, price 3s. 6d. in extra cloth, gilt edges. (*Now ready.*)

Mozley.—A Review of the Baptismal Controversy. By J. B. Mozley, B.D., Vicar of Old Shoreham, late Fellow of Magdalen College, Oxford. 8vo. 9s. 6d. (*Now ready.*)

Greswell.—The Three Witnesses, and the Threefold Cord; being the testimony of the Natural Measures of Time, of the Primitive Civil Calendar, and of Antediluvian and Postdiluvian Tradition, on the principal questions of fact in sacred or profane Antiquity. By Edward Greswell, B.D., Fellow of Corpus Christi College, Oxford. 8vo. 7s. 6d. (*Now ready.*)

Williams.—The Beginning of the Book of Genesis, with Notes and Reflections. By the Rev. Isaac Williams, B.D. Printed uniformly with Mr. Williams's Harmony and Commentary on the Gospels, in small 8vo. 7s. 6d.

Devotional.—The Threshold of Private Devotion; containing Prayers, and Extracts from the Holy Scriptures and from Various Authors. 18mo. 2s. (*Just published.*)

Williams.—Female Characters of Holy Scripture; in a Series of Sermons. By the Rev. Isaac Williams, B.D., late Fellow of Trinity College, Oxford. *Second Edition.* Small 8vo. 5s. 6d. (*Just published.*)

RIVINGTONS, WATERLOO PLACE, LONDON.

Clabon.—Praise, Precept, and Prayer; a Complete Manual of Family Worship. By J. M. Clabon. In One large Volume, 8vo. 16s.

Wordsworth.—The Holy Year; or, Hymns for Sundays and Holydays, and for other Occasions. By Chr. Wordsworth, D.D., Canon of Westminster. Small 8vo. 4s. 6d. in extra cloth, or 10s. 6d. in morocco.

Knowles.—Notes on the Epistle to the Hebrews, with Analysis and Brief Paraphrase; for Theological Students. Dedicated by permission to the Lord Bishop of Oxford. By the Rev. E. H. Knowles, late Michel Fellow of Queen's College, Oxford. Crown 8vo. 6s. 6d.

The Annual Register; or, a View of the History and Politics of the Year 1861. 8vo. 18s. (*Now ready.*)

Alford.—The Greek Testament; with a critically revised Text: a Digest of Various Readings: Marginal References to Verbal and Idiomatic Usage: Prolegomena: and a copious Critical and Exegetical Commentary in English. For the Use of Theological Students and Ministers. By Henry Alford, D.D., Dean of Canterbury.

In 4 Vols. 8vo., price 5l. 2s.; or, separately,

Vol. I.—The Four Gospels. *Fourth Edition.* 28s.
Vol. II.—Acts to II. Corinthians. *Fourth Edition.* 24s.
Vol. III.—Galatians to Philemon. *Third Edition.* 18s.
Vol. IV.—Hebrews to Revelation. *Second Edition.* 32s.
The fourth Volume may still be had in Two Parts.

Peile.—The Miracle of Healing Power. Christ in His Man's Nature through Death Man's Quickener into Life in God: an Argument from Scripture only. By Thomas Williamson Peile, D.D., Incumbent of St. Paul's, Hampstead, late Vicar of Luton, Beds, and sometime Fellow of Trinity College, Cambridge. 8vo. 5s.

Markby.—The Man Christ Jesus; or, the Daily Life, and Teaching of our Lord, in Childhood and Manhood, on Earth. By the Rev. Thomas Markby, M.A., lately Afternoon Lecturer at St. James's, Paddington. Crown 8vo. 9s. 6d.

Boyle.—The Unsealed Visions of Daniel; their Age, their Authenticity, and their Fulfilment. With a Rectification of Ancient Chronology, adjusting it to the Christian Æra. By W. R. A. Boyle. 8vo. (*In the press.*)

Douglas.—Sermons. By Henry Alexander Douglas, M.A., Dean of Cape Town. 12mo. 4s. 6d. (*Just published.*)

Green.—Brief Memorials of the late Rev. Charles Green, M.A., of Worcester College, Oxford; Missionary and Secretary of the Society for the Propagation of the Gospel. Small 8vo. 2s. 6d.

Crosthwaite.—Eight Lectures on the Historical Events and Characters in the Book of Daniel: to which are added, Four Discourses on the Doctrine of our Mutual Recognition in a Future State. Inscribed, by permission, to his Grace the late Archbishop of Armagh. By the Rev. J. C. Crosthwaite, M.A., Rector of St. Mary-at-Hill, London. 12mo. 7s. (*In the press.*)

American Church.—Recent Recollections of the Anglo-American Church in the United States. By an English Layman, five years resident in that Republic. In Two Vols., post 8vo. 18s.

Wordsworth.—The New Testament of our Lord and Saviour Jesus Christ, in the Original Greek. With Notes, Introductions, and Indexes. By Chr. Wordsworth, D.D., Canon of Westminster. *New Edition.* In Two Vols., imperial 8vo. 4l.

Or separately,
Part I.: The Four Gospels. *New Edition.* 1l. 1s.
Part II.: The Acts. *New Edition.* 10s. 6d.
Part III.: The Epistles of St. Paul. *New Edition.* 1l. 11s. 6d.
Part IV.: The General Epistles and Book of Revelation; with Indexes. *New Edition.* 1l. 1s.

Simon.—The Mission and Martyrdom of St. Peter: or, Did St. Peter ever leave the East? containing the Original Text of all the Passages in Ancient writers supposed to imply a Journey into Europe, with Translations and Roman Catholic Comments; showing that there is not the least sign in antiquity of the alleged fact. By Thomas Collyns Simon. Second Edition, with corrections and additions. 8vo. 6s.

Arnold.—A Practical Introduction to Latin Prose Composition, Part I. By the Rev. T. K. Arnold, M.A., late Rector of Lyndon, and formerly Fellow of Trinity College, Cambridge. *Twelfth Edition.* 8vo. 6s. 6d.

<small>This work is at once a Syntax, a Vocabulary, and an Exercise Book: and considerable attention has been paid to the subject of Synonymes. It is now used at all, or nearly all, the public schools.</small>

Goulburn.—An Introduction to the Devotional Study of the Holy Scriptures. By Edward Meyrick Goulburn, D.D. *Fifth Edition.* Small 8vo. 4s. 6d.

Roman Biography. — De Viris Illustribus Urbis Romæ, a Romulo ad Augustum. An Elementary Latin Reading Book, being a Series of Biographical Chapters on Roman History, chronologically arranged; simplified from the Text of Livy and other Roman writers; adapted, with Annotations and a Vocabulary, from the work of Professor Lhomond. By the Editor of the "Graduated Series of English Reading Books." Small 8vo. 3s.

Atkins.—Six-Discourses on Pastoral Duties, preached before the University of Dublin; being the Donnellan Lectures for 1860. By William Atkins, D.D., formerly Fellow of Trinity College, Dublin; Rector of Tullyagnish, Diocese of Raphoe; and Examining Chaplain to the Lord Bishop of Derry. 8vo. 6s.

Glover.—England, the Remnant of Judah, and the Israel of Ephraim. By the Rev. F. R. A. Glover, M.A., Chaplain to the Consulate at Cologne. 8vo. 6s. 6d.

Miller.—Parochial Sermons. By the Rev. J. K. Miller, late Vicar of Walkeringham, Notts, and formerly Fellow of Trinity College, Cambridge. Small 8vo. 4s. 6d.

NEW WORKS AND NEW EDITIONS.

Hawkins.—The Limits of Religious Belief: Suggestions addressed to the Student in Divine Things. By the Rev. Wm. Bentinck Hawkins, M.A., F.R.S., of Exeter College, Oxford. Small 8vo. 2s. 6d.

Alford.—Reminiscences by a Clergyman's Wife. Edited by The Dean of Canterbury. Crown 8vo. 5s.

Wordsworth.—The Inspiration of the Bible; Five Lectures, delivered in Westminster Abbey. By Christopher Wordsworth, D.D., Canon of Westminster. Post 8vo. 3s. 6d.

Wordsworth.—The Interpretation of the Bible; Five Lectures, delivered in Westminster Abbey. By the same Author. Post 8vo. 3s. 6d.

Galloway.—Ezekiel's Sign, Metrically Paraphrased and Interpreted, from his Fourth and Fifth Chapters; with Notes and Elucidations from the Sculptured Slabs of Nineveh. By W. B. Galloway, M.A., Incumbent of St. Mark's, Regent's Park, and Chaplain to the Viscount Hawarden. Small 8vo. 2s. 6d.

Byng.—Sermons for Households. By Francis E. C. Byng, M.A., Rector of Little Casterton. Crown 8vo. 3s. 6d.

Arnold.—A Practical Introduction to Greek Accidence; with Easy Exercises and Vocabulary. By the Rev. T. K. Arnold, M.A. *Seventh Edition.* 8vo. 5s. 6d.

Henley.—The Prayer of Prayers. By the Hon. and Rev. Robert Henley, M.A., Perpetual Curate of Putney. Small 8vo. 4s. 6d.

Warter.—The Sea-board and the Down; or, My Parish in the South. By John Wood Warter, B.D., Vicar of West Tarring, Sussex. In Two Vols., small 4to., with Illustrations. 28s.

RIVINGTONS, WATERLOO PLACE, LONDON.

Trevelyan.—Quarr Abbey, or the Mistaken Calling; a Tale of the Isle of Wight in the Thirteenth Century. By Frances A. Trevelyan, Author of "Lectures on English History." Small 4to., price 1s. 6d., or in cloth, with Illustrations, 2s. 6d.

Arnold.—Spelling turned Etymology, Part I. By the Rev. T. K. Arnold, M.A. *Second Edition.* 12mo. 2s. 6d.

Arnold.—The Eighth Edition of a Second Latin Book, and Practical Grammar; intended as a Sequel to "Henry's First Latin Book." By the same Author. 4s.

⁎ This work is a *Practical Latin Grammar, with Reading Lessons and Exercises.* Particular attention is given to the principles on which derivative words are formed.

Monsell.—Parish Musings; or, Devotional Poems. By John S. B. Monsell, LL.D., Vicar of Egham, Surrey, and Rural Dean. *Fifth Edition.* 2s.

Hooper.—The Revelation of Jesus Christ; expounded by Francis Bodfield Hooper, Rector of Upton Warren, Worcestershire, Author of "A Guide to the Apocalypse," and other Works. In Two Vols., 8vo. 28s.

Hodgson.—Instructions for the Use of Candidates for Holy Orders, and of the Parochial Clergy, as to Ordination, Licences, Induction, Pluralities, Residence, &c. &c., with Acts of Parliament relating to the above, and Forms to be used. By Christopher Hodgson, M.A., Secretary to the Governors of Queen Anne's Bounty. *Eighth Edition.* In 8vo. 12s.

⁎ In this Edition such alterations have been made as appeared to be necessary in consequence of recent amendments in the laws relating to the Clergy.

Giles.—Village Sermons, preached at some of the chief Christian Seasons, in the Parish Church of Belleau with Aby. By J. D. Giles, M.A., late Rector. Small 8vo. 5s.

RIVINGTONS, WATERLOO PLACE, LONDON.

PAMPHLETS LATELY PUBLISHED

BY

MESSRS. RIVINGTON.

Parochial Mission-Women; their Work and its Fruits. By the Hon. Mrs. J. C. Talbot. Small 8vo. Price 2s. in limp cloth.
The object of this little book is to give a sketch of a work which has now for two years been carried on among the lowest classes of the population of London and some other great towns, under the direct control of the Parochial Clergy, and which appears to have succeeded in a remarkable manner.

"The Waiting Isles." A Sermon preached at the Farewell Service of the Mission to the Sandwich Islands, in Westminster Abbey, July 23, 1862. By the Right Rev. the Bishop of Honolulu. 8vo. 1s.

Case whether Professor Jowett's Essay has so distinctly contravened the Doctrines of the Church of England, that a Court of Law would pronounce him Guilty; with the Opinion of the Queen's Advocate thereon. 8vo. 6d.

An Apology for the Beard; addressed to Men in General, to the Clergy in Particular. By Artium Magister. Small 8vo. 1s. 6d.

A Charge delivered at his Sixth Visitation of the Archdeaconry of Buckingham, in June, 1862. By Edward Bickersteth, M.A., Archdeacon of Buckingham, and Vicar of Aylesbury. 8vo. 1s. 6d.

A Charge addressed to the Clergy and Churchwardens at the General Visitation of the Archdeaconry of Bristol held by Commission in July, 1862. By Thomas Thorp, B.D., Archdeacon of Bristol. *Second Edition.* 12mo. 6d.

Soundings of Antiquity: a New Method of applying the Astronomical Evidences to the Events of History; and an Assignment of true Dates to the Epochs of the Church. By the Rev. H. M. Grover, Rector of Hitcham, Bucks. 8vo. 1s.

Five Short Letters to Sir William Heathcote, Bart., M.P. for the University of Oxford, on the Studies and Discipline of Public Schools. By George Moberly, D.C.L., Head Master of Winchester College. 8vo. 2s. 6d.

The Spirit of Truth, and the Spirit of the World; a Sermon preached before the University of Oxford. By R. C. Coxe, M.A., Archdeacon of Lindisfarne, and Canon of Durham. Second Edition. 8vo. 1s.

Hold fast the Form of Sound Words. An Argument on Creeds and Confessions of Faith, in a Sermon, by the same Author. 1s.

A Reply to the Christian Observer's Review (August, 1862) of "Three Letters on Justification." Small 8vo. 1s.

The Doctrine of Justification and the Harmony of the Apostles Paul and James considered, with particular reference to the Treatise of Bishop O'Brien. In three Letters, reprinted from the British Magazine. Designed for the Use of Students in Divinity. Small 8vo. Price 1s. 6d. *in limp cloth.*

The Teachers of the People; a Tract for the Time: with an Introductory Address to the Right Hon. Sir John Taylor Coleridge, D.C.L. By the Rev. Derwent Coleridge, M.A., Principal of St. Mark's College, Chelsea, and Prebendary of St. Paul's Cathedral. 8vo. 2s. 6d.

Four Sermons preached at the Anniversary Festival of the Consecration of the Church, on Sunday, Sept. 29, and Oct. 3, 1861, at St. Michael's, Tenbury. 8vo. 2s.

Lectures on the Office and Duties of Churchwardens, Chapelwardens, and Sidesmen, Parish Clerks, and Sextons, delivered to the Students of the Theological College, Lichfield, by James Thos. Law, M.A., Chancellor of the Diocese, and late Special Commissary of the Diocese of Bath and Wells. 8vo. 3s.

A Bicentenary Sermon on the Book of Common Prayer; preached in Westminster Abbey. By Chr. Wordsworth, D.D., Canon of Westminster. 1d.

An Essay on the Angels of the Churches: Rev. ii. iii. By the Rev. George Holden, M.A. 6d.

Twenty Reasons for an Increase of the Home Episcopate. 1s. *per dozen.*

Church Extension in St. Pancras. A comparative Statement of the Increase of Population and Church Accommodation in that Parish, from 1801 to 1851; with a Summary of the measures in progress to provide for its spiritual wants. By William Rivington. *Third Edition.* 8vo. 6d.

The Hardships and Sufferings of the Poor Clergy. A Sequel to "Startling Facts." By the Rev. W. G. Jervis, M.A. 6d.

A Few Words on our Calling of God to Salvation in the Church of England. By the Rev. C. J. Heathcote, M.A., late Incumbent of St. Thomas's, Stamford Hill. 1s.

Mazzaroth; or, The Constellations. In three Parts. Royal 8vo. 10s.

A Dissertation on the Sacrament of Baptism. By the Rev. W. Meara, B.A. 8vo. 2s. 6d.

Occasional Paper of the Oxford, Cambridge, Dublin, and Durham Mission to Central Africa; containing Letters from Bishop Mackenzie, Dr. Livingstone, and others. 8vo. 1s.

Third Report of the Columbia Mission, 1861. 8vo. 6d.

TRACTS
ON
CONFIRMATION, THE SACRAMENTS, THE CHURCH CATECHISM, AND OTHER SUBJECTS.

The Rite of Confirmation Explained. By the Rev. D. J. Eyre, M.A., Sub-Dean of Sarum. Price 4d., or 3s. 6d. per dozen.

Questions and Answers on Confirmation. By W. F. Hook, D.D., Dean of Chichester. Price 2d., or 15s. per 100.

A Plain Catechism before Confirmation. By the Ven. Archd. Dodgson, M.A. 2d.

Manual on Confirmation. By Chr. Wordsworth, D.D. 1s.

On the Sacrament of the Lord's Supper. By the Plain Man's Friend. Price 4d.

A Companion to the Lord's Supper. By the same Author. 8d. bound.

The Happy Communicant; or, the Soldier Armed. A true Story. By the Rev. John James, D.D., Canon of Peterborough. Price 3d., or 2s. 6d. per dozen.

The Benefit of the Sacrament of the Lord's Supper Explained. By Edward Burton, D.D. Price 2d., or 15s. per 100.

Infant Baptism, and the Mode of Administering it. By R. Twopeny, B.D. 6d.

Plain Remarks on Infant Baptism and Confirmation. By W. J. Edge, M.A. 3d.

Infant Stories on Holy Baptism, the Visitation of the Sick, and the Burial of the Dead. By a Lady. Price 4d.

The Infant Christian's First Catechism. By Mrs. Parry, of Barbados. Price 3d., or 2s. 6d. per dozen.

It is Written: or, the Catechism teaching from Scripture; a Manual in Question and Answer. By the Rev. C. J. Heathcote, M.A. 6d., or 5s. per dozen.

Help and Comfort for the Sick Poor. By the Author of "Sickness: its Trials and Blessings." Price 1s.

Prayers for the Sick and Dying. By the same Author. Price 2s. 6d.

Eyes and Ears; or, the History of one who was Deaf and Blind. Price 2d., or 25 for 3s. 6d.

"It is Well with the Child," or, Reasons for Resignation under the Loss of beloved Children. By the Rev. Edmund Tew, B.A. Price 6d.

Instructions for the Relief of the Sick Poor in Diseases of frequent Occurrence. By the late R. Pearson, M.D. 18mo. Price 1s. 6d.

The Cottage Bee-Hive. Price 3d., or 2s. 6d. per dozen.

An Exhortation to the Lord's Day. By the Ven. R. W. Evans, M.A., Archdeacon of Westmoreland. Price 1s. 6d.

How Lent may be kept both by Rich and by Poor. By the Rev. C. E. Kennaway. Price 2d., or one dozen and a half for 2s. 6d.

The Christian Servant Warned: being the substance of a Village Sermon. By the Rev. Francis Phillott, M.A. Price 6d.

Pastoral Counsels to Servants. By the late Rev. Henry Pritchard, B.D. 4d.

Advice to a Public School Boy. By the Rev. F. Poynder, M.A. 18mo. Price 6d.

The Holy Bible the One Design of One Eternal Mind. By the Rev. David Laing, M.A., Incumbent of Trinity, St. Pancras. Price 1s.

Brief History of the Book of Common Prayer. By the same Author. Price 1s.

An Explanation of Dr. Watts's Hymns, in Question and Answer. Price 8d., or 7s. per dozen.

Publishing Quarterly, at 3d. per Number,
IN CONNEXION WITH
THE INCORPORATED SOCIETY FOR PROMOTING
THE ENLARGEMENT, BUILDING, AND REPAIRING OF CHURCHES
AND CHAPELS IN ENGLAND AND WALES,

The Church Builder,

AN ILLUSTRATED JOURNAL OF
CHURCH EXTENSION IN ENGLAND AND WALES.
Supplied post-free to all Subscribers of One Shilling and Fourpence per annum, paid in advance.

The Editor solicits the co-operation of Churchmen in his efforts to render this Periodical subservient to the interests of the Church Building Society, and to the work of Church Extension generally in England and Wales. All Communications should be addressed to the Editor, No. 7, Whitehall, London, S.W.

Nos. I. to IV. are published.

———⋈———

Quarterly, at 1d. per Number,
CHURCH-WORK AMONG THE MASSES; in connexion with the London Diocesan Church Building Society.
Nos. I. to IV. are published.

———⋈———

Quarterly, at One Penny,
The HOME MISSION FIELD of the CHURCH of ENGLAND; in connexion with the Additional Curates' Society.
Nos. I. to XVI. are published.

———⋈———

RIVINGTONS, WATERLOO PLACE, LONDON.

PSALMS AND HYMNS
ADAPTED TO THE
SERVICES OF THE CHURCH OF ENGLAND.
BY THE REV. W. J. HALL, M.A.,
late Priest in Ordinary to Her Majesty, and Vicar of Tottenham.

From the great care bestowed upon this collection (under the immediate supervision of the late Lord Bishop of London), that it should be sound in doctrine, spiritual in tone, and practical in tendency, it has been most extensively adopted throughout this country, as well as in our Dependencies and Colonies, in America, and also in most of the English Churches abroad. Nearly a million and a half have been sold altogether of the various Editions.

THIS WORK IS PRINTED IN THE FOLLOWING SIZES :—

	s.	d.
32mo, Nonpareil type, cloth limp, cut flush	0	8
——— ——— ——— cloth, boards	1	0
——————————— sheep	1	2
——————————— roan, with gilt edges	1	6
32mo and 48mo, Fine Paper, Pearl type, cloth, gold mitre, g. edges	2	0
——————————————————— purple morocco	4	0
24mo, Bourgeois type, cloth limp, cut flush	1	3
——————————— cloth, boards	1	6
——————————— sheep	1	8
——————————— roan, with gilt edges	2	0
24mo, Fine Paper, Bourgeois type, cloth, with gold mitre	2	0
——————————————— purple calf	3	0
——————————————— purple calf, extra, gilt edges	3	6
——————————————— morocco, gilt edges	4	6
18mo, Pica type, cloth, with gold mitre	3	0
——————————— roan, with gilt edges, or purple calf	4	0
——————————— purple calf, extra, gilt edges	4	6
——————————— morocco	5	6
Octavo, Pica type, cloth, with gold mitre	8	0
——————— morocco, gilt edges	12	0

Messrs. RIVINGTON keep several sizes of the Psalms and Hymns, bound with the Book of Common Prayer.

A SELECTION of PSALM and HYMN TUNES, *with Chants*,
Sanctuses, &c. harmonized for FOUR VOICES, *by* JOHN GOSS, ESQ., *and especially adapted to this Work.*

	£	s.	d.
Royal 8vo, cloth	0	12	0
——— half-bound in calf	0	14	0
——— bound in whole calf	0	16	0
——— calf extra, gilt edges	0	18	0
——— purple morocco	1	1	0

Also a HAND-BOOK edition of the above for Congregational use. 3s. 6d.

A Considerable Allowance made to the Clergy, Organists, and for Charitable Purposes.

WORKS

EDITED FOR THE SYNDICS

OF THE

CAMBRIDGE UNIVERSITY PRESS.

SOLD BY RIVINGTONS,

CAMBRIDGE WAREHOUSE, 32, PATERNOSTER ROW,

AND 3, WATERLOO PLACE, LONDON.

Pearson's Exposition of the Creed; edited by Temple Chevallier, B.D., Professor of Mathematics in the University of Durham, and late Fellow and Tutor of St. Catharine's College, Cambridge. Second Edition. 8vo. 10s. 6d.

Select Discourses, by John Smith, late Fellow of Queens' College, Cambridge. Edited by H. G. Williams, B.D., Professor of Arabic in the University. Royal 8vo. 10s. 6d.

The Works of Isaac Barrow, compared with the Original MSS. enlarged with Materials hitherto unpublished. A New Edition, by A. Napier, M.A., of Trinity College, Vicar of Holkham, Norfolk. 9 vols. 8vo. 4l. 14s. 6d.

A Treatise of the Pope's Supremacy, and a Discourse concerning the Unity of the Church. By Isaac Barrow. 8vo. 12s.

The Mathematical Works of Isaac Barrow, D.D. Edited by W. Whewell, D.D., Master of Trinity College. 8vo. 15s.

Wheatly on the Common Prayer; edited by G. E. Corrie, D.D., Master of Jesus College, Examining Chaplain to the Lord Bishop of Ely. 8vo. 12s. 6d.

The Gospel according to Saint Matthew in Anglo-Saxon and Northumbrian Versions, synoptically arranged: with Collations of the best Manuscripts. By J. M. Kemble, M.A., and Archdeacon Hardwick, late Christian Advocate. 10s.

CAMBRIDGE UNIVERSITY PRESS BOOKS. 15

Cambridge Greek and English Testament, in Parallel Columns on the same page. Edited by J. Scholefield, M.A., late Regius Professor of Greek in the University. Fourth Edition. Small 8vo. 7s. 6d., or 12s. in morocco.

Cambridge Greek Testament. Ex editione Stephani tertia, 1550. Small 8vo. 3s. 6d.

Ciceronis de Officiis Libri tres; with an English Commentary, and Copious Indices, by H. A. Holden, M.A., Head Master of Ipswich School, late Fellow of Trinity College, Cambridge. Post 8vo. 9s. 6d.

Ciceronis Oratio pro Milone; with English Notes, by J. S. Purton, M.A., President and Tutor of St. Catharine's College. Post 8vo. 3s. 6d.

Grotius de Jure Belli et Pacis; with the Notes of Barbeyrac and others; accompanied by an abridged Translation of the Text, by W. Whewell, D.D., Master of Trinity College. 3 vols. 8vo. 42s. The Translation separate, 14s.

The Homilies, with Various Readings, and the Quotations from the Fathers given at length in the Original Languages. Edited by G. E. Corrie, D.D. 8vo. 10s. 6d.

Archbishop Usher's Answer to a Jesuit, with other Tracts on Popery. Edited by J. Scholefield, M.A. 8vo. 13s. 6d.

Wilson's Illustration of the Method of explaining the New Testament, by the early opinions of Jews and Christians concerning Christ. Edited by T. Turton, D.D., Lord Bishop of Ely. 8vo. 8s.

Lectures on Divinity delivered in the University of Cambridge. By John Hey, D.D. Third Edition, by T. Turton, D.D., Lord Bishop of Ely. 2 vols. 8vo. 30s.

Theophylacti in Evangelium S. Matthæi Commentarius. Edited by W. G. Humphry, B.D., Prebendary of St. Paul's, and Vicar of St. Martin's-in-the-Fields, London, late Fellow of Trinity College. 8vo. 14s.

Tertullianus de Corona Militis, de Spectaculis, de Idololatria; with Analysis and English Notes, by George Currey, B.D., Preacher at the Charter House, late Fellow and Tutor of St. John's College. Crown 8vo. 7s. 6d.

A more complete List of the Publications of the Cambridge University Press may be had on application to Messrs. Rivington.

BIBLES,

COMMON PRAYER BOOKS,

&c.,

PRINTED AT

The Cambridge University Press.

MESSRS. RIVINGTON

BEG LEAVE TO ANNOUNCE THAT THEY HAVE BEEN APPOINTED AGENTS FOR THE SALE OF THE ABOVE EDITIONS,

WHICH MAY BE SEEN AT

No. 3, WATERLOO PLACE, PALL MALL,

AND AT THEIR CAMBRIDGE WAREHOUSE,

No. 32, PATERNOSTER ROW, LONDON.

GILBERT AND RIVINGTON, PRINTERS, ST. JOHN'S SQUARE, LONDON.